MW01632953

NEW AGE BIBLE & PHILOSOPHY CENTER
1139 Lincoln Blvd.
Santa Monica, CA 90403

REPRINTED 1986

Esoteric Music

Corinne Heline

BASED ON THE
MUSICAL SEERSHIP OF

RICHARD WAGNER

In this study, the placement ot Wagner's music-dramas has been determined not by their date of composition or production, but in accordance with the steps they portray in the progressive spiritual development of the individual and the race.

The more I know my Wagner, the more convinced I am that this is the most wonderful artist-mind the world has ever seen. From the liking of Wagner as a musician, I have gone to adoration.

—*Ernest Newman*

NEW AGE WRITINGS BY CORINNE HELINE

New Age Bible Interpretation

Old Testament

Vol I - Five Books of Moses and Joshua
Vol II - Part I. Solomon and the Temple Builders
Part II. Books of Initiation
Vol III - Part I. The Promise
Part II. The Preparation

New Testament

Vol IV. Preparation for coming of the Light of the World
Vol V. The Christ and His Mission
Vol VI. The Work of the Apostles and Paul and Book of Revelation
Vol VII. Mystery of the Christos

Other Books on Bible Interpretation

Tarot and the Bible - Mythology and the Bible - Mystic Masonry and the Bible -Occult Anatomy and the Bible - The Bible and the Stars - Sacred Science of Numbers - Questions and Answers on Bible Enigmas - Supreme Initiations of the Blessed Virgin - Blessed Virgin Mary, her Life & Mission.

Other Works

Magic Gardens - Star Gates - Color and Music in the New Age - Music: the Keynote of Human Evolution - The Cosmic Harp - Healing and Regeneration through Color - Healing and Regeneration through Music - Esoteric Music of Richard Wagner - Beethoven's Nine Symphonies - The Twelve Labors of Hercules - Mysteries of the Holy Grail

NEW AGE WRITINGS BY THEODORE HELINE

America's Destiny, The American Indian, The Archetype Unveiled - Capital Punishment - Esoteric Drama Studies - Romeo and Juliet - The Merchant of Venice - Saint Francis and the Wolf of Gubbio

****

CONTENTS

Part I

Esoteric Music Based on the Musical Seership of Richard Wagner

INTRODUCTION

THE MUSIC DRAMAS ESOTERICALLY INTERPRETED

PART I

Esoteric Brotherhoods and Schools of Initiation

THE FLYING DUTCHMAN (Der Fliegende Hollander)

How Good Overcomes Evil

THE MASTERSINGERS (Die Meistersinger)

Musical Schools of Initiation

Contents - Part II

Individual Attainment

TANNHAUSER—The Drama of Human Regeneration
The Degree of Purification

LOHENGRIN—The Knight of the Swan
The Degree of Conscious Invisible Helpership

TRISTAN AND ISOLDE—The Rite of the Mystic Marriage
The Degree of Equilibrium

PARSIFAL—The Initiate - Teacher
The Degree of Mastership

Contents - Part III

Cosmic Evolution

THE RING OF THE NIBELUNGS
(Der Ring des Niebelung)

THE RHINEGOLD (Das Rheingold)
The Water Path

THE VALKYRIES (Die Walkure)
The Air Path

SIEGFRIED
The Earth Path

THE TWILIGHT OF THE GODS
(Die Gotterdammerung
The Fire Path

ILLUSTRATIONS

RICHARD WAGNER'S DREAM
(Reading the Akhasic Records)
From the painting by Schweniger

INTRODUCTORY

The Man and His Work

I have found true Art to be at one with true Religion.
—Richard Wagner

RICHARD WAGNER was a New Age Messenger of music, so a full understanding of the mission and purpose of his work belongs to the World of Tomorrow.

His magnificent operas are attuned to the rhythms of the coming Air Age and play directly upon the inner or finer vehicles of man, awakening and stimulating certain latent centers which pioneers of the New Aquarian Age are even now in process of developing. An understanding of Wagner's operas should form, therefore, a part of the equipment of every serious student of the Mysteries since each and all of them mark definite steps in esoteric development.

An aspirant working upon the inital step of *Purification* will be greatly assisted in the process by drawing close to the music of *Tannhauser*. The music of *Lohengrin* will be especially helpful in the attainment of the next step, which has to do with the development of *Conscious Night Memory*. The following Degree of the Mysteries pertains to the *Rite of the Mystic Marriage,* the spiritual significance of which is embodied in the rhythms of *Tristan and Isolde.* The most advanced work, that of a Conscious Temple Initiate, is given in *Parsifal.* The close connection between *Tristan and Isolde* and *Parsifal* is indicated by Wagner in the statement that Tristan was reborn as Parsifal, and that he returned to earth as one whose high attainment privileged him to labor as a teacher and a saviour of men.

The Flying Dutchman defines and clarifies the distinction between a White and a Black Magician, outlining the path followed by each. Closely related to this theme is *The Mastersingers of Nuremberg* which dramaticaly describes medieval Schools of Musical Initiation and so becomes a sort of prelude to *Tannhauser,* setting forth something of the methods of training used in these Schools and certain processes involved in esoteric development.

The work of *The Ring* forms a vast kaleidoscopic picture of the past, present and future development of the entire human race. Man's misuse of both spiritual and physical riches is plainly outlined. The consequences following upon such misdirection appear in *The Twilight of the Gods,* which depicts the darkness of materiality now engulfing the world. But the way out, the Path of Initiation through Love that leads mankind back into the light of spirit, is also traced with equal clarity in Wagner's works for the benefit of all who will take pains to discover it in all its major stages. These major stages, also frequently referred to as "Steps" or "Degrees," together with the music keyed to their several requirements, are given in the operas *Tannhauser, Lohengrin, Tristan and Parsifal.*

Some of Wagner's earliest critics spoke more wisely than they knew when with mild scorn they jestingly referred to his work as "music of the future." This it truly is. The time is coming when Schools of Spiritual Illumination will make use of Wagner's music in their initiatory curriculums. That Wagner himself was aware of this deep spiritual content and purpose of his work is clearly indicated by lines of his own composition which he placed within the cornerstone of his Temple-Theatre at Bayreuth. Wrote he:

I bury here a secret deep,
For centuries long to lie concealed;
Yet while this stone its trust shall keep,
To all the secret stands revealed.

In the atmosphere of peace, sanctity and beauty pervading Bayreuth in the days before the present world upheaval, many wonderful powers of music, well-known to the Ancients but for long years lost and forgotten, were in process of being restored. No doubt they will be in days to come when order and tranquillity is re-established on earth. The place was of Wagner's own choosing, remote from city throngs and in the very heart of unspoiled nature. Here he saw himself, and others after him, working with the hidden powers of nature to bring forth musically a cosmic symphony whereby man and planet could rise to higher levels of being.

Judging Wagner by his own works, there can be no doubt that he was an emissary sent to earth from the great inner-plane Temple of Music. In that exalted center of learning musical Initiates acquire sensitivity to hear the music of the spheres. Some of this celestial harmony has been transcribed for mortal man's hearing by master musicians. Such is Wagner's Grail and Temple music.

Among those who have come to earth as emissaries from the glorious Music Temple on High, Beethoven was probably most perfectly attuned to rhythms of the Celestial Hierarchies. This being so, his deafness became a blessing in disguise because it shut away all discordant noises and helped him to become a perfectly sensitized channel for receiving and transmitting heavenly harmonies.

Wagner recognized the authenticity of Beethoven's soul contact with music of higher spheres and turned to him for his supreme inspiriation in musical composition. Thus, in the early beginnings of his career, Wagner writes: "I hardly know for what I was orginally intended. I only remember that I heard one evening a symphony of Beethoven's; that I thereupon fell ill of a fever, and that when I recovered I was a . . . musician." Wagner further states that as a young lad the music of Beethoven had the effect of enabling him to see mystic constellations and weird shapes.

Wagner tells how, when he was eighteen, he went to bed with Beethoven's Sonatas and arose with his Quartettes. Later he writes, "As soon as one of Beethoven's divine Symphonies is heard, the phenomenal world vanishes into nothingness. In his music stands written the eternal symbols of a new and different world."

Richard Wagner united within himself the rare gifts of poetry and music. Had either talent been denied expression, the other would have placed his name upon immortal scrolls. He was also a philosopher and a prophet. Musically, he was so far ahead of his time that it took nearly half a century for his music-dramas to find general favor among the public at large; and it will take, perhaps, another half century before there will be general recognition of their deep spiritual values and esoteric content.

Much has been written about Wagner's quixotic habits, his irritability and nervous disposition. These are weaknesses to be sure. But until perfect, full-rounded mastership has been attained in the whole of his nature, it could scarcely be otherwise with a sensitive artist such as Wagner, especially when one considers the intense force and power of his inspiration. To keep a physical instrument in tune with celestial harmonies and, at the same time, sufficiently insulated to withstand discordant impacts from the outer objective world has always constituted a serious problem for highly sensitized, creative artists.

The world can never be sufficiently grateful that this mighty genius remained in physical embodiment long enough to bring through a glorious new method of musical Initiation, climaxed by his crowning work, *Parsifal*, with its transcription of angelc music! This music Wagner rightly designated as belonging to the "Art of the Future."

Wagner was acutely conscious of the fact that his mission was to help man recover his lost realization of the sanctity and uplifting influence of music. Says he, "I believe in God, Mozart and Beethoven, and in their disciples and apostles; I believe in the Holy Ghost and the truth of art—one and indivisible; I believe that this art proceeds from God and dwells in the hearts of all enlightened men."

Further amplifying his credo, he writes: "I believe that whoever has revelled in the glorious joys of this high art must be forever devoted to it and can never repudiate it. I believe that all men become blessed through this art, and that therefore it is permitted to anyone to die of hunger for its sake; I believe that I shall become most happy through death. I believe that I have been on earth a discordant chord that shall be made harmonious and clear by death. I believe in a last judgment that shall fearfully damn all those who have dared on this earth to make profit out of this chaste and holy art—who have disgraced it and dishonored it through badness of heart and the coarse instincts of sensuality. I believe that such men will be condemned to hear their own music through all eternity. I believe on the other hand that the true disciples of pure art will be glorified in a divine atmosphere of sun-illumined, fragrant concords, and united eternally with the divine source of all harmony. And may such a merciful lot be granted to me. Amen."

Wagner was working on the development of a suitable curriculum for his esoteric musical training school at the time of his passing. This course of instruction was being planned to cover a period of approximately six years.

The first of these six years of training was to provide general preparation. The second year the student was to devote himself to his own compositions and *their particular mode of rendering*. (The italics are Wagner's.) The third year was to be given to study of *The Flying Dutchman, Tannhauser* and *Lohengrin.* The fourth year was to include *Tristan and Isolde* and *The Mastersingers.* The fifth year was reserved for *The Ring of the Nibelungen;* the sixth year to *Parsifal,* which contains in outline processes leading to the attainment of Spiritual Illumination or Initiation.

Wagner placed his very own soul signature upon performances of his Bayreuth Theatre. They were not mere theatrical offerings but Temple rituals, designed to serve the spiritual life of those who came to absorb their beauty and to find refreshment in their inspiration. No worker, from scene shifter to star, received any remuneration other than mere living expenses. The performers came, as it were, on a soul pilgrimage, as did the understanding attendants. The sacrifice of the personal for the sake of the ideal always creates a soul quality not otherwise attainable.

The aim of the founder of this Temple-Theatre was to develop within and about it a vibrant, luminous aura that would radiate a healing, uplifting influence into the lives of all who came within its environs. Wagner well knew that in order to do this it was important, in fact, necessary, to take certain protective measures. Applause, for instance, was prohibited since it shatters the beautiful astral patterns that are created by the music instead of leaving them to continue in the atmosphere as living images with healing and blessing in their wings.

As previously stated, Wagner chose to erect his Temple in a place detached from the world's maddening throng. It was for the few who would seek it out to partake of the soul service it was designed to perform. It was spiritually charged and dedicated. Since *Parsifal* was, above all his other music-dramas, a sacred festival composition, he specifically provided that its presentation be confined solely to his own specially dedicated Temple-Theatre. He believed that when a disciple was ready to become a Master and to be inducted into the Holy of Holies where he, too, could listen to celestial music, then he was ready for the Parsifal Initiation attuned to rhythms of the inner-plane Temple and its hosts of attendant Angels; and that he should come to the Bayreuth Temple for the event.

Wagner thus refers to the deep inner purposes of Bayreuth at the time of its dedication: "The skill of the architect has produced a certain indefinable effect of distance which causes the tableau to retreat from the spectator as in a dream; meanwhile the music as it comes forth like a spirit voice from the 'mystic gulf,' or like the vapor rising from the sacred bosom of Earth beneath the tripod of the Pythia, induces in him that spiritualized state of clairvoyance wherein the scenic representation becomes the perfect image of real life."

Wagner designates this as the "Art-work of the Future," a work which, he averred, "*only the life of the future* can enable us to produce."

In his letters dealing with music of the future, this great musician-seer paints a glorious picture of the inner significance of music and of its ultimate development in the more highly evolved and spiritualized civilization of the New Aquarian Age now dawning.

Wagner issues a challenging call to all disciples of the Musical Ray to go foward along the path he pioneered, bravely proclaiming by their inspired art the deep significance of music in the spirtual development of the race. Writes he:

> Dash boldly into the full waves of the sea of music, hand in hand with me, you can never lose connection with that which is fully intelligible to every man. For through me you

> **stand forever on the basis of dramatic action and this action at the moment of its scenic presentation is the most directly intelligible of all poems. Extend melody fearlessly so that it may flow through your whole work like an uninterrupted stream. Do you speak that upon which I keep silence, for you alone can say it, and I, though silent, will yet say it all—for I lead you by the hand.**

A modern poet paid fitting tribute to this great musical Initiate and his work when he said, "In some far-off time humanity shall scan these dim, dead centuries for some trace of immortality and say, He stands alone—His living symphonies echo tonight along the Milky Way and still the dwellers on the Pleiades."

PART I

Introductory

I. THE FLYING DUTCHMAN
Workings of the Brotherhoods

II. THE MEISTERSINGER
Black and White
Musical Schools of Initiation

CHAPTER I

The Flying Dutchman

(Der Fliegende Hollander)

How Good Overcomes Evil

THERE is all too general a tendency in this materialistic age to discount the reality of esoteric Brotherhoods, both "White" and "Black," so-called. Their existence has come to be regarded as the veriest superstition by the majority of people; while among a very small minority who do accept their reality there are comparatively few who have the understanding and insight to distinguish operations of one from the other. Thus most people are subject to influences, good or bad as the case may be, which they do not believe to exist or do not properly understand.

The Schools here spoken of are institutions belonging to the inner or spiritual realm and not exoteric organizations of this physical world. The great difficulty for many people is to understand the relationship between the spiritual and physical worlds. These two are not separate but exist in a united state, the higher interpenetrating but extending beyond the lower. They are continuously reacting upon one another, for the Wheel of Rebirth turns unceasingly, carrying the embodied into psycho-spiritual levels and the so-called "dead" back into embodiment and materiality.

Where there is no real division there can be no actual gulf except in consciousness, and great esoteric Brotherhoods exist which are dedicated to the work of making truths of the Soul World known to incarnate men. Their work does not cease when an individual dies. The ego who has joined their ranks continues in their care when it takes up its work in that wonderful land of soul which ancient Greeks said lay "beyond the sunrise."

In the lower levels of the Soul World, on the borderline between material and psychical consciousness, "etheric" Temples of the esoteric Brotherhoods are built. Such is the Temple referred to by Wagner in both *Lohengrin* and *Parsifal.* These etheric Temples are almost physical. Sensitive people sometimes feel they are in a strange and magnetic atmosphere when they approach one, even if they do not know what it is that affects them. The etheric Temple of the Brotherhood of the Rose Cross, for example, is said to interpenetrate the home of the Brothers which, in its physical form, is simply a private dwelling. But to psychic vision it is revealed as a magnificent Temple, somewhat in the nature of an Art Temple, and the ceremonials taking place there are art-forms embodying a living Idea.

The head of the order in these esoteric Temples is never seen by Initiates who attend the services and participate in the work; but his presence is felt the moment he enters, and this is the signal for commencement of the ceremony. It is for this reason that at their annual festival, Manicheans were accustomed to place *an empty chair* for their Master, Mani, who was known to be present but visible only to their Perfecti. Likewise in the Grail Castle, Titurel, the august Founder, remains invisible in the background while his disembodied voice is being heard by the assembly.

There are two general types of humanity: the Mystic and the Intellectualist. The Mystic learns to transcend reason altogether. He strives through love to reach God and thinks of nothing else, thereby attaining to that Divine

Wisdom which is far superior to all worldly knowledge. On the other hand, the Intellectualist, who dominates the modern scene, seeks Truth. He must *know,* not merely *feel,* so for him a scientific way is prepared by the Hierophants of the Mysteries.

It is the aim of all Temple Teachings to reunite science, religion and art, so that Truth, Goodness and Beauty work together to the ultimate salvation of mankind. Many creative artists of all professions have chosen to serve in the Ministry of Beauty, knowing that Beauty is in very truth Immanuel or *God-with-us.* In *Die Meistersinger* Wagner gives us a picture of an Art Brotherhood organized around this Divine Idea, for Wagner himself was an emissary from the Temple of Beauty.

Unfortunately there are Black" as well as "White" Brotherhoods, because spiritual power can be used for either good or evil. In Christian lands all of the White Brotherhoods are spoken of as "the White Grail," while cults devoted to evil are spoken of as "the Black Grail." It is an occult axiom that, as shown in *Parsifal,* we cannot reach the Castle of the True Grail without passing through the country of the Black Grail with its many temptations.

The White Grail is nourished, sustained and strengthened by the right feeling and true thinking of mankind, together with its will to good and its actual service to the common weal. The Black Grail feeds upon those negative and destructive passions that plague fallen humanity, and draws upon those who pass from this life while yet given to greed, hate, cruelty and carnality. While they remain on the lower astral plane, such discarnate egos add tremendously to the power of the Black Brotherhood. In our day we see these powers issue forth from their secret lairs, openly combating the Forces of Light as they strive to win the world to their wicked ways.

The habit of continually thinking in terms of material interests contributes powerfully to the strength of the

Black Grail. This is because of the effect such thought has on the etheric double, the interpenetrating vehicle that vitalizes the physical body. That etheric body is a fourfold structure composed of four kinds of ether. The most attenuated of these are called the Light Ether and the Reflecting Ether. They are channels for spiritual and mental forces, and their power of transmission increases as they are strengthened by the exercise of the higher mind and by devotion to noble ideas. Since the materialist uses chiefly only the lower or concrete mind and is concerned principally with things that contribute to physical sensation, he draws to himself very little of these rare and beautiful ethers. Hence, in his etheric double the two lower ethers predominate. Through them but little inspiration can enter from higher regions of the Soul World, with the result that he becomes more susceptible to influences of the Black Grail.

Then, too, it often follows that psychism, being a sense-faculty, may be developed into super-physical powers and placed at the service of the Black Grail. The two lower ethers—technically known as Chemical and Life Ethers—which nourish the body, grow abnormally, gaining a tenacious grasp on physical life and the body of flesh, until at length, after many lives spent in ministry of the Black Grail, a spurious immortality is achieved. Since no soul qualities are evolved there is no urge toward the spiritual world in which the soul powers are amalgamated by spirit. The result is that the ego becomes earthbound, unable to leave its immediate environs even in death. This is the occult foundation for legends such as Wagner embodies in *The Flying Dutchman,* and which are also treated, from another aspect, in the character of Kundry in *Parsifal.* The ancient legend of the Wandering Jew is of like import. In it a Jew who abused the Christ on His way to Golgotha is sentenced to physical immortality upon earth until the end of time. Israelites told a similar tale of the Pharaoh who oppressed their ancestors in Egypt, while Christians seem to hold a like belief in regard to the cruel Nero.

A more common form of this condition we call "earth-bound souls" who, even after death of the body, continue to haunt the earth, striving by many occult means to build a material body for themselves and sometimes succeeding in materializing for longer or shorter periods of time by the aid of persons still in the flesh. This problem is not represented in any of the Wagnerian dramas, however, unless we choose to give *The Flying Dutchman* such a secondary interpretation.

There are also those who, like the biblical heroes Enoch and Elijah, are "lost to death" under the ministry of the White Grail. These servants of the White Grail become so imbued with the powers of the Universal Spirit (symbolized in *Parsifal* by the White Dove which descends upon the Chalice) that they are conscious of their unity with life on all planes. In them consciousness is uninterrupted; life and being are experienced in unbroken continuity. They cannot "die" for they have demonstrated Life Eternal and Love Immortal.

The etheric double of such an Illumined One is composed almost entirely of radiant blue and gold spiritual ethers and his physical body is truly the Body of Transfiguration, emanating rays of light and love and healing for all to draw upon as they can and will.

Therese Neumann, the Catholic Stigmatist, is an example of the Mystic who is sustained by the Grail. Ancient Mystery Teachers of primitive Christianity had already received, prior to the Christ's advent, a perfect technique for inducing the "stigmatic" consciousness, and one of the Gnostic sacraments was that of Stigmatization. These Stigmatists of the esoteric Schools, however, developed the stigmata invisibily. Whatever was to be endured of pain and suffering in the early stages of their development was endured stoically, in silence and even without the knowledge of those nearest them as to what was taking place. The Church refuses to credit the Stigmatization of Catherine of Sienna because her stigmata were invisible, as she says, at her own request; and it is of profound occult import to observe that in her case after a time these invisible stagmata ceased to be painful and became instead a source of strength and joy and spiritual power.

In esoteric unfoldment the Initiate of the Grail himself becomes the Grail—the "stone of tincture" of the alchemists, whose touch or mere presence confers healing and imparts strength for successfully waging the lattle of life. The Eucharist of the Manicheans exemplified this principle, which is a radical departure from the orthodox concept of transubstantiation. It was during the twelfth century, when many of the Grail epics were written, that this problem of the Eucharist occupied the attention of the orthodox Church, but it was not until 1215 that the Doctrine of Transubstantiation was officially decreed as an established teaching of the orthodox Church. Wolfram von Eschenbach's *Parsifal* belongs to this same period, showing how deeply Europe was moved by the spiritual problem of the Eucharist. The materialization of the Eucharist concept in this thirteenth century reveals how far the orthodox Church had wandered from its earlier esoteric source, and was a foreshadowing of the darkness of materiality which had already begun to descend upon the world.

The Brotherhoods of Light and Shadow are today engaged in such a terrific contest for world domination as has occurred but few times in the whole course of human evolution. The purpose of the Dark Forces is, as it has always been, to create suspicion, envy, disruption, conflict and destruction throughout the world. The counteracting work of the White Brotherhood is to generate goodwill and to establish right relations and peace upon earth. "That you may love one another even as I have loved you" is the keynote of the Blessed Presence who is the supreme Leader of the Forces of Light.

Wagner's operas, beginning with *The Flying Dutchman,* exemplify various stages of spiritual development in the individual and the race. At first he was not clearly conscious of his life plan, but a higher wisdom guided him. In retrospect we can observe the path by which he climbed to the eminence of his mission to our Age. In *The Flying Dutchman* we are shown that the magic formula for overcoming all evil lies in the practice of selfless love.

Interpretation of the Music Drama

PREFATORY NOTE

The familiar saying that "coming events cast their shadows before" is applicable to *The Flying Dutchman* in its relation to Wagner's later musical creation. This opera gives us our first intimation of Wagner the Immortal. Here for the first time we meet with those fascinating motifs, that dramatic and symphonic treatment, which are essential characteristics of his mature operatic works. In the weird and menacing motif of the lonely wanderer of the seas, in the brooding mysticism of the lovely Senta, in the drama of their first enraptured meeting and the tragedy of their separation, in Senta's self-immolation and the promise of after-life reunion, we glimpse the tremendous dramatic potentialities of a budding genius which later shines forth most resplendently in *The Ring* epic and in *Parsifal.*

Wagner's utilization of descriptive musical motifs opened a new phase of musical psychology. It was with a kind of clairvoyance that the great composer saw new and dramatic possibilities of the operatic form by introducing into it musical patterns that correspond to characters and situations in the music-drama. Recent developments in the use of sound and color, and their effects on mind and body, are now reaching a point where they verify the scientific soundness and accuracy of Wagner's musical seership.

Writing to a friend many years after his youthful production of the *Flying Dutchman,* Wagner comments: "I have made a new close for the Overture of *The Flying Dutchman* which pleases me much. It was only after I had written Isolde's last transfiguration that I could find the right close for *the Flying Dutchman Overture.*" He also expressed at this time the desire to rewrite earlier operas including *The Dutchman, Tannhauser* and *Lohengrin*. What a priceless heritage the world has missed! These earlier works, inestimable as they are, retouched by the magic of the great master-seer of *Tristan, The Ring* and *Parsifal!* Wonderful beyond measure would this gift have been.

A stormy experience on the North Sea inspired Wagner to compose *The Flying Dutchman*. For three weeks the small boat upon which he had taken passage was buffeted by a terrific storm and was finally forced to seek shelter in a bleak and desolate Norwegian harbor, the little village of Sandvike. Wagner wrote: "The passage through the narrows made a wondrous impression on my fancy. The legend of *The Flying Dutchman* was confirmed by the sailors and the circumstances gave it a distinct and characteristic color in my mind."

The atmosphere of the far northern country, fraught with mystic silence and heavy as with impending doom, breathes through the entire opera.

Wagner wrote the libretto of *The Dutchman* and gave it to the director of the Paris Opera, who was interested in the work but engaged another composer to write the music. The opera was produced but it was an instant failure.

The following spring (1841) Wagner took a cottage near Paris and there, in seven weeks, rewrote the poem and composed all of the music with the exception of the overture. In his autobiography he says of this experience: "In order to set about this composition, I required to hire a pianoforte, for after nine months interruption of all musical production, I had to try to surround myself with the needful preliminaries of a musical atmosphere. As soon as the piano arrived, my heart beat fast for very fear; I dreaded to discover that I had ceased to be a musician. I began first with the Sailors' Chorus and the Spinning Song. Everything sped along as on wings and I shouted for joy, as I felt within me that I was still a musician."

Again he writes: "With *The Flying Dutchman* began my new career as a poet. I was now no longer a writer of operatic libretti. Henceforward in my dramatic capacity I was in the first place a poet; not until the poem came to be fully worked out did I again become a musician. But as a poet I fully divined the power which music possessed for enforcing my words."

Too often the story of civilization has been written in blood. In *The Flying Dutchman* we have a silent, bloodless revolution—but one not unattended by suffering. It was a revolution in the realm of music that was of unimaginable importance to the history of the soul, a revolution born out of Wagner's own experience at a critical time in his career, when he was suffering as only the young can suffer. The storm of the wild North Sea was, in fact, an objectification of his own inner turmoil. In working out the story of the wandering Dutchman he reached far down into the depths of his inner being and found there the pearl of great price.

THE LEGEND

In its original form the legend of the Flying Dutchman reaches back into time immemorial, as do all folk tales embodying elements illustrative of the cosmic laws of life and being.

This particular folk story recounts the adventure of a Dutch sea captain who, upon finding his ship obstructed by adverse gales near the Cape of Good Hope, set up his own human will as superior to the Divine and swore that he would finish his course though all hell should try to stop him. This daring oath was registered in Cosmic scrolls, and the Devil, the personification of all adverse powers in nature, took up the challenge. Like the biblical Adversary of Job, he acted as the agent of Cosmic Law and wreaked punishment upon the presumptuous mariner by condemning him to sail the seas forever. Every port was barred against him, the only mitigation of his sentence being that he was permitted to land once in seven years to seek for a woman who would love him and be faithful to him—for it was by means of a love as constant as the oceans were inconstant that he should find redemption.

Fascinating as the legend may be, it takes on added color and significance in Wagner's treatment of it in operatic form with musical motifs. The story was transformed into a mythical allegory of the soul, for Wagner, like Goethe before him, had become interested in occult and mystic studies at an early age. Thus the unceasing and fateful journeying of the Dutchman represents the ego's restless journeying on the sea of mortal life, and the constantly repeated cycles of rebirth from which there is no release until all earth's lessons have been learned. The sea typifies the pulsating and rhythmical currents of life which ofttimes become tempestuous in travail and sorrow. The sound of the restless, surging ocean of life, upon which the soul is driven to and fro seeking the haven of Love Eternal, forms the dominant theme of the opera.

At the expiration of each seventh incarnation, Cosmic Law grants a lifetime of rest. This is always a period of relative repose and well-being, when the soul can contemplate past losses and gains and make preparation for the cycle of lives to come. It is an incarnation in which the ego is free from paying cosmic debts and under no impelling urge or compulsion to learn new lessons. It is simply retrospecting, recapitulating, assimilating into soul power the experiences of the past. It is a sabbatical period and as such, free from trial or pain.

This represents the normal life pattern. However, repeated earth lives dedicated to the pursuit of evil can destroy the normal design and place the ego under the power of the Brothers of the Shadow—represented in this legend by the Devil. In this lamentable state the ego will, through repeated earth lives, move farther away from the normal incarnational pattern. If he be not rescued through the mighty transforming power of love, he gradually loses touch with his own life wave and is drawn back into Chaos, there to await a new evolutionary impulse into which he may enter and begin once again a long cycle of earth pilgrimages.

Fortunately, such a tragic fate is not a common one. Its possibility, however, is kept alive in legends such as *The Journeyings of Ulysses, The Wandering Jew* and *The Flying Dutchman.* "The soul that sinneth shall die" is an occult axiom bearing a far deeper meaning than is generally suspected.

God is Love . . . . and God is Law. In harmony with the Divine Plan for every human emergency there is a way out. This way lies wholly in the Love-Light of the soul which reveals it.

It is significant that Wagner never chose legends for use in his immortal operas merely because they are pretty or fanciful. True beauty always has meaning. That prettiness which is of the outer form side only but is empty within is not the whole Signature of God. But beauty flowing outward from the soul is indeed truth, for it is the embodiment, the revelation of Divine Intelligence. It is only by this divine understanding within us that we can perceive beauty at all, in any of its manifestations.

Wagner chose, as the basis for his operas, themes which illustrate profoundest truths. They cover every phase of the evolutionary progress and development of mankind. Taken as a whole, the Wagnerian operas constitute the most complete outline of Initiation through music ever revealed to our race.

Without doubt this method of development would have been introduced into the model School of Music which Wagner attempted to establish in Munich and would have been a later addition to the work he established at Bayreuth. He was often heard to declare that Bayreuth was destined to become the art center of the world. His passing almost immediately after the first presentation of *Parsifal* terminated the hope of bringing into actuality his dream of an Art Temple. Its fulfillment, however, was only postponed, not defeated. A new generation will one day appreciate the true worth of this greatest of musical seers, and a new world will see the establishment of a school such as Wagner dreamed of, wherein definite processes of soul illumination will be unfolded in harmony with Wagnerian music. This will be done step by step as he has carefully outlined them in his operas, with the music of each score setting the keynote of the particular aspect of soul development portrayed by the story. Though misunderstood in his own day, Wagner was perceptive enough to know that another and wiser age would understand, appreciate and utilize the profound musical truths he came to impart to the world.

THE OVERTURE

The Overture to *The Flying Dutchman* contains a musical summary of the opera as a whole. It is somber in tone and expressive of tempestuous emotions and a strange, sinister influence. Wagner describes it thus:

> Driven along by the fury of the gale, the terrible ship of the Flying Dutchman approaches the shore and reaches the land, where its captain has been promised he shall one day find salvation and deliverance We hear the compassionate tones of this promise which affect us like prayers and lamentations. Gloomy in appearance and bereft of hope, the doomed man is listening to them also. Weary and longing for death, he paces the strand, while his crew, worn and tired of life, are silently employed in making all taut on board. How often has he, ill-fated, gone through the same scene? How often has he steered his ship on ocean's billows to the inhabited shores on which, at each seven years' truce, he has been permitted to land? How many times has he fancied he has reached the limit of his torment, and alas, how repeatedly has he, terribly undeceived, been obliged to betake himself again to his wild wanderings at sea? In order that he may secure release by death he has made common cause in his anguish with the flood and the tempests against himself; he has driven his ship into the gaping gulf of the billows, yet the gulf has not swallowed

it up; through the surf of the breakers he has steered it upon the rocks, yet the rocks have not broken it to pieces. All the terrible dangers of the sea at which he once laughed in his wild eagerness for energetic action now mock at him. They do him no injury. Under a curse he is doomed to wander over the ocean's waste in quest of treasures which fail to reanimate him, and without finding that alone which can renew him.

Swiftly a smart looking ship sails by him. He hears the jovial, familiar song of its crew as returning from a voyage they make jolly on returning home. Enraged at their merry humor he gives chase and comes up with them in the gale, and so scares them that they become mute and take to flight. From the depths of his terrible misery he shrieks out for redemption. In his horrible banishment from mankind it is a woman alone who can bring him salvation. Where and in what country tarries this deliverer? Where is the feeling heart to sympathize with his woes? Where is She who will not turn away from him in horror and fright like those cowardly fellows who hold up the cross at his approach?

A lurid light now breaks through the darkness; like lightning it pierces his tortured soul. It vanishes and again beams forth. Keeping his eye upon his guiding star the sailor steers toward it over waves and floods. What is it that so powerfully attracts him but the gaze of a woman, who, full of divine sadness and sublime sympathy, is drawn towards him? A heart has opened its uttermost depths to the awful sorrows of this ill-fated one; it cannot but sacrifice itself for his sake, and breaking in sympathy for him annihilate itself in his woes. The unhappy one is overwhelmed by the divine appearance; his ship is broken in pieces and swallowed up in the gulf of the billows, but he, saved and exalted, emerges from the waves, with his victorious deliverer at his side, and ascends to Heaven, led by the rescuing hand of sublimest Love.

When Wagner translated his original dramatic poem of *The Flying Dutchman* into the opera he divided it into three parts or acts. The first is called *The Coming of the Phantom Ship* and introduces its mysterious Captain. The second is descriptive of the Norwegian girl, Senta, the foreordained woman in whose quest the strange mariner has sailed for uncounted years across so many seas. This second part is therefore termed appropriately *The Recognition*. The third and final act of the drama describes the proving of Senta, the young maiden, faithful to her pledge, even unto death and–beyond. This third part is called *The Immortal Pact.*

In their application to human life, the first act deals with the workings of the Law of Retribution as it operates in the life of one who sets his human will above Divine Will; the second act reveals how, through suffering and remorse, the higher nature (the woman) is discovered and recognized at first sight; the third and final act shows the indissoluble union of the human with the Divine. The attainment of this union is the purpose of all earthly incarnations. When finally effected it is proof against time, place and condition. Death has no power over it for it belongs to eternity.

Ernest Newman, in his *Stories of the Great Operas,* writes that the Overture to *The Flying Dutchman* is the finest piece of work in its genre the world has known since the great overtures of Beethoven. He also states that it is a worthy forerunner to the overtures to *The Mastersingers* and *Tannhauser.*

We shall take occasion in the course of these interpretations to stress the importance of Wagner's work from the viewpoint of musical psychology. For example, in *The Flying Dutchman* two principal motifs underlie the operatic score, the first expressing the anxious and reckless questing of the Dutchman–the Ocean theme–and the other, the transcendently beautiful theme of Redemption which highlights the entire work.

The Dutchman motif, sounded in the horns, is generally followed by the malediction which pursues the homeless seafarer. The latter is expressed in a curious dissonance sounded by the wood winds. This is followed by a repetition of the theme conveying the Dutchman's restless search and the agony accompanying it as death continues to elude him.

As the Norwegian ship approaches, the wood winds give forth rollicking strains of the Sailors' Chorus. This is followed by the Dutchman's motif sounded in the horns as, raging with envy and remorse, the Flying Dutchman pursues the speeding ship through the wild storm.

Suddenly the wailing minor tones are changed to major. The unhappy man has glimpsed a vision of the woman. As this vision proclaims the turning point in his life and marks the beginning of his upward climb, the Overture music now sounds forth the glorious theme of Redemption. As the Overture draws to a close, the Dutchman's motif, until now sad and sorrowful, takes on the strains of joyous triumph.

Thus did Wagner, at the early age of twenty-eight, depict in music an entire incarnational cycle.

ACT I

The first act is pregnant with the atmosphere of the sea. There are great cliffs and a rugged shoreline upon which huge waves hammer unceasingly. The Norwegian sailors sing their lusty "Yeho! Yeho! Yeho! Land ho!" as their Captain, Daland, scans the stormy landscape and thinks longingly of his daughter Senta and his nearby home.

The genial appearance of Daland's ship and the happiness of his crew are in strange contrast to that of the Phantom Ship and its ghostly sailors. Silently, yet swifter tnan the wind, sails this strange black craft with its blood-red sails and its brooding, melancholy Captain, dressed in a black Spanish costume and wearing long dark flowing tresses. This contrast is strikingly marked in the music where we hear the jolly Sailors' Song from one ship and the dark sinister Dutchman's motif from the other.

The wild passion of the music mounts as the anguished Dutchman prays alternately for death or salvation. Defiantly he challenges the mighty ocean that ever changes while his pain is eternal. His passionate agony is voiced in his cry: "Cursed am I for aye! For love and faith unchanging in vain I pray!" As he falls exhausted by suffering, the passion of the orchestra ebbs to quivering notes of the basses and kettle drums. His final hope is the destruction that must eventually overcome the earth and so bring him to the peace and rest of death. Mournfully his erstwhile silent crew chant after him, "Endless destruction upon us all."

We have already commented on the fate which sometimes overtakes a few souls, fortunately rare, who by continued pursuit of evil through many lifetimes cut themselves off from the human race and must take up their evolution in some new and strange life wave of the future. Such a lot is intimated in the Dutchman's speech concerning the final destruction of the earth. That soul which binds itself to the earth must of necessity perish with the earth. But note well, this statement is made of the *soul*, not of the *spirit*. Soul is the product of spirit working in and through bodily form. Forms are fleeting, perishable. The soul is relatively immortal but may be "lost." Spirit, a portion of the Divine Whole, is indestructible. It possesses absolute immortality.

Wagner has magnificently set forth in musical contrasts the condition of those following the normal life pattern and those dark spirits who have come under control of the Brothers of Shadow.

It is inevitable that Daland and the strange Captain should meet. Heaps of gold and rare jeweled treasure are spread before Daland's astonished gaze when he speaks of his daughter, Senta. "Perhaps she is an angel," murmurs the Dutchman as he makes ready to accompany the Norwegian Captain to his home.

ACT II

The setting of the second act is a room in Daland's home. His daughter Senta sits in dreamy, abstracted silence, gazing upon a portrait of the Flying Dutchman hanging on the opposite wall. Senta is surrounded by a group of merry girl companions who, as they sit working at their wheels, sing the famous Spinning Song. This music is beautifully harmonious and lyrical in its composition, yet it is fraught with indefinable mystery and half-revealed meanings. The ceaseless hum of the spinning wheel with its winding threads symbolizes Destiny or Fate which spins, measures and binds all moral existence.

Senta seems altogether removed from the laughing, carefree girls. She neither spins with them nor does she join in their song. Later, however, she sings of the sad fate of the Flying Dutchman; and then, rising to a state of exaltation, she declares she has been appointed to bring his redemption: "O may God's angel hither speed thee, my love, to grace again I'll lead thee!"

Wagner said that Senta's song contained the principal psychological interest of this opera. "It was," he declared, "the picture *in petto* of the whole drama as it stood before my soul."

The young maidens so much in love with things of this world typify average humanity. Senta, the girl remote and detached from all wordly things, praying only that she may sacrifice herself to save another who has entered the downward path, represents the aspirant upon the Way of Illumination.

Until this moment Senta has been looked upon as betrothed to young Eric, who has loved her for many years but has been away on a journey. She has, however, forgotten him in her spiritually romatic love for the Dutchman whom she has never seen. Eric represents all that is normal and natural in human love, good in itself but an obstruction on the Path of Holiness when once a soul has been awakened by the call of Spirit to its disciplines.

As Senta passionately declares that she is chosen to sacrifice herself for the Flying Dutchman, her companions spring to their feet in terror. Eric, who has entered the room in time to hear Senta's declaration, says he will save her from herself for she is mad. He announces that Daland's ship is in sight, and the girls, forgetting Senta, rush laughing and shouting from the house to greet their lovers.

Eric seizes this opportunity to press his suit. In a soft, lovely aria he pleads for Senta's love. She rejects his pleas, telling him her one purpose is to redeem the Dutchman from his endless suffering

Eric recounts a dream he has had in which he witnessed the coming of Senta's strange love and their sailing away together. The girl cries, "Oh he seeks for me! His fate I must share!" As Eric desparingly leaves her, saying, "I have lost her! My dream was true!" Senta gazes at the portrait of the Flying Dutchman and beseeches heaven to grant the prayer that her life and love may save him. With her final words the door opens and her father and the man of mystery stands before her.

When Daland enters the room accompained by the fateful stranger, the orchestra sweeps into à joyous rhythm as a look of soul recognition passes between Senta and the Dutchman. Beautifully expressive is the duet in which they sing of their recognition and at-one-ment. Then the music slips into minor strains as he warns her of the heavy cost of renunciation, but once again soars in happy majors as she pledges her faith for all time and eternity: "Him whom I choose, I choose forevermore."

Senta now appeals to heaven for strength to remain steadfast to her pledge. Here she voices a new and higher note than she has sung before in "What power is this that through and through doth thrill me!" The Dutchman repeats this note as he sings: "Thy voice is music in my night of woe." Then their voices are united in divine ecstasy. The transmutation of his lower nature has begun. Hand in hand they vow eternal fidelity. Daland enters and the act concludes with a bright and happy trio "Come to the Wedding Feast. Today let all rejoice."

ACT III

In the beginning of the third act the new and exquisite note of Senta's Ecstasy hovers above the carefree abandon of the Sailors' Song. The sailors are joined by village maidens who have brought food and drink, and soon the deck of the ship is ringing with merriment as they sing and dance.

In contrast again is the silent and ghostly bark of the Flying Dutchman, with its great black hulk and blood-red sails—described by the orchestra in dark and somber arpeggios.

The sailors, in an excess of jollity and merrymaking, mischievously taunt the crew of the gloomy craft: "They are old and grey, their hearts are lead, and all their sweethearts a long time dead." A weird, blue light appears on the spectral ship, its beams agitating nearby waters although the vast expanse of ocean round about is quiet and still. A violent wind sweeps through its sails as out of its depths are heard the supernatural voices of its ghostly sailors: "What care we how fast we go! Satan fills our sails! Yeho!"

The joyous Sailors' Song from the Norwegian ship is in C major. With the opening of the spectral Chorus the music changes to a plaintive wail in C sharp minor. Wagner, in accord with the laws of esoteric music, uses minor keys to depict the supernatural and subjective, major keys to describe the normal and objective. Intermingling with the music of the Sailors' Song and the spectral Chorus is heard softly in the deep basses an echo, as it were, of the Dutchman's motif, followed still more softly by the soothing motif of Redemption, whereupon the Norwegian sailors, awed and hushed, make the sign of the Cross.

Senta appears to strains of the Redemptive music, followed by Eric who pleads again for her love and beseeches her to renounce the Dutchman. The latter approaches and, hearing Eric accuse Senta of faithlessness, is overwhelmed with despair. He cries out "Lost all my hopes of Heaven!"

Senta calls to Eric, "I must no longer think of thee for a higher duty calls." Then, with face alight in high and holy resolve, she turns to the Dutchman: "Thy bitter sorrow now shall have an end. 'Tis I whose love shall bring thy Redemption." Here again the strains of the Dutchman's motif are heard, followed and blessed, as it seems, by the soft clear notes of the Redemptive music.

The Dutchman now speaks to Senta in a voice filled with the sorrow of long centuries, bidding her stay with her human love and leave him to his sad and terrible state. He wishes to save her from the curse of a like fate which would surely be her portion were she to break her troth with him. This curse is "eternal damnation," but only in the sense previously defined as the loss of one's humanity, not the hell fire of orthodox concept.

As the dark and gloomy figure turns to his ship and bids the sailors depart, he says that he is the Flying Dutchman whose very name has sent terror into human hearts. Then the ghostly ship departs, its crew singing their wild unearthly chorus.

Senta, the only one in the assembled crowd who is unafraid, seeks to follow the Dutchman but is restrained by Eric and her father. However, as the ship puts out to sea, she looses herself from them and throws herself from a high cliff into the waters, crying. "My life is nothing to me unless thou be redeemed."

With Senta's sublime act of renunciation the strange ship suddenly disappears from sight—symbolic of the complete submergence of the physical in the spiritual. The terrestrial has become the celestial.

As the dark ship disappears the sunrise of a bright new day floods sky and sea, and the Dutchman, his face transfigured and with Senta clasped in his arms, rises from the waves and ascends toward heaven to the accompaniment of his own motif, now softened and beautified, together with the motif of Redemption sounding from wood winds and harps—the sublime culmination of human Transfiguration set to music.

Wagner says of this opera:

> The Flying Dutchman is a mythical creation of the folk. A primal trait of human nature speaks out from it with a heart-enthralling force. This trait in its most universal meaning is the longing for rest after the storms of life. The sea in its turn became the soul of life; yet no longer the land-locked sea of the Grecian world but the great ocean that engirdles the earth. The fetters of the older world were broken, the longing of Ulysses for home and hearth and wedded life, until it became a yearning for death that had mounted to the craving for a new and unknown home, invisible as yet, but dimly boded. This broader feature confronts us in *The Flying Dutchman,* that seaman's poem of the world-historical age of journeys of discovery. Here we discover a remarkable mixture, a blend effected by the spirit of the folk, of the character of Ulysses with that of the Wandering Jew; the Hollandic mariner in punishment for his temerity is condemned by the Devil to do battle with the unresting waves for all eternity. Like Ahaseurus, he longs for his sufferings to be ended by death. The Dutchman, however, may gain this redemption by the hands of a Woman who for very love shall sacrifice herself for him. The yearning for death thus spurs him on to seek this Woman; but she is no longer the home-tending Penelope of Ulysses, as courted in the days of old, but the quintessence of womankind; and yet the still unmanifest, the longed-for, the dreamed-of, the infinitely womanly—let me express it in one word—The Woman of the Future.

In the esoteric musical Schools of the future music will come to be widely employed as a purifying and transmuting agent. Already in psychological experimentation, the power of music to cure mental disorders is known and demonstrated. It remains with the esotericist to use this wonderful power to heal the soul and liberate its hidden potentialities. The Redemptive motif and that of Senta's Ecstasy are medicines of immortality in the truest sense of the words and will be so used in these New Age Schools, particularly as we come to understand more perfectly the nature and function of the "Eternal Feminine" of Goethe, the "The Woman of the Future" of Wagner.

As Wagner has said, the "entire opera evolved spontaneously from a single dramatic germ"–Senta's Ecstasy motif in the second act. This he wrote first, and he said of it that "It contains the whole conception of the opera in essence." Thus it is shown that the redemption of the lower nature by means of the higher is the central purpose of all earthly pilgrimages. In one way or another, it lies with the Divine Feminine to lead mankind upward to the eternal Consummation. From Ariadne to Senta we see this principle exemplified in the folk lore of all nations.

CHAPTER II

The Mastersingers

(Die Meistersinger)

Musical Schools of Initiation

INNER-PLANE MUSICAL SCHOOLS AND THEIR INSPIRED MINSTRELSY

THOSE who are accustomed to regard everything from the material point of view find it difficult to think of the realm of the soul as being no less substantial to its inhabitants than the physical world is to them. They cannot realize that the soul has an ethereal body with senses peculiar to itself (our organs of psychism), and that even while we are incarnate in physical bodies we are really living souls, with a spiritual nature that to some degree permeates and overshadows our outer personality. In the ordinary course of events this soul-self is released only by the Death Angel, at which time it matures.

But there are techniques whereby the higher self may be liberated during the lifetime of the physical body. As earthly physicians labor physically to assist in the birth of a babe, so do unseen physicians and teachers work lovingly and skillfully to bring a soul to birth in their realm.

Some of these teachers and physicians are of the so-called "dead;" some are members of various angelic Hierarchies; others are men and women Initiates who have learned to dwell simultaneously in the worlds of matter and soul, and are deeply desirous that their fellowmen share their privileges. For the treasure of the soul grows by sharing, so there is no object in retaining for themselves alone their precious wisdom.

When we understand that the soul is not a mere wraith, but that it has a soul-body and soul-senses (psychic powers), we are in a position to realize what is meant when our great teachers tell us that on inner planes there are schools for the promulgation of the arts just as there are upon the earth.

Among the Art Schools of the soul world, the one centered in musical consciousness—or on the Musical Ray, as we term it in esoteric parlance—is basic to all others. There is no art which cannot be resolved into music whereas music cannot be interpreted to a like degree in techniques of other arts.

Thus, the inner plane School of Music is of paramount importance. It reflects in its structure the cosmic pattern revealed in the stars. Its musicianship is acquired under the tutelage of Angels and Archangels who "step down" the divine harmonies intoned by the twelve zodiacal Hierarchies and who assist a soul to hear the "music of the spheres" belonging to its own planetary chain. The earth also has its keynote and its cosmic song, from which earthly musicians draw their inspiration.

Musicians of the higher plane have built their own Temple of Initiation, and every true musician on earth contributes to the beauty of this structure, whether he is aware of it or not. When he has reached that point in his soul's maturity where he is ripe for induction into the higher world, an emissary from the Brotherhood is sent to instruct him in necessary techniques and to assist him in his entry into their company as a Lay Brother.

Following the cosmic pattern, their Temple is under the supervision of twelve Masters who, from time to time, send forth representatives to earth. Such a messenger was Richard Wagner.

In biblical times the exalted Masters of the Temple worked through Schools of the Prophets founded by Samuel, the great Initiate-Singer of his day. Prophets wooed the Divine Mother Wisdom with song and dance, in order to induce the trance of ecstasy by which their soul was liberated from the body. After Samuel, David was the great Initiate of the bibical School. His harp has become its symbol. We read that Elisha—the great prototype of Jesus as Elijah was of John the Baptist—was accustomed to play upon his harp when he sought to enter the prophetic state. And it was a saying of Israelite Seers that the Shekinah (Christians called Her *Sophia)* avoided gloominess and tears and, further, would bless with Her Presence only the soul which came to Her in gladness and joy. Her coming was said to have been heralded by the glory of light and by joyous ringing of little silver bells. (The beloved Saint Theresa also believed that gloom and piety were incompatible).

Arabic poets organized their great Schools with the same idea in mind. During the time when Moslem civilization was at its height, Islamic poetry was composed with the deliberate aim of lifting the soul into a state of ecstasy. In fact, scholars tell us that the dervish cults of the Arab are similar to Schools of the Prophets of ancient biblical times.

The Renaissance in Europe was the fruitage of Moslem influence, first through Spain and Southern France, and then through the Crusades which brought Christians into direct contact with Moslem culture in its own world. From ancient Druidic times European minstrels had been wandering singers and teachers. During the Middle Ages they visited every part of the known world; and medieval minstrelsy in Europe showed marked Islamic influence, especially of its Persian branch, from first to last. The downfall of Toledo made available to the Christian world in general the great libraries of the Moors and started a new wave of thought in Europe. Toledo was famous for its schools of magic and alchemy. Legends tell us that the first version of the Legend of the Holy Grail was discovered in manuscript in the Toledo library. Also according to legend, the Grail Castle was built on a high eminence in Spain. Wagner locates his Castle in *Parsifal* on the border between France and Spain.

The south of France was the original paradise of the Troubadours or Love Singers. Their regime came to an end with the bloody Albigensian Wars, when the esoteric School founded by the great Persian Master, Mani, was wiped out, and the civilization of Southern France with it. It is not known for how many centuries the Manichean Church was present in the south of France, but it suddenly flowered in the twelfth century and swept like wildfire over that sunny land, seriously threatening the survival of the Church of Rome. Even the Catholics in the land were influenced by the presence in their midst of a highly esoteric Mystery Religion whose supreme Head was for a time located at Babylon and then at Samarkand, and has been identified by some with the mysterious Prester John, King of the Holy Grail of Christian legend.

Certain it is that the Troubadours were strongly influenced by this colorful Persian Christianity, and when the Albigensian Wars brought the flourishing Southern civilization to an untimely end, these Singers scattered throughout Europe, preaching and singing rebellion against Rome. Many found sanctuary with the German King, and formed the nucleus from which there developed in that land the principal European School of initiatory music. From Wolfram von Eschenbach, whose *Parsifal* shows Manichean-Islamic influence, to Richard Wagner, Germany has produced more esoteric musicians than any other country in the world. It was these Troubadours and their comrades, the Minnesingers, who fomented the Reformation, which was achieved in the sixteenth century, the period in which *Die Meistersinger* is laid. Hans Sachs, the mastersinger of this opera, was one of Luther's supporters.

When an emissary from the Hierarchy is sent into the world, he establishes such organizations as he deems necessary to carry out the divine purpose for that period. Thus, when the art of creative music was no longer the exclusive property of the nobles, as in the times of the Troubadours and Minnesingers, but had broadened to include craftsmen, Guilds were organized to serve as Schools and Mystery Temples. In fourteenth century France, for example, there was the *Consistoire du Gai Savoir*, whose founders were "learned, subtle, and discreet," and who defined their object as a desire to serve "that excellent and virtuous Lady Science so that she might furnish and give them the gay art of writing in verse and teach them to make good poems so that they might speak and recite good and remarkable words . . . in praise of God, our Lord, and his glorious Mother and all the saints of paradise for the instruction of the ignorant, for the restraint of foolish lovers, and in order that all might live in joy and happiness and dispel boredom and sadness, the enemies of the Gay Science." All these objectives are realized most beautifully in *Die Meistersinger*.

In Germany the Guild of Mastersingers at Nuremberg was a society similar to that just described. Nuremberg was long venerated as the repository of the Sacred Lance which, together with the Grail, were the holiest relics of Christendom.

The Guild of Mastersingers consisted of three general divisions or degrees, and five steps or grades with twelve

Masters at the head. The three general Degrees were Apprentices (students), Companions (neophytes) and Masters (Initiates). The five grades were (1) pupils; (2) school friends, who must know something of the *Tabulatur* (rules) and a certain number of tones and poems; (3) singers, who were able to sing without error a given number of these; (4) poets, who must make new poems on the old models; (5) Masters, who won their title by inventing a new tone and a new mode. There were two kinds of singing, free and chief. Secular subjects were permitted in the former and the song meetings were held in inns. The latter were always convened in a church on Sundays or on certain festival days. The annual Trial Contest for Mastersingers was held on high and holy St. John's Day in the sacred season of the Summer Solstice.

The Master Songs were always unaccompanied and could not be printed or sung in public. They were looked upon as sacred and were given a holy Baptism under the sponsorship of certain chosen godparents selected on the basis of their spiritual qualifications.

The Song Contests held by these Guilds with so much pomp and ceremony were originally examinations preparatory to various degrees of Initiation by Music. When the neophyte became a Master his opportunities for service were greatly enhanced. Through his knowledge of musical therapy he could bring peace, harmony and healing where needed. Thus he became both priest and physician in his exalted rank of Mastersinger.

The badge and banner of the Mastersingers' Guild were emblazoned with an image of King David and his sacred harp, the harp bearing a special meaning in connection with the Degree of Mastership. Like the lyre of Orpheus in the Greek Mysteries, the seven strings of David's harp typify the seven psychic centers of the soul body—corresponding to the planetary notes of the cosmic scale—whose awakening in man brings self-mastery.

The harp is, therefore, a fitting symbol of heavenly harmony, "the music of the spheres," which resounds in nature as the sun passes each month through a different constellation of the zodiac. This divine harmony underlies the creation of all natural beauty. The Order of the Universe falls into its perfect patterns according to the cosmic keynote, a blend of the twelve tones of the twelve celestial Hierarchies. Esoteric musicians know that music or tone is central to the whole creative process and is the primary factor in the expression of all that is beautiful.

As Age yields to Age, training offered in Schools of Initiation gradually changes in accordance with men's development. New ideals are implanted in humanity from generation to generation by qualified emissaries from the Great White Lodge. If they are to succeed in their undertaking, all such pioneering leaders must have an inner conviction of the righteousness of their mission, which will give them strength and courage to go forward in spite of hostile opposition by those who do not understand new and added revelation. Only a comparatively few are ever ready to accept the message of a pioneer. It requires time for the masses to outgrow those ideas which, by tradition and custom, are accepted as belonging to an unchanging order of things. But every form is, by its very nature, transient. The creative spirit is ever expanding and must, therefore, periodically renew and enlarge the forms through which it expresses itself. When, for this reason, more advanced egos withdraw from forms, institutional or ceremonial, that have been outgrown, they lose this sustaining power and eventually become mere empty shells devoid of life and significance. Then they are a hindrance rather than a help to those who still adhere to them, fearing to let go of the old for the new. All forms and beliefs that have lost their inner meaning ultimately disintegrate, since neither man nor institutions can stand still. They either move forward or fall backward.

It must be admitted, however, that even in retrogression ceremonials created by Seers and Initiates continue for a long period to carry something of the initiatory impress, just as paintings of great masters continue to shine with the spiritual power originally imparted to them though the canvas itself is in process of disintegration. Ceremonials of the Church and of certain lodges are not without value from the standpoint of their initiatory vibration which may help an individual unseal founts of power.

Those who remain heads of organizations that have become static because they have lost contact with their original spiritual impulse, are generally the strictest adherents to established forms which they regard with superstitious awe. They therefore guard them jealously against any change whatsoever. If perpetuated, such a condition would lead to complete crystallization and decay. Masters of wisdom endeavor to forestall this by sending forth from time to time emissaries bearing a new message keyed to humanity's growth and changing needs. These messengers are vibrant with life from the Source of divine power. Such was the mission of Walter von Staltzing to the ancient and conservative Guild of Mastersingers of Nuremberg and he received the treatment always accorded pioneers by warders of the old order. And so was Wagner received when he came to bring his New Age musical gospel.

The high spiritual knowledge possessed by Knightly Orders as described in *Tannhauser* (the true Minnesingers or Love Singers) also fell into more materialized conventions when the craftsmen in cities formed themselves into Guilds of Mastersingers with a rigid *Tabalatur*.

The Minnesingers journeyed through many lands disseminating their secret truths as honored guests of kings and nobles, their interest centering primarily in the life of their immediate communities. Thus, it may be seen how easy it was for the latter to become narrow and pedantic, and to lose the true spirit and purpose of their work in form and rote. Yet these Mastersingers were close to the masses of people and, with all their faults, they did bring esoteric truth to folk who otherwise would never have had it. Besides, they unquestionably fostered a great impulse toward religious freedom which culminated in the Reformation under Luther.

The Mastersingers of Nuremberg traced their origin to Heinrich von Meissen who founded a Society of Minstrels in Mainz. (It was at Bierbich, just westward across the Rhine from Mainz, that Wagner composed *Die Meistersinger.*) Dissentions in the Guild at Mainz caused the minstrel Nestler to withdraw and, with his followers, to establish the Nuremberg Guild of Mastersingers. This was the group of which Hans Sachs later became leader and chief source of inspiration. Sachs began his work at the age of nineteen, and left to his followers thousands of songs and poems, farces and fables.

Wagner used authentic historical material in *Die Meistersinger.* He writes in one of his letters that the tones and modes used in this work are genuine and that some of the wording in the choruses is taken from the original works of Hans Sachs.

Interpretation of the the Music Drama

PREFATORY NOTE

The immortal pianist, Ignace Paderewski, has been quoted as saying that he considered *Die Meistersinger* "Not only the greatest work of genius ever achieved by a musician, but the greatest ever achieved by any artist in any field of human activity."

It was in his comparatively early years that Wagner made his initial sketch of *Die Meistersinger.* It must have been almost immediately after his completion of *Tannhauser.* In his autobiography he gives a most colorful and vivid account of the opera's inception.

In 1845 he writes that when *Tannhauser* was completed he went for a holiday to the medicinal baths at Marienbad, Bohemia. He took with him the medieval poems of Wolfram von Eschenbach together with the annonymous epic, *Lohengrin.* There, in the deep brooding silence of pine forests, he dwelt in a dream world—in company, as he tells us, with Titurel, Parsifal and Lohengrin. This high state of contemplation produced in him such intense creative excitement that to calm his nerves he sought relaxation in working out a musical study based on the lives of the Mastersingers of Nuremberg. Nothing more was done with this opera, however, for many years to come.

While visiting friends in Venice one summer Wagner, standing in contemplation before Titian's *Assumption of the Virgin,* became aware that "it exercised a most sublime influence upon me. . . . My old powers flashed through me, and as though by a sudden flash of inspiration I determined at once to begin to work upon *Die Meistersinger.*" During a train journey from Venice to Vienna he began work upon the score, still unfinished from the Marienbad days of sixteen years previous. "At this time," he adds, "I conceived with the utmost distinctness the principal part of the Prelude in C Major."

From Paris Wagner wrote, "I often laugh aloud when I raise my eyes from my work and see from my window the Tuileries and Louvre straight opposite, for you must know that my real self is now roaming the streets of Nuremberg and mixing with somewhat blunt and square-cornered folk." He also says that it was while strolling through the galleries of the Palais Royale, on the way to the Taverne Anglaise, that he conceived the melody for the great chorale with which the populace in the final act greets their beloved Mastersinger, Hans Sachs.

Cosima Wagner wrote to her father, Franz Liszt, sensitively and feelingly regarding this work: "*Die Meistersinger* is to Wagner's creations what the *Winter's Tale* is to Shakespeare's other works. Wagner's imagination has made an excursion into realms of mischievous gaiety and has so conjured up medieval Nuremberg with its guilds and corporations, its craftsmen poets, its pedants and its knights, as to call forth in the sublimest and most noble way the laughter that does most to emancipate the spirit. Its artistic conception," she continues, "may be compared with the tabernacle in the Church of St. Laurence; like the sculpture of the tabernacle, the musician has here achieved the purest and most graceful form. And just as at the base of the tabernacle Adam Krafft bears up and supports the whole structure with an expression of grave and concentrated reverence, so in *Die Meistersinger* it is the figure of Hans Sachs that dominates and directs the action with a cheerful and lovable serenity."

Another time Cosima writes, apropos of the same subject: "If I could send you the wondrous music I am hearing! It is like a deep musical radiance. In this sunlit transport one does not know whether one is listening to light or seeing sound." And so saying, she puts into inspired words the joyous charm which is this opera's most distinctive quality—the golden translucence which is not color, which cannot be said to shine, but nonetheless pervades the atmosphere with its exquisite radiance and gives us a true perception of the beauty and peace and happiness known to the Mastersingers at their best. Against the background of this golden air, we behold in *Die Meistersinger* a colorful pageant of the later Middle Ages which is, to the layman, enjoyable as pure music and rich drama, while to the instructed it reveals mysteries of the deepest spiritual import.

THE PRELUDE

The Overture or Prelude to *Die Meistersinger* is magnificent. The opening chords are stately and dignified, a musical representation of the twelve Mastersingers of Nuremberg. Mingling with this, the theme of the Old, is a theme of the New, introduced by Walter, which has in it elements of immortality since it is centered in Love, the greatest of all powers. This motif runs throughout the opera. It sparkles and shimmers with vibrant delicacy, illuminating the whole work, so is termed the "Waking Tone."

This Prelude has been rated the finest Overture ever written. The entire score has been passed upon by critics as flawless. In Wagner's own words, it contains "the drama's leading thoughts, but not the individual fate of single persons."

The Prelude is composed of five principal themes. Two of these are descriptive of the pompous and stately Mastersingers; the other three pertain to the love and wooing of Walter and Eva.

The opening motif, that of the Mastersingers, admirably depicts their attitude—self-important and pedantic. This is followed by the Masters' fanfare in brass, woodwind and strings. Wagner adapted this theme from one of the original Meistersinger melodies.

The Master Song of Walter is now introduced faintly—an echo, as it were, of what is to come. This is followed by the Love motif, heard in its fullness during the Song Contest. Then appears the dainty and beautiful Call of Spring, the motif used by Walter in his first Trial before the Masters when Hans Sachs recognizes his great poetic and musical genius. The exquisite strains of this motif now merge into a lighter version of the Mastersingers, wherein the quarrelsome and ludicrous Beckmesser motif is most pronounced.

The Prelude's magnificent finale is largely a kaleidoscopic musical display of the happenings of St. John's Day: the failure of Beckmesser amid the laughter of the people; the crowning of Walter and the people's chorus in appreciation thereof; the homage of the Masters and the people for Hans Sachs.

Writes Wagner in his autobiography: "As from the balcony of my home is a sunset of great splendour. I gazed upon the magnificent spectacle of Golden Mayence with the majestic Rhine flowing along its outskirts in a glory of light, the prelude to my Meistersinger again suddenly made its presence closely and distinctly felt in my soul. Once before had I seen it rise before me out of a lake of sorrow like some distant mirage. I proceeded to write down the prelude exactly as it appears today in the score, that is, containing the clear outline of the leading themes of the whole drama. I proceeded at once to continue the composition, intending to allow the remaining scenes to follow in due succession."

The Overture ends in an uplifting climax, the themes of the Old and the New triumphantly blended. So it is that the Overture is a musical summary of the story, showing in miniature how the disdain and antagonism of the Mastersingers becomes acclaim and homage upon Walter's rendition of his Prize Song.

ACT I

In the cast of *Die Meistersinger* Wagner used the names of actual persons who held membership in the Nuremberg Guild, as evidenced by a descriptive document compiled by J. C. Wegenseil and published in 1697 in Altdorf. Two of the motifs, The Banner and The Art Brotherhood, are also taken from actual "Prize Mastertones" from the same source.

The principal characters of the opera are: Hans (German for John) Sachs, leader of the Guild of Mastersingers and Teacher of neophytes who aspire to become Masters; Walter Von Stolzing, messenger of the New and candidate for the Degree of Mastership in the Guild; Pogner, a goldsmith, second in importance to Hans Sachs among the Mastersingers; Eva, Pogner's daughter and the beloved of Walter, represents the Divine Feminine, without whose inspiration man can never attain the heights of Mastership; Beckmesser, the town clerk, a member of the Guild and aspirant for Eva's love, represents the lower nature which, throughout the action of the story, is expressed as envy, jealousy, dishonesty and untruthfulness; David, apprentice to Hans Sachs.

As previously observed in connection with the Prelude, Wagner gives to each of his characters a particular motif descriptive of the person's essential nature. This motif always accompanies the character and becomes, as it were, a musical signature. For example, Walter is presented to the Mastersingers to the accompaniment of the Love motif, well describing his handsome person and pleasing manner. The motif of Beckmesser is characterized by dissonances indicative of his evil and quarrelsome nature.

The motif of Hans Sachs is noble, soothing and elevating, in accordance with his greatness of soul and his tender, compassionate nature. David's motif is as bright and merry as the lad himself. His light tones alternate with the stately Meistersinger measures. With a consciousness of his own self-importance, he essays to coach Walter for the Song Contest.

The locale of the opera is sixteenth century Nuremberg. The opening scene is laid in the interior of the Church of St. Katherine where the morning service is in progress. The solemn and stately measures of the choral of St. John are heard, sung by the congregation. There is a long pause after each line of the choral during which the worshippers' attention may occasionally wander. At one side of the church, leaning against a pillar, the young Knight, Walter, is seen. He is evidently much attracted by the beauty and charm of Eva, who is not unaware of his presence. After the service Walter, a stranger in Nuremberg, makes inquires about Eva and learns that her father, the goldsmith-Mastersinger Pogner, will give his daughter in marriage to the winner of the Song Contest to be held the following day, provided the contestant proves acceptable to Eva. Walter at once desires to enter the contest; but as this is open only to Mastersingers, a degree to which he has not yet attained, he must first qualify for entrance before he can compete for the prize and, what to him is more, Eva.

Attending Eva in the church is her nurse, Magdalena. For Eva's sake she calls upon her sweetheart, David, apprentice to Hans Sachs, to instruct Walter in the rules of composition. He loses no time in doing this, for a Song Trial is to be held almost immediately in the forecourt of the Church. Even now apprentices are arranging furniture for the meeting.

David condescendingly inquires of Walter if he has passed the degrees of Poet and Singer or merely that of School Friend. Greatly surprised to discover that Walter knows nothing of these terms, he says curtly, "Take warning from me and abandon your Master dream, for Singer and Poet you must be if you would enter into Mastership."

Under these circumstances the apprentice considers himself too superior to instruct a mere aspiring singer who is without formal training. The fact that Walter is proved to be a true genius is utilized by Wagner to express his conviction that too long established conventions and procedures in the lives of individuals and institutions become so static and rigid that there is little chance for any person or enterprise to receive fair consideration unless the same conforms to established rules and regulations, and measures up to fixed standards. When one like Walter comes along, regardless of how gifted he may be, he is denied an opportunity if he does not fall into the customary pattern; and he is judged, not by innate ability but by arbitrary standards which fail to accommodate themselves to the ever-changing needs of man's unfolding and expanding creative spirit. In the opera Walter recognizes this situation and refuses to accept David's admonition. He declares with the determination of him who knows his own inherent powers that there is only one final reward: to find the "true tone" to fit his verse.

Every creative artist will recognize the unconquerable spirit that underlies a challenge and a resolve like Walter's. Such a spirit holds within its grasp the power of successful fulfillment, no matter how great external odds against it may be. But there is also a deeper significance to this circumstance pertaining to initiatory development. Naught but the ability of the Mastersinger to fit his verse with *its proper keynote,* his own, confers the powers of Mastership; and only "living the life" develops these powers, not mere affiliation with an organization which may lose its usefulness by too strict adherence to externals while neglecting to nourish the inner Light.

To the dignified motif of the Assembly, the twelve

Mastersingers march in and solemnly take their places for roll call, after which Pogner announces that he offers his daughter's hand in marriage to him who wins on the morrow, provided the winner proves acceptable to her. Walter boldly asks permission to enter the trial. His request is granted and the Mastersingers proceed to explain something of the Guild's hard and fast rules which must be punctiliously observed by all candidates.

For each Song Trial a "marker" was elected. His office was to set down with chalk upon a blackboard all the mistakes of the candidate-singer. If the errors exceeded seven the candidate was disqualified for entering the Contest, being declared "outsung" and "outdone."

It is significant that Beckmesser, indicative of man's unregenerate nature, is the "marker" for aspirants in their Trial examinations. It is the degree to which this lower nature has been brought under control and transmuted that determines whether or not a candidate has qualifications for entering upon the work that leads directly to the Degree of Mastership. Throughout the remainder of the first act this struggle on the part of the candidate to make another grade is conveyed musically by the orchestra apparently struggling with the two conflicting motifs representing the higher and lower natures of man, the Walter and Beckmesser of the opera.

Walter, undaunted, improvises a lovely Hymn to Spring, free in style and soaring joyously above the cramping forms and regulations of the Guild. In this song he summarizes his early life and environment among the beauties of nature. He recounts feelingly the youthful aspirations which led him to enter the present Song Contest. His sparklingly beautiful Hymn is accompanied by the yearning, tender motif of awakening love.

According to the Guild's decrees the singer sits for the contest; but to the consternation of the members, Walter, animated by the beauty and inspiration of his subject, stands up as he sings the second stanza of his song.

When he has finished, Beckmesser appears with the slate entirely covered with disqualifying marks as the orchestra graphically expresses in the uneven measures of the Beckmesser motif the vindictiveness with which errors were chalked down against the aspirant.

Hans Sachs alone recognizes something unique and promising in Walter's song. Its novel beauty greatly impresses him and, as the realization dawns in his consciousness that a true artist-in-the-making has entered their midst, his emotions find expression in the beautiful Renunciation motif. Sachs not only renounces his love for Eva, but humbly acknowledges a spirit of unquestionable genius in Walter. He realizes that Walter's song is new and different, but that these are not sufficient reasons for barring it from sympathetic consideration. Moreover, he also recognizes that Walter's song is not a disorderly departure from the accepted style and manner but that it gives evidence of being fashioned after a sound inner pattern, so it is the duty and privilege of their School to examine it with due care.

As the Guild is thrown into a high state of excitement by Walter's song, Beckmesser's angry voice is heard accompanied by his uneven motif and the scratching of chalk. Walter, encouraged by Sachs, now mounts the chair again. Defying the Masters who agree with Beckmesser that the young Knight is definitely "outsung" and "outdone," he sings the third stanza of his song. Half contemptuously, he improvises the story of an owl that swooped down into a stygian thicket and awakened from their long sleep a flock of dark and gloomy ravens. Not finding his rightful place here, the owl lifts himself up and encounters a bird with golden pinions that points the way toward heights into which the owl soared despite the croaking of the ravens. The point of this story was not missed by his irate listeners.

As Walter leaves his chair and goes out of the hall the company is in a tumult. Apprentices delight in singing their mocking song as they dance about the room removing chairs and setting the place in order. Only Hans Sachs is wise enough to probe the meaning of events. As he ponders the situation thoughtfully and solemnly, the exquisitely tender strains of Walter's Hymn to Spring (the Voice of the New) sounds in the orchestra, followed immediately by the measured notes of the Meistersinger motif (the Voice of the Old). Sachs, wise teacher that he is, realizes that the New must supercede the Old, and that Walter has set the former's impress upon his beautiful Hymn.

A beautiful esoteric truth is brought out in connection with Walter's song. Each human being sounds his own individual keynote, which is attuned to one of the planets of our solar system. One of the requirements for the Third or Master's Degree is ability to tune in to the musical key of the inmost spirit. This requires sensitivity and spirituality of a high order, plus the ability to enter so deeply into meditation that all external sounds are closed out and one's inner ear is perfectly attuned to the keynote of his own being. Sachs is the only one of the twelve Mastersingers with the spiritual development enabling him to recognize that Walter had done this and, therefore, is qualified to try for the Master's Degree by composing his Prize Song, or Master Work, around his own archetypal keynote.

ACT II

A bright and merry Prelude, largely an abbreviation of the St. John motif, introduces Act. II, the setting for which is a street scene in Nuremberg. On one side of the street is the pretentious house of Pogner and his daughter Eva; on the opposite side, the humble dwelling of Hans Sachs, the local shoemaker.

Apprentices, or First Degree students in the Mastersingers' Guild, make their home with the Masters with whom they study. The most important of these apprentices is David. He lives with Hans Sachs from whom he receives instruction in both cobblery and music.

Third Degree work is rewarded by the bestowal of a crown upon the fortunate contestant. The possession of this crown is the goal of every apprentice and is ever-present before his mind's eye. Wagner has fittingly described the musical motif of these youths as "the Crown." It is a lively, tripping air, symbolic of carefree, aspiring, idealistic youth.

Sachs, generous, compassionate and unselfish by nature, sits in his workshop. To the accompaniment of his own motif he reviews the events of the day. In his reverie the music of Walter's Hymn to Spring and its message keeps haunting him. He muses, "No rule would fit it, yet it was faultless." As he ponders on the elusive magic and witchery of the song he declares it to be "filled with ancient truths that seemed so new, like songs of birds in Springtime."

Informed by Magdalena of Walter's failure before the Masters, Eva is in a state of great pertubation because she is not sure of Sach's aid after her recent interview with him.

To the accompaniment of the Knight's motif, Walter approaches Eva. She greets him with the excited exclamation, "You are both hero of the Prize and my only friend!"

Walter answers her sadly, "Only thy friend, for they will not name me Master, therefore my longing is in vain for the lady's hand."

Impatient with the narrow and bigoted attitude of the Masters of the Guild, he entreats Eva to flee with him and so escape the terrible fate of becoming a Master's bride.

The poignantly tender song by Sachs at this time has great significance in its twofold meaning. He sings of his Muse who raises him so far above earth that he can be both shoemaker and poet. This is the attitude of every true Master. Disregarding the evaluations of an uncomprehending world, he fulfills himself in the humblest menial employment, discovering in his work a significance touching his inner life and, therefore, dignifying it with virtues and graces of the spirit.

With most delightful irony, Wagner sets the Old over against the New in a scene introducing musical contrast between Beckmesser and Walter. Beckmesser comes to serenade Eva but, unknown to him, it is Magdalena who appears at the window. His serenade, while it meets all conventional requirements and regulations of the Guild, is nevertheless a hodge-podge—a travesty on true beauty and fine feeling, a striking contrast to the free and untrammeled loveliness of Walter's exquisite song improvised under guidance of Mastersingers from higher planes.

The force and influence of the lower nature, as symbolized by Beckmesser, is powerful and far-reaching. Wagner demonstrates this truth in a most interesting way. The noise, confusion and inharmony produced by Beckmesser's serenade awakens townspeople in adjoining houses. Clad in their night dresses they rush out into the street. David, thinking that the serenade was intended for Magdalena, begins to beat Beckmesser, whereupon the confused people, swayed by the inharmonious currents, maul one another until pandemonium reigns. Wagner depicts this upheaval with extraordinary cleverness. Nearly all the musical motifs of the various characters are introduced. One hears the notes of Sachs, Walter, the Mastersingers and the apprentices, while underlying each motif is heard an undercurrent of Beckmesser's crude and inharmonious serenade. This is Wagner's way of saying that the discord and confusion in life springs from the disruptive elements in man's own lower nature. Beckmesser, expressing the low, could not reach Eva, the higher nature. Instead, he produced only disturbing conditions on his own level of expression.

Sach's efforts to prevent the elopment of Eva and Walter have a much deeper meaning than that of frustrating the plans of two love-lorn young people. The neophyte of every Mystery School is taught early in his work that personal desires must be sacrificed to the exacting demands of spirit. This ideal underlies Sachs' Renunciation motif previously referred to. The deeper philosophical meanings written into all of Wagner's dramas are missed if the student fails to look beyond the merely personal aspects of the love stories around which the action revolves.

Uproarious confusion in the erstwhile quiet street is finally stilled as a faithful town crier sings out his familiar call, "Ten o'clock, lights out! All's well, praise God." This call is accompanied by a singularly beautiful melody, *Peace of the Summer Night.* This theme, the very heart song of nature, restores quiet and harmony as it floats in heavenly benediction over the ancient village.

ACT III

As the curtain rises on Act III it is early morning. Hans Sachs is seen in his workshop, seated in an armchair and entirely absorbed in reading *The Chronicle of The World.* Without interrupting his profound concentration he speaks to his young apprentice. The boy departs, leaving him with head bowed in melancholy meditation over the great book.

Wagner states that the pivotal theme of the prologue came to him suddenly as he was sitting alone one day. It is Sachs' despairing monologue "Vanity of vanities, all is vanity." This thought is contained in various moods to the triumphant choral of the populace at the close of the third act. This motif, played by itself, is fully developed, then dies away in the somberness of the Renunciation theme. Then the horns take it up softly as though heard from a distance and one hears the solemn chant with which Hans Sachs saluted Luther and the Reformation, and which brought the poet great popularity.

After the first strophe, the stringed instruments, in a very soft, slow movement, repeat the theme of the shoemaker's true song as if the man has raised his head from his work to look upward and lose himself in sweet and tender memories. The horns break into the most exalted tones of the Hymn of the Mastersingers, to which the people of Nuremberg joyously, and with thunderous applause, greet Sachs as he makes his appearance at the fete. Again the first motif, played by the strings, expresses with vigor the emotions of a strong soul profoundly moved; then the music gradually becomes more serene until it finally describes the peace of a sweet and holy resignation.

Sachs now bursts forth into the aria *Wahn! Wahn! Uberall Wahn!*, Mad! Mad! The whole world is mad! Walter enters the workshop and tells the Master of a "wondrous lovely dream" he had during the night in which he dreamed both words and melody of a marvelous song. Sachs replies that "to treasure and expound his dreams is just the poet's work. Heed my counsel," he adds, "and bend your mood to a Master Song."

Walter wants to know what "Master Song" means, and Sachs explains to the accompaniment of musical themes that illustrate the points he wishes to emphasize. These include the Renunciation motif, the theme of his meditation, the Midsummer Night theme, beautiful and mystic, and echoes of Walter's Hymn to Spring, the voice of the New. Sachs goes on to say that many are endowed with the gift of song who use it as they are inspired by passion, but that only when one is able to draw inspiration from a source higher than the earth is it possible to create a Master Song.

The early Initiate bards sang solely of heavenly realms; their "Dream Songs" recounted experiences while functioning on inner planes. In later centuries this high art addressed itself to secular subjects singing chiefly of human loves and achievements. It is to help restore bards to their former high estate that Walter comes into their midst. Sachs, recognizing this, bids Walter take pen and paper and first, *make his rules;* then *follow them.* In other words, he is telling Walter he is a creator in his own right and is, therefore, expected to give free expression to his own genius, but in strict adherence to the law of his own being. Such is the admonition of every true spiritual teacher to disciples who are striving to come into complete attunement with their own divine self.

Both the Prelude and the music with which the third act opens are embellished with the musical picture of Hans Sachs. It depicts a person who is wise, understanding and compassionate, and whose demeanor is grave and dignified. The theme used has been called one of human wisdom. Its majestic strains gradually blend with the gay, tripping motif of David, the young apprentice, who arrives to take part in the Song Contest that is in preparation for celebrating Midsummer Day.

Midsummer Day is the Summer Solstice, one of the four major turning points in the course of the Sun's annual procession through the twelve signs of the Zodiac. Like the other three—the Winter Solstice and the two Equinoxes—this is a time when cosmic currents of spiritual power impinge upon the earth with special force. In harmony with this sacred seasonal rhythm Christmas falls on the Winter Solstice, Easter at the time of the Spring Equinox, while the Summer Solstice is dedicated to the memory of the holy St. John.

At the Summer Solstice the earth is attuned to the keynote of the zodiacal sign of Cancer, called the Gateway of Heaven. Consequently, it is a time especially propitious for any worthy aspirant to make inner plane contacts, and for observing those rituals which accompany the elevation of a worthy neophyte to the status of Mastership.

So it is that Walter's Dream Song, which has to do with heaven-world experiences, is delivered at this sacred season. With the experienced assistance of Hans Sachs, Walter's offering becomes a finished, inspired song that carries away the prize.

Walter's Dream Song is divided into three parts corresponding to the three steps or Degrees leading to Mastership. It recounts the experiences through which he passed in each of these three stages leading to Initiation. The first part describes the beauty and light of inner planes as a garden of radiance and soul delight. The second tells of the luminous Tree of Life in the midst of the Garden and of a beautiful maiden, resembling Eva—representative of the "Eternal Feminine" of Goethe that "draws us ever upward and on." This maiden leads him to the wonderful Tree of Life, through the branches of which he beheld a multitude of twinkling stars adorning the Tree like fruit.

This Tree represents the soul or celestial body of the Initiate whose centers are alight and radiant with the Fire of the living spirit. This state is not attained until the soul has passed through processes of purification and transmutation leading to the Mystic Marriage, whereby the Divine Feminine principle is conjoined to the redeemed Masculine. Then it is that the awakened centers of the illumined body shine with all the brilliance of heavenly stars. Music can play an important part in bringing about this exalted state, as Sachs intimates in his last instructions to Walter before the latter's entry into the Song Contest.

There are three parts to Walter's Dream Song, but he cannot rehearse the last one in public. Dealing as it does with the highest of the three Degrees, it is reserved for the Contest. It reveals the experiences which accompany the candidate's own individual development.

When Walter has passed the Second Degree in the Song Trial and is being arrayed in the festal garments, representative of the luminous soul body of one entering upon the Third Degree, his mentor observes significantly that "A little dove has surely shown him the nest wherein his Master dreams." These words are accompanied by an ethereally ascending motif, carried by first violins and flutes, denoting the exalted state of consciousness necessary to

Initiation; and the dove spoken of by Sachs is a symbol of Initiation. This beautiful motif occurs again at the Festival as Sachs calls upon Walter to sing his Prize Song.

As Walter retires to the accompaniment of his Love motif, Beckmesser enters to his discordant and quarrelsome Beating motif. Discovering the score of Walter's composition and thinking it to be the work of Sachs, the great teacher, he surreptitiously seizes it and departs jubilantly with his precious find.

Eva now comes in, beautiful in her betrothal robe and accompanied by her own motif which mounts to a full and glorious climax. Walter returns in coronation attire and for the first time sings his Prize Song in its entirety. This event, marking the culmination of the Great Work which Walter has accomplished, is possible only in the presence of the white-robed, exalted Feminine, represented by Eva.

At this point Sachs proposes a "Baptism of the New Mode." Magdalena and David, both in festal array, are summoned as witnesses. Sachs serves as godfather and Eva as godmother. This high moment in the drama is accompanied by some of the most sublime music ever composed by Richard Wagner. It is called the Quintet of Baptism. The glorious music rises to high levels belonging to the sacred Rite. To its strains and under the direction of the teacher, Hans Sachs, Walter is raised to the Third or Master's Degree, while David, a First Degree Apprentice, is raised to a Second Degree Companion. Eva and Magdalena typify the Feminine principle or soul-status of the First and Second Degrees, Master and Companion respectively.

An ancient formula descriptive of this mystic Rite of Union declares that "In every individual of every species there are four elements comprising two males and two females; by the proper union we get a dual being, a new individual." Here is the key to the Mystic Marriage or Third Degree.

The concluding scene in the drama is the Song Contest.

It takes place in a meadow in the environs of Nuremberg. Boats laden with townspeople in gala attire approach the river bank to be welcomed by Apprentices and Companions. This lovely scene is accompanied by an equally delightful motif called Nuremberg *en fete.* But indicating the sacred purpose of the happy gathering are orchestral strains of the Song of St. John's Day and the profound Hans Sachs motif woven delicately into the fabric of the Fete motif.

To the majestic strains of the Mastersinger motif the twelve august Guild Fathers enter. Eva accompanies her father and occupies a seat of honor in the foreground. When the Apprentices have called for silence, the leader, Hans Sachs, arises to describe the importance and sacredness of the occasion and to declare that contestants must prove their past record to be without blemish or stain. Sachs is accompanied by his own motif together with those of the Mastersingers and of St. John. The people in turn pay him homage by singing a beautiful and touching Choral named in his honor.

Beckmesser is the first contestant. His theme, adapted to the stolen words of Walter's song, is uneven, discordant and, as it progresses, actually ridiculous. He is hooted from the stage by the jeering of the assemblage. That Backmesser appears in the Song Contest at all is indicative of the fact that subtle forces of the lower nature are with an aspirant to the very doorway of Mastership, ever seeking to turn the accumulated forces of soul knowledge and power—represented by the Prize Song—to their own unworthy and self-centered ends. The utter defeat and withdrawal of Beckmesser reveals the spiritual attainment of the victor, the celebrated Knight, Walter von Stoltzing.

As the high moment of his Prize Song arrives, Walter, having passed all inner tests, is directed by Sachs to take his rightful place among the Masters. He does so to the accompaniment of his Love motif, then stands before the Mastersingers and sings the Prize Song. In its three parts he recounts, as previously indicated, his inner realm experiences. First he tells of the wondrous Tree beneath which appeared the vision of the *fairest* of women, Eva in Paradise. In the second stanza he tells of climbing a steep elevation leading to the sacred spring beneath the star-studded Tree, where he saw in a "waking poet's dream" the *holiest* of woman, who baptized him in the spring. In the final verse he describes the Paradise of his poet's dream as this opened to him after baptism in the sacred waters had shown him the Path. And now, in the full glory of the day and through the victory of his song, he enters into that Paradise.

Walter's Prize Song foreshadows the Path of Progress for all mankind. Rightly understood, it is the Prize Song of every soul's ultimate attainment. Each of the three initiatory Degrees is attuned to its appropriate rhythm and all three are in harmony with the keynote of the initiatory School represented. This is shown in Walter's Song by the choral response of the listeners at certain intervals.

In early Schools of Initiation music was used to awaken psychic centers visible to clairvoyant sight as focal points of light or wheels of glittering color in specific parts of the etheric and astral bodies. Each of these centers of force responds to a definite musical tone, the tone varying with the individual. Masters of initiatory orders sang in chorus, and this volume of sound imparted its vibration to a corresponding psychic sense center, thereby accelerating its motion and heightening its powers of perception. Fragments of such ancient and half-forgotten truths are clearly discernible in Wagner's operas. They were incorporated therein for the purpose of restoring them to the modern world. It is this aspect of Wagner's work which constitutes its greatest value and holds for the occultist its deepest fascination.

To the accompaniment of the Love motif, the keynote of the third part of the Prize Song, Eva places the victor's crown of laurel upon Walter's head. Then follows the triumphant chorus of the Mastersingers and the assembled company.

Sachs next comes forward to clasp around Walter's neck the insignia of the order, a medal bearing the image of King David with his magic harp. Walter, however, hesitates to accept membership in the ancient order which, to this young pioneer of the New Day, appears crystallized and outmoded. As he declares when the Mastersingers reject his improvization on spring at his first appearance before them, he intends to soar far beyond their "low vaulted" concepts into dimensions they know not of. "Over the croaking ravens and magpies soars a golden bird," he says. "I shall follow him where mastercrows no longer cackle, and sing my lady's praises."

But the wise Hans Sachs points out that the New ever builds on the Old; that from the past must be conserved elements that have enduring worth. Only that which has become a hindrance is to be left behind. Into the New must be incorporated the essence of all the good that the past has developed. Thus is the creative process continued unbroken, the New ever transforming and illumining worthwhile factors of the Old that can be transferred.

And so Hans Sachs points to future revivals of certain long-lost powers of poetry and music that must be recovered by pioneers of the New Age.

Standing hand in hand with Eva, Walter is received into the order of the Mastersingers, as the air of the exquisite Love motif, conjoined with the majestic notes of the Meistersinger theme, reaches a brilliant climax of tonal color and beauty.

So concludes this fascinating rendition of an ancient initiatory Rite.

That Ernest Newman, the erudite interpreter of Wagner and his work, realized the deep import of this music-drama is indicated by his self-answering query, "Can we term *Die Meistersinger* a comedy when it contains so much that is the quintessence of inner beauty, of profound philosophy and of serious wisdom?"

THE CROWNING OF PARSIFAL

PART II

Individual Attainment

I. TANNHAUSER
The Degree of Purification

II. LOHENGRIN
Conscious Individual Helpership

III. TRISTAN AND ISOLDE
The Rite of the Mystic Marriage

IV. PARSIFAL
The Degree of Mastership

Tannhauser

THE LEGEND

THE Tannhauser legend, like that of Parsifal, belongs to the Knight-Troubadour period of the early thirteenth century; since it has some degree of historical fact behind it, it is often regarded as an historical legend.

All of the characters in Wagner's *Tannhauser* were suggested by actual historical personages. These were, however, adapted by the musical dramatist to suit the spiritual purpose they were designed to serve. The Tannhauser of the opera, for example, combines the semi-historical Heinrich von Ofterdingen with Tannhauser, a Swabian Troubadour. The historical Tannhauser at the court of Duke Frederick II of Austria was a dissolute Knight and minstrel who squandered his wealth and his health, but died at last in the arms of the Church. His family estate was located near Vienna, but after its loss he found protection with Otto II of Bavaria. Medieval poets attributed noble works to Tannhauser, such as the composition of the *Lay of the Nibelungen,* although this is not borne out by modern findings.

Historians do not look upon the Song Festival at the Wartburg as historically authentic, but the characters mentioned are real people. The Landgrave Hermann, Landgravine Sophia (who, with St. Elizabeth, became the original of Elizabeth in the opera), Wolfram von Eschenbach (author of Parsifal and Germany's foremost authority of his time on Provencal literature), Reinmar der Alte, Heinrich von Rispach, Biterolf, Heinrich von Ofterdingen and Klingsor, who was said to have been a black magician, were all flesh and blood characters. It is related that Ofterdingen sought the protection of Klingsor (said to be the nephew of Virgilius of Naples) and that the Landgravine sheltered him under her cloak when he was hard pressed by his fellow Knights.

The Tannhauser legend was transmitted through folk ballads—among them a carnival play by Hans Sachs—and was evidently part of a propaganda campaign against the Church of Rome which culminated in the Reformation, when Luther was hailed as "the one who was to come." The Pope, Urban IV, who refused absolution to the repentant Knight, is actually condemned to hell by the poet; and Wagner, in his concluding scenes of the opera, also points up the moral that there is no limit to the mercy and love of God, who can set aside any human decree which is not consistent with divine compassion. This was anti-papal propaganda typical of the Troubadours after the Albigensian Wars. The attitude of the Church toward the Troubadours is shown in the legend of Faust, where Mephistopheles assumes the guise of a Troubadour and accompanies his knightly master on his journeys, acting as the latter's representative in his affair with Marguerite.

The Troubadours of the twelfth century and the early part of the thirteenth were noble Knights, usually so born but sometimes elevated to the nobility as a reward for their brilliant achievements. They were attended by one or more minstrels who were often novices learning the art of music from their Knight. They might be hired by their instructor to sing and play his compositions if he himself was not especially an expert in these accomplishments. If from the lower classes, the minstrels might thus have an opportunity of becoming ennobled.

During the entire twelfth and thirteenth centuries, when the Troubadours were still noble Knights, the Order of the Temple had been growing apace, exactly paralleling the growth of Grail literature, with which it was closely connected in the popular mind. It was from the beginning an esoteric Order. Wolfram von Eschenbach was a prominent member of the German branch. The "religion of love" professed by the Templars was the love of humanity; the Virgin, whose image stood on their altars, was in fact the Secret Wisdom—or Sophia, as the early Church knew her—the Divine Feminine of Arcane Doctrine.

Troubadours had developed a secret language of their own. That Knights in the Order of the Temple also knew this Mystery Tongue is suggested in Wolfram von Eschenbach's *Parsifal*. The mysterious Prester John, Eastern King of the Grail, was popularly associated with the head of the Templars at Jerusalem. There is reason to believe that this Order had, indeed, as its objective to make Jerusalem the Christian capital in the place of Rome—which purpose incurred the disfavor of the Church and thus led to its defeat.

The fully initiated Knights were called "Perfect." They were given a golden cup or Grail, symbol of Initiation, and "a kiss by a most beautiful lady," representing the awakened Divine Feminine, in token of their accomplishments.

The romantic terminology of the Troubadours' songs was actually the secret symbolical phrasing of the Christian Mysteries, of which they were exoteric representatives. All references to love and women are to be understood in this sense. Thus, the "Courts of Love" of Southern Troubadours become Lodges of the Templars. The Grail legends developed in the North of France, the South of Germany and the Netherlands. The Minnesingers, or Love Singers, of Germany also understood the double significance of this romantic wording.

There were two broad divisions in the Order: the Knights Troubadour who took their message to courts and kings, and the humbler minstrels who brought enlightenment to the common folk. The Arthurian legends, which were most closely associated with England, were also part of this Mystery cycle. The Roundtable, featured in these legends, admitted to seats as members only those who had attained to the status of Perfect Knight.

Early in the thirteenth century, when France was being ravaged by the Albigensian Wars, Hermann of Thuringia held at Wartburg Castle the Singer's Contest wherein many eminent poets took part, as related in Wagner's Tannhauser.

Wagner follows a late version of the Tannhauser legend, but he adds the Elizabeth episode and the Contest at the Wartburg from the Ofterdingen legends. In this ballad Tannhauser wanders into the forest to seek adventure in the knightly tradition and to "see wonders." He comes upon a group of dancing maidens in the Court of Venus (Frau Frene or Freya) and remains there for some time, "dreaming under Frau Frene's fig tree," the fig tree symbolizing sex. But Tannhauser, sickening of sensual indulgence, dreams that he must renounce his sinful life, whereupon he tears himself free of enchantment and proceeds to Rome to seek absolution. The Pope declares, "Your sins are as little likely to be forgiven as this staff is to turn green." On hearing this hopeless verdict Tannhauser departs in despair, though praying to the Christ to look upon him with mercy and forgiveness. Three days later the Pope's staff is covered with leaves. Seeing this, he sends for Tannhauser, only to learn that in desperation the Knight had returned to the Court of Venus.

It is evident that although Wagner based his *Tannhauser* on both history and tradition, like every great artist he used them freely in order to introduce deeply esoteric truths belonging to Initiation.

The late eminent music critic, Laurence Gilman, gave a perfect statement of the message of *Tannhauser* as "a tragic parable of the endless conflicts in the soul of man between those impulses which are earthbound and sensual and those which are, as St. Paul described them, the 'fruits of the spirit'."

The story of Tannhauser deals largely with subtle emanations from the psycho-spiritual stratum called the Desire World, the heaven and hell of orthodoxy or the Soul World of the mystic. It is the realm of secret desires of the heart which, if good and true, relate the soul to the heaven world; if evil and base, to the purgatorial region. This Soul World is no mere abstraction. It is visible and tangible to inner senses. The lower desires appear to extended vision as restless, surging undulations of a deep crimson hue, represented musically in the agitated Venusberg music of the opera.

Inharmonious Desire World rhythms find their most effective expression in the jazz of our day. In primitive times these rhythms found a corresponding expression. They then served the useful evolutionary purpose of arousing humanity from its vegetative state of consciousness into the next higher animalistic state, the emotional nature being quickened from a static to a dynamic condition in accordance with evolutionary requirements. But the jazz of our time serves no such constructive purpose. On the contrary, it is destructive since it inflames the desire nature which is now overdeveloped and is leading humanity, against its better knowledge and higher will, into ways it should not go. Jazz is not for an age that has so far succumbed to uncontrolled passions as to lead humanity into two world wars within a single generation, leaving it struggling desperately for such rational controls as will bring peace.

The discordant rhythms of jazz are especially harmful to children and growing youths. Their sensitive natures are more easily "jangled out of tune" than are those whose inner and outer bodies have reached maturity. The harm suffered by the young in their formative years reacts disastrously both physically and morally. Well may one ask how discordant lines of force that have become embodied in these sensitive, growing organisms can ever be completely eradicated. The importance of this subject from a social, moral and spiritual point of view can scarcely be over emphasized.

For the spiritual aspirant, *Tannhauser* contains the key to the first step of unfoldment: Purification, or the Great Overcoming. *Self-control* is the keyword given every neophyte of every Mystery School as the primary requisite to further attainment.

THE OVERTURE

The Overture to Act I presents a summary of the opera in its two leading themes, the Pilgrim's Chorus and the Venusberg music. These themes weave their tonal magic about the listener as he follows the struggle for supremacy between the higher and the lower natures in man, as Richard Wagner depicts it.

The Overture opens with the majestic measures of the Pilgrim's Chorus sounded in the woodwinds with soul calm and gradually increasing in intensity until the entire orchestra proclaims it triumphantly. As often occurs in human experience, when holy inspiration reaches a climax, temptations of the desire nature intrude themselves. At this point in the Overture the intoxicating strains of the Venusberg music are heard. The Finale, however, proclaims the eventual triumph of spirit over the senses for the Overture concludes with the majestic strains of the Pilgrims' Chorus.

Wagner was much criticized for introducing the agitated Venusberg motif into this chorus. But the objectors fail to recognize that Wagner sought from the very beginning to depict the conflict which takes place within every aspirant on the Path of Initiation between his lower nature that would keep him chained to earth and his higher nature that would set him free.

ACT I

In the opening scene, Tannhauser, a Minstrel-Knight, is riding through a trackless forest in deep meditation. He lifts his thoughts in anguished prayer and supplication: "Is there no panacea in heaven or earth to stem the fiery passions which, however much they are gratified, yet leave the heart dry and dusty with unassuaged desire?" As he ponders sadly, a strange bird flies straight into the face of his horse. This so frightens the steed that it plunges madly forward and soon loses its way in the pathless woods.

In the language of symbolism a horse represents unbridled desires. For example, the early Viking custom of sacrificing a horse by throwing it from a high cliff signified the overcoming of the lower nature.

After a time Tannhauser hears strains of soft, seductive music and finds himself enveloped in a radiant red-gold mist. Siren forms of enticing beauty dance in this strange light; and Tannhauser, enraptured, is guided to a luxurious bower hung with deep crimson roses. In their intoxicating fragrance his senses become steeped as in wine, while his dazzled gaze beholds the seductive loveliness of the Goddess Venus. She greets him in tones as sweet as the song of morning birds: "Tannhauser, minstrel and my love, my heart has waited for you these many days." On hearing these seductive words, the enamoured Knight swoons as though he were in a sea of fire.

At this point Tannhauser illustrates the danger that ofttimes confronts an earnest and sincere aspirant who succeeds in rending the veil and passing into inner realms before he has been "duly and truly prepared." Nothing is more dangerous than to attempt to investigate unseen worlds before spiritual stabilization has been attained. To do so leads inevitably to tragedy, as it does in the case of Tannhauser.

In appraising the Overture to Tannhauser, Laurence Gilman, previously quoted, declared it to be "a moving and beautiful work. But," he added, "the Bacchanale is colossal and without precedent. Nothing like this blazing torrent of orchestral tone has ever been released from a musician's imagination. Its overpowering intensity has added a novel and perturbing page to the literature of music."

The long crescendo with which the meeting of Tannhauser and Venus concludes, and which also introduces the dialogue between them that follows, contains some of the loveliest music Wagner ever wrote.

After having revised his early *Tannhauser* score, Wagner wrote to a friend from Paris regarding the second version, which he had embellished from the deepening wisdom of years: "The only scene I meant to recast entirely is that between Venus and Tannhauser. I find Venus stiff, a few good features, but no true life. I have added a fair number of verses . . . The Goddess of Delight herself has become affecting and Tannhauser's agony real, so that his invocation of the Virgin Mary bursts as a cry of anguish from his deepest soul. At that period [meaning fifteen years before when the opera was written in Dresden] I could never have made a thing like this . . . . It required a greater mastery, by far, which only now I have attained At the time I wrote *Tannhauser* I was quite unable to portray the passionate inwardness, the full intensity of woman . . . . In fact I'm horrified at my former 'property' Venus! . . . But the blithe and gay side of Tannhauser is all good and there I can alter nothing; it had in it the distilled essence of everything that bears the flavor of the legend, although I have touched up features now and then."

After a year has passed Tannhauser is surfeited with the sensual delights of the Venusberg. There are indications noticeable to the astral vampire that he would like to be free from her magnetic hold. In her most alluring manner she tries to keep his thoughts centered on her. "Beloved, say, where strayeth thy thought?" she asks. To which Tannhauser replies by crying out, "Oh, that I might now awaken!" Venus, caressing him, pleads again that he share with her his hidden longing. Tannhauser now makes confession of the source of his troubled thoughts by telling her that he has just heard something so long strange to him—he has heard the sound of church bells.

During the earlier part of this scene, while the hypnotic spell of Venus is still unbroken, the orchestra flames into sensuous tones to which fauns and nymphs play in mad abandon. It is the amorous strains of the Siren's Chorus that now sound forth.

When Tannhauser's conscience is touched by the promptings of his higher self, the flutes and oboes convey the chiming of church bells, the hearing of which brings the Knight to his right senses. "How long," says he, "since I have heard their tones. I know not how to measure time since I have dwelt here with thee. Of days and months I have lost count, no longer do I see the sun, nor the friendly stars above. No longer do I see the tender grass with its promise of summer, no longer do I hear the nightingales singing that spring is nigh. Oh, shall I never see and hear these again?"

In an effort to regain her hold on her disillusioned lover, Venus reminds Tannhauser of the balm that her love brought him in his days of sorrow. She pleads with him to be reconciled to the good he now enjoys and to take up his harp and sing as he had done before, in praise of love. He agrees, but no sooner has he begun than the remembrance of the bell call to his soul causes him to stop short. He begs

Venus for his freedom. Impatiently she exclaims: "He praises love and yet from love would flee!"

No, not from love, replies Tannhauser, but from her all too powerful charm he would flee.

As this struggle between the higher and lower nature in Tannhauser is going on, denizens of Venusberg do their utmost to beguile him as sirens sing: "Come to these bowers." Venus joins them with the appeal, "Drink draughts divine, drink of love's own wine."

The ravishing music becomes even more enchanting as Venus whispers: "Tell me, beloved, wilt thou fly from me?" Tannhauser, now swept away on tides of emotion, vows with passionate ardor that he will ever be her true and fearless champion.

But again his higher nature asserts itself and the struggle continues. Venus is exasperated. Angrily she bids him return to the world he scorned when he came to her; yet she tries to dissuade him from actually doing so by assuring him that on his return he will be met by so poor a welcome that he will wish himself back with her—and will, moreover, come seeking her in sorrow and humiliation only to be rejected by her also. "Not to slaves but to heroes only do I open my heart," she declares.

"My pride that last distress shall spare thee," replies Tannhauser, "to see me kneeling in dishonor, for he who now leaves thee, will never more return."

In despair Venus sobs that if he returns not, her curse shall rest on him. "The earth shall be a desert when the goddess smiles on it no more."

Tannhauser is resolved. "In my heart," says he, "I bear now only death and the grave. By repentance and penitence alone shall I find peace—not with thee, goddess of delights—my hope is in Mary alone." Then it is that he cries aloud to the Virgin Mary to save him. As he speaks that sacred name, the magic spell of Venus falls away. All the lovely enticements of her red-gold bower melt into nothingness—and Tannhauser is free.

As the illusory beauties of the Venusberg disappear, Tannhauser finds himself in a peaceful vale. The blue sky is above him and the sun is shining. In the distance is the Wartburg, and a path from it leads downward to the valley. In the foreground on a small eminence is a shrine to the Virgin Mary, before which Tannhauser kneels. From the heights the sound of sheep bells is heard, and also the piping music of a young shepherd. A band of penitents pass by, chanting their hymn of faith in God. From his altar of prayer, his voice choked with tears, the sad and sorrowing Tannhauser joins in the hymn as the voices of the pilgrims sound softly from the distance.

Suddenly a joyous trumpeting announces the approach of Landgrave Hermann of Thuringia, accompanied by his minstrels. They observe the kneeling Tannhauser and Wolfram, his closest friend of olden days, is the first to recognize him with a glad welcoming cry: "It is Heinrich!" The minstrel Knights are on their way to the Festival of Song to be given in the Wartburg Castle of Prince Hermann.

The Landgrave asks Tannhauser what his return portends, and Walther von der Vogelweide queries, "Comest thou as friend or foe?" Biterolf demands grimly whether he is peaceable or dreaming of further strife.

The gentle Wolfram protests their questionings. Is Tannhauser's attitude that of pride or humility? he asks. Warmly clasping the forlorn minstrel's hand, he tells him that all too long has he absented himself from their ranks. To this Tannhauser, his brow furrowed in pain, makes reply: "There is a long path leading from where I have been to the goal I now seek. I am not worthy to come with you. Let me go away alone in prayer and penance."

Wolfram, the most spiritually advanced among the Knights, perceives the fierce struggle which rends the soul of the penitent and whispers gently to him: "If you will not come for us, then come for the sake of the fair Elizabeth who, during your year's absence, has not once graced our

Festival. Come with us now that we may again know the inspiration of her gracious presence."

Elizabeth represents the power of the awakened spirit, the Divine Feminine. With mention of her name the very light of heaven shines about Tannhauser and he hears the voices of Angels singing. With uplifted head and exultant look he cries out: "For the sake of Elizabeth! To the Wartburg!"

In a glorious burst of concerted harmony, the Knights ride joyously away, up the path leading to the Castle and the Festival of Song.

In order to realize the full import of Tannhauser's sin it is necessary to understand just who these minstrel Knights were, and how important it was that they should set an example of noble living before the people.

Their beginnings are shrouded in a misty past. As early as the seventh century B.C., in Ireland the highest honors were paid to the physician, the poet and the harp player. Medieval minstrel Knights were the spiritual teachers of their time, and their Festivals of Song were sacred assemblies in which high spiritual truths were taught to the most advanced of the people—as shown, for example, in *Die Meistersinger*. The action of the Tannhauser legend is in the thirteenth century, yet even today only a few are ready to receive inner teachings given in that far-off time.

These minstrel Knights were regarded as holy men. Monks and abbotts often left their cells to join them for a time, and the minstrel might officiate in the offices of the church upon occasion. They were received with honor and reverence everywhere. As a token of identification, the king of the country gave a golden harp and the queen, a richly jewelled ring or cup to those who possessed the essential qualifications for this service. These qualifications included a peculiarly sensitive temperament together with "second sight." The first poets laureate were bards having memory of inner-plane experiences and the ability to best describe them in verse.

There were different degrees of spiritual attainment introduced into the Tournaments of Song. By the magic of their music some were able to produce and control the spirits of the four elements, Fire, Earth, Air and Water. Others could leave their bodies at will. These were termed the Secrets of the Bards and belonged to higher degrees than those given in the Tannhauser legend.

Many landed barons, such as Prince Hermann for example, retained twelve minstrel Knights, one for each month of the year. Prior to the sixteenth century materialism was not so pronounced as it is now. People were sensitive to the changes in the psychic atmosphere of the earth as the sun passed from one to another of the zodiacal signs. These changes were observed with music in harmony with the zodiacal keynotes of the incoming month.

Minstrelsy was, therefore, a holy calling, one not to be degraded in any way. The themes chosen for Tournaments were always sacred, dealing largely with the lives of the Blessed Virgin and her Holy Son. Often bands of Angels, as true seers among them could testify, came to these Tournaments and added the beauty of their celestial music to that of the Knights.

In the light of the foregoing, it can be seen that Tannhauser had fallen a long way from the purity and sacredness of his former life. This realization created consternation among the assembled company and was productive of dire consequences in his own life as well as in the lives of those who had looked up to him with respect and reverence as a spiritual teacher.

ACT II

The second act begins with an orchestral Prelude depicting the happiness of Elizabeth at the return of Tannhauser. This is succeeded by the even deeper thanksgiving note of the returned Knight himself. But this jubilation is soon interrupted by a dark and sombre note from the woodwinds, termed *The Warning,* that foreshadows the tragic event soon to transpire within the Hall of Song.

When Tannhauser enters he is welcomed by the Princess Elizabeth, who comes flushed and eager to greet him. As he kneels before her she tells him that he must never kneel before the heart wherein he reigns. And then she inquires why he has absented himself for so long from his friends.

Tannhauser, like many another, is susceptible to the influence of environment. In the company of Venus he revels in desire; in the presence of the pure Elizabeth he is equally eager but for things of the spirit.

Answering Elizabeth's question as to his absence, Tannhauser speaks sadly and with deep emotion: "Between the past and the goal which I now seek there stretches a dark oblivion." He confesses to having lost all hope of ever seeing her again, so unworthy did he know himself to be. Surely, he says, it is by some great wonder that he is again in her blessed presence.

"Then I praise this wonder," exclaims Elizabeth joyfully.

In questioning her own emotions, she asks of Tannhauser what it is he has done to her, to which the greatful Knight replies by assuring her that it is the love of God that brought him back to her and that all is well. Then they sing together joyously: "Oh blessed hour of meeting." Tannhauser now pleads for her love, saying that without her he cannot save himself. Here their love music is deeply emotional and singularly beautiful.

The grand march which precedes the entrance of the Knights and their Ladies is one of the most magnificent Wagnerian scores. Silver trumpets herald their coming, cymbals and harps welcome the company as they find their places in the great hall, brilliant and beautiful in lighting and coloring.

In a stately chorus the Nobles and Knights sing praises of the hall in which they are assembled, and in song extend their grateful greeting to their beloved ruler and patron, Landgrave Hermann of Thuringia.

It must be remembered that this company is made up of neophytes who have come to be instructed and to receive inspiration from the minstrel Knights.

As previously stated, these contests were not mere concerts but occasions for imparting and receiving spiritual instruction pertaining to the Path that leads to Illumination. At these spiritually charged gatherings there were those who acquired the gift of healing by means of music. One who possessed such power was the beloved St. Francis of Assisi. When he journeyed from hamlet to hamlet accompanied by his little band of brother minstrels, and sang for the people in the open market places, he was serving in the best tradition of the "Love-Singers."

When the songfest is about to begin the contestants take their places before the assemblage. Each man places his name in a silver plate which an attending page passes to Elizabeth. She draws one of the names and hands it to the page, from whom we hear the proclamation: "Wolfram Von Eschenbach, begin the strife of the Great Overcoming."

The subject of the contest, which has been announced previously by Prince Hermann, is "Love's meaning and its celestial grace."

There are two types of love in the world—pure altruistic love which lifts one to higher spiritual levels, and the lust which draws one down to the plane of selfish, carnal desire. The former is voiced by Wolfram; the latter, by Tannhauser. Wolfram's ideal of love is centered in service; it is outgoing; it is selfless surrender. Tannhauser's ideal, as voiced in his song, is self-centered. Its keynote is possession. Wolfram's love leads to liberation from bondage to sense life. Tannhauser's brings sadness, sorrow and suffering, as the unfolding drama sets forth with unforgettable clarity and forcefulness.

It is love in the Uranian octave that inspires Wolfram as he addresses his ideal with the words: "When I gaze upon your tender beauty, my heart is filled with holy, prayerful dreams. To love and serve thee is all that I desire." "The meaning of my song," he concludes, "is plain to see; the essense of true love is Purity."

One cannot remain for long submerged in low desire and feel at home in high and holy company. Tannhauser is strangely ill at ease during Wolfram's song. Its theme appears pale and lifeless as he contrasts it with the seductive delights of the Venusberg. Grasping his harp impatiently, and with a far-off gaze as though looking into other realms, Tannhauser begins to sing a song strangely sweet and yet strangely horrible. Faint echoes of the Venusberg music sound as an accompaniment to his song, the theme of which is: "Love is passion, Love is pleasure." Exultantly he sings: "I would not approach the margin of love unless passion filled my being. Oh, tides of love, let me possess thy splendor."

Louder and fiercer grows his song! Deep crimson lights flash through the hall. The assembled people spring to their feet in bewilderment and consternation as Tannhauser, in high frenzy, addresses himself to Wolfram and exclaims: "That of which you sing is but a pale effigy! If you would really know love, go to the Venusberg."

A man speaks in accordance with his true nature. What he really is will inevitably find expression. In the words of

Emerson: "I cannot hear what you say for what you are is shouting so loudly in my ears."

In the confusion following Tannhauser's outpouring, swords are drawn as the minstrels surround him. A shining blade would have found its way into his heart but for Elizabeth who stands before him. When the Knights remonstrate with her, she cries: "I think not of myself, but of his soul's salvation. Even though he has taken my happiness and flung it away, my life will be one long prayer that he may be saved from his error and his sin."

The Knights then sing their beautiful chorus: "An angel has from heaven descended. Thou gavest her death. She pleadeth for thy pardon."

Prince Hermann now speaks to Tannhauser: "A foul, dark crime has been committed here and heaven would curse the roof that sheltered thee for long. There is one way open for your redemption. Over my province pilgrims are gathering to attend the Festival of Grace in Rome. Will you join them and promise never to return unless forgiveness be granted thee?"

Tannhauser, who meanwhile is overwhelmed with contrition and humiliation, is kneeling abjectly at the feet of Elizabeth. As he kisses the hem of her garment, he murmurs brokenly over and over, "God forgive my arrogance and my sin."

Prince Hermann again addresses Tannhauser, advising him to join the band of penitents for Rome and there seek forgiveness for his terrible sin. Says he: "The old men on their way have started. Still lingers here a youthful band. For slight and trifling misdeeds only they leave their home and friends behind and take the pilgrim robe and staff, in Rome forgiveness to find. With them now shalt thou go to the City of Grace."

After hearing these grave words, Tannhauser, with one long look of anguish and appeal to Elizabeth, quickly leaves the hall, crying out as he goes: "To Rome!"

As the penitent Knight disappears, far down the valley sounds the solemn call of the Pilgrims' Chorus, the hymn of the contrite soul seeking the path of repentance and redemption.

ACT III

Act III opens with an orchestral introduction which carries the title, "Tannhauser's Pilgrimage." The music begins with measures from the Pilgrims' Chorus, followed by the motif of Elizabeth's intercession in the Hall of Song. Then sad, brooding, yet fraught with striving, is the musical picture of Tannhauser's struggle with sin and his consequent suffering. This dark picture is brightened toward the end with the introduction of a new motif, Heavenly Grace, in which is to be found the glorious keynote of transmutation, the theme upon which the entire opera is based.

It is autumn in all its crimson beauty. Elizabeth is kneeling in supplication for Tannhauser before the shrine of the Blessed Madonna. Wolfram is seen watching her adoringly as she kneels in prayer. There is silence, broken at length by returning penitents singing the Pilgrims' Chorus. As they draw near, Elizabeth goes eagerly to greet them, scanning each face anxiously in the vain hope of finding Tannhauser among their number. Disappointed, she sobs brokenly to music throbbing with intense sorrow: "He will return no more."

Elizabeth then turns again to the shrine, bending like a flower before a storm, and sings the exquisite aria, Elizabeth's Prayer: "Oh, let me come to heaven with thee as Thy handmaid to kneel before Thy throne and pray for him." This is a poignant lament of the higher nature for the erring personality.

At length, Elizabeth turns homeward. As she goes slowly up the path toward the Castle Wolfram offers to accompany her, but she gently motions him away. Her grief is too deep for speech. Pointing heavenward, she indicates to Wolfram that her solace now lies only in the love that comes to her from above. Her slow ascent to the Wartburg is made to the orchestral accompaniment of Wolfram's tender and exquisite theme of selfless and renunciatory love. As Elizabeth mounts higher and higher, the music becomes more ethereal and heavenly, until in the woodwinds it is lost to human hearing.

Left alone, Wolfram gives vent to his great sorrow in the tender strains of his harp, and twilight falls over the valley. In its darkening shadows he sees a symbol of death coming to claim one who would fain exchange earth for heaven; but in the sky above he sees the Evening Star, the Love Star, shining with a radiance that robs both night and death of their terrors. Solemnly and tenderly he bids this Love Star greet the pure maiden as she "leaves this sad vale of earth and soars aloft to peace unending."

All true music tends to link heaven and earth, but there are certain compositions that are especially effective in bridging the inner and the outer worlds. Among these is The Evening Star sung by Wolfram. So, too, are the Pilgrims' Chorus and Elizabeth's Prayer.

The powers that can be communicated to earth by means of music are as yet scarcely suspected by the average individual, but the time is fast approaching when man will select his music with the same intelligent care and knowledge he now uses to select his food. When that time comes music will become a principal source of healing for many individual and social ills, and human evolution will be tremendously accelerated.

When Wolfram finishes his sublime song to the evening star he sees approaching a strange figure whose garments are torn and travel-stained and whose weariness seems but a single step from death itself. To Wolfram's amazement and sorrow, he discovers the sorry figure to be none other than the returned Knight, Tannhauser. The haggard pilgrim is accompanied by a dark and gloomy motif, the Curse, carried by horns and strings.

Wolfram addresses the sad and dejected wanderer, asking if he knows who it is that is speaking to him. Tannhauser replies in embittered tones, "I know thy name right well. Thou art Wolfram, the skillful minstrel."

Deeply moved, Wolfram starts forward, exclaiming, "Heinrich! Why unforgiven hast thou returned? . . . You did not go to Rome?"

As Wolfram advances toward him, Tannhauser motions him to stand apart and warns him not to come too near. "The very ground I tread is accursed," says he fiercely.

Tannhauser is a strong soul who does nothing by halves. Having come to a realization of the full enormity of his transgression through the redemptive power of Elizabeth's love, he throws the full strength of his intense nature into the work of self-purification and the transmutation of animal passion into spiritual power. How desperately he has tried to become worthy of the pure love of Elizabeth is the burden of his story to Wolfram. He tells of his journey to Rome as a penitent seeking forgiveness. Says he: "When my companions walked on the soft green meadows, I trod on stones. When they made their prayers to heaven, I bared my arms and gave my blood. When their thirst was quenched by cool forest streams, I drank only of the fiery sun and when they were warmly couched in the beds of the hospice, I made my bed of ice and snow. It was thus I reached the city and begged of him whom I supplicated to free me from these bonds of fire. He listened to my story and then he answered: 'You are damned for all eternity. Sooner this dry staff upon which I lean shall burst into bloom of tender green, than that God's grace shall bloom for thee.'"

Tannhauser relates further that when he heard this terrible verdict he swooned, and that when he awakened, morning was shining over the square and in the distance he heard the triumphant chorus of the pilgrims as they were wending their way homeward, redeemed.

"Now," Tannhauser continues despairingly, "there is no heaven for me but the Venusberg and no love but Venus."

As he utters these words the red mists of enchantment begin to fill the valley. Siren forms appear dancing to alluring music, and Venus sings in her softest, sweetest tones, "The founts of joy are open eternally; never again shall you leave me."

Realizing the subtle danger that now confronts Tannhauser, Wolfram springs between him and the Goddess. Just as Tannhauser is about to be engulfed in the sinister, red-gold Venusian mist, Wolfram calls on Elizabeth for help. As he utters her name, Tannhauser turns and beholds the funeral procession of Elizabeth approaching to the accompaniment of solemn music. The procession is headed by the oldest minstrels, who are followed by the younger men bearing the open bier. Behind them come Prince Hermann, the Knights and Nobles. In chorus they sing: "Blessed be the pure one who appears with the Saints around the throne of the Lord."

Kneeling beside the lifeless form of his true and highest love, Tannhauser sobs out, "Saint Elizabeth, in heaven pray for me."

As the Knight makes this appeal to Elizabeth, who represents his higher self, Venus, representative of his lower self, realizes she has lost her supremacy over the heart of Tannhauser. With resignation she wails, "He is lost to me forever."

As previously stated, Wagner utilizes a specific motif to describe the essential nature of each of his principal characters. Elizabeth's Prayer is a tonal picture of her beauty and purity; the Venus music is enticingly seductive. The Evening Star reveals Wolfram's spiritual nobility. At first Tannhauser is depicted musically by the dark and threatening Damnation motif; after his journey of repentance to Rome, this is transformed into a sweet and healing motif called The Pardon or healing through grace. The Curse or Damnation is not used in the orthodox sense of eternal punishment, but has reference to the soul's subjection to base desires and animal passions which continue until it is set free by the transmutation of lower sensual impulses into a higher expression of the spirit.

As Tannhauser kneels in complete dedication beside the bier of Elizabeth a band of pilgrims approach, carrying aloft a staff wreathed in flowers—the staff that budded in token of Tannhauser's redemption. Joyously they chant as they enter, holding aloft the flowering staff: "The world is redeemed by heavenly love. The Lord at midnight's holy hour in a miracle revealed his power. The dry baton in priestly hand has turned into a living tree. A sign of mercy this shall be. High o'er this world the Lord [Spiritual Law] doth reign. Let none His endless love disdain."

Thus the judgment of man, which declared that this redemption could not be, is rendered null and void by the power of the Christ that is awakened within—the glorious truth that forms the central theme of this beautiful soul myth.

It is the young pilgrims that bring back the budding rod indicating Tannhauser's forgiveness. With their appearance the sun rises in glory, heralding a new day and a new racial consciousness. The old penitents who returned without sign of Tannhauser's redemption typify the ancient karmic law of "an eye for an eye and a tooth for a tooth" which is superseded by grace in Christ—figured in the young pilgrims who come bearing the flowering staff—for in Christ all things are made new.

In early centuries the Christian Church was a true School of the Mysteries. None occupied the Pope's chair who was not an Initiate. His staff was symbolic of the sacred creative fire of the body which, when uplifted through the regenerative life, ascends along the spinal canal and quickens successively the several etheric centers along its path. This results in unfolded psychic and spiritual powers. It is the Flowering Staff. The Pope's three-tiered crown represents the purification of the physical and emotional natures and spiritualization of the mind.

The Tannhauser myth is one of the most beautiful of all transmutation legends which have come down from medieval times. Elizabeth is the higher nature or the spirit. She is in heaven; in other words, the principle she represents is the Kingdom of God within man himself.

Tannhauser is the personality which, through surrender to a misdirected love impulse, falls into error and suffers the unspeakable tragedy of being shut off from his beloved Elizabeth, his higher self. Through repentance he effects a renewed contact by means of transmutation, symbolized by the rod that budded. Thus, the legend reveals the story of the fall of man and the process by which his final redemption is achieved.

Wagner climaxes this great opera with a magnificent musical epilogue in which a chorus is heard singing triumphant alleluias of faith and hope. The music rises in shimmering crescendos until the very stars of heaven seem to add their blessed benediction upon a soul reborn. Wagner thus sounds the musical keynote of the New Age around which much of the "miracle-music" of the New Christed Dispensation will be written.

• • •

Many were the vicissitudes and trials which beset the path of that brave and indefatigable spirit, Richard Wagner, before success crowned his work. When he was finally permitted to present *Tannhauser* at the Paris Opera he was commanded to add a ballet, as the subscribers were more interested in ballet than music. When he had added the ballet to the first act he received further orders to change it to the second act, because subscribers never arrived in time for the first act! Small wonder he called the opera directors "The Jockey Club."

On the night of its premiere, the opera house was filled with hecklers of a hostile press. Cat-call and horse-laughs greeted the exquisite music, which was dismissed by some critics as "musical hodge-podge." Because they could neither understand nor appreciate it, they scoffingly called it the "music of the future." Little did they realize the truth they spoke in scorn.

Wagner encountered the same lack of understanding among musical critics of his day when he chose to have his theatre built in a secluded retreat where his purpose might best be served. Some remarked at the time that only an escaped lunatic or an ignoramus could have planned so senseless a project. This was sneeringly referred to as "the theatre of the future."

Truly, it was just that, and that it still is. The world does not yet recognize the lofty concept Wagner entertained in establishing at Bayreuth an institution in which there was to be restored something of the sublime Temple Mysteries of ancient days.

Since the high office which this "Art-Temple" was designed to fulfill was of a sacred character, it was desirable that it be situated in the quiet, serene country and in purity of atmosphere and beauty of setting which only unspoiled nature can provide. All this Wagner found at Bayreuth. It was not a place to attract crowds seeking entertainment, but it was a retreat inviting those who loved the arts in their finest and purest form, and who sought the spiritual upliftment that such could provide.

At its dedicatory ceremonies, which occurred on May 22, 1872, Beethoven's Ninth Symphony was performed by an orchestra made up of many of Europe's foremost musicians. The choice of this, Beethoven's most sublime Symphony, was in perfect accord with the purposes to which the theatre was dedicated. Verily, it opens the doors to heaven worlds where the music of the spheres can be heard, doors through which the neophyte may pass from this plane into realms where dwell angelic hosts.

Speaking at the dedication of his "Art-Temple," Wagner said that "even architecture has to acquire a new meaning under the influence of music" and that "the myth of the Amphion building the walls of Thebes by the notes of the lyre has a deep meaning."

Bayreuth lost its spiritual power after Wagner's passing. That which the musical seer imparted to it was gone. The key to its deeper purposes, initiatory in character, was lost.

Had Bayreuth continued to function in the manner and for the purpose envisioned by Wagner, it would have become so enveloped in a spiritual aura of its own creation that it would undoubtedly have been protected from the late war's ruinous bombing. But as it had lost its inner spirit, its outer form became subject to the physical forces that destroyed so many of Europe's structures.

Wagner well knew that he was the transmitter of values that were all but totally unrecognized in his day, and that they would, in all probability, remain so for a long time to come. This belief, or perhaps more correctly, this knowledge he conveyed to both his contemporaries and posterity in the words he had inscribed on the cornerstone of his theatre at Bayreuth:

I bury here a secret deep.
For centuries long to lie concealed,
But while this stone its trust shall keep,
To all this secret stands revealed.

CHAPTER II

Lohengrin

The Degree of Conscious Invisible Helpership

The immortal soul does not participate in the weaknesses of matter; during the sleep of the body it spreads its radiant wings and travels, God knows where! What it then does, no one can say, but inspiration sometimes betrays the secret of its nocturnal wanderings.

—Schiller

CIRCUMSTANCES ATTENDING THE MUSIC-DRAMA'S COMPOSITION

IT IS significant that when Wagner first began to feel the inflow of inspiration which was to take its embodiment in the romantic opera, *Lohengrin,* he was spending a holiday in a certain place impregnated by the vibratory rhythm of a mighty occult Brotherhood, its initiatory Temple being located in that vicinity. He tells us he had been sent there for complete rest and quiet, but found it impossible to relax because of the "volcanic" soil around him which exercised a most exhilarating effect upon his sensitive nerves. Daily he wandered in the woods, reading the old Lohengrin epic and recreating in his mind's eye the world of its transpiring.

The result was an ever-increasing and distressing state of excitement. Recalling the experience, Wagner tells us that "Lohengrin suddenly stood fully before me down to the smallest detail of the dramatic construction." Remembering his doctor's advice to keep as quiet as possible, he tried to drive *Lohengrin* from his mind by taking up a less exciting subject, the Master Singers. In the latter he sought respite from the high nervous tension which always accompanies creative work, especially when done under first-hand instruction and when the influx of psychic energy is almost too much for a physical instrument to bear.

Under such pressure Wagner labored. Even when taking a prescribed medical bath, the creative inspiration so impelled him that, as he wrote, "I was unable to remain in the bath for the stipulated hour, jumped out after a few minutes, and barely giving myself time to dress, ran like a madman to my lodging to put on paper what was crying out for expression within me. The same thing," he added, "occurred for several days until *Lohengrin* was sketched out complete." Under such circumstances it is not surprising to learn that his doctor gave him up as a hopeless case.

Wagner's creative restlessness continued to increase for some time, during which he resorted to long and fatiguing walks as the only means for working off his superfluous energy.

It was during this period when the *Lohengrin* music-drama was in the making that Wagner's fortunes reached, perhaps, their lowest ebb. He had separated from his first wife, with whom he appears to have been entirely incompatible. He was in direst poverty, hounded by debtors, and nervously ill and depleted; besides all this, he was surrounded by lack of appreciation and understanding.

Despite such distressing circumstances his soul found sanctuary in inner-plane communion, during which he transcribed for earthly ears the celestial music of the Grail. By his life as well as his music, Richard Wagner teaches the great lesson that in the crucible of one's own sorrow it is always possible to find strength with which to rise to spiritual heights and thus gain surcease from misery and inspiration for service to others. Surely the medieval alchemists must have had this idea in mind when they inscribed upon their crucibles the sign of the cross—whence the vessel derives its name.

THE LEGEND

The story of Lohengrin is not unrelated to German history. Schwangau, "the district of the Swan," is the home of the Dukes of Bavaria. During the twelfth century literature passed from ecclesiastical into knightly hands, and the tide of poetry flowing in from France entered Germany principally by way of the Netherlands, where lay both Flanders and Brabant. Elsa von Brabant is the heroine of Lohengrin. Lohengrin himself belongs to the Swan country of Bavaria where Knights of the Swan built their castles high on wooded hills. It was from one of these castles that Lohengrin went forth to aid Elsa of Brabant.

Wagner's own life history touched upon this historic stream, for King Ludwig II, his patron, grew up in these environs, familiar with and loving its hauntingly beautiful legends. It is said that Ludwig's father, Maximilian, while on a hunting trip one day saw the ruined old castle of Schwangau. He was so fascinated by the ancient dwelling place of his own ancestors, the Dukes of Bavaria, that he bought the castle and had it rebuilt; then had its walls decorated with scenes drawn from German history and legend.

King Ludwig loved this castle and countryside. Later he built his own fairytale castle, Neuschwanstein, on a rocky peak across from Hohenschwangau, on the very eminence which legend pronounced to be the site of Tannhauser's castle. Neuschwanstein's salons are vivid with frescoes depicting scenes from *Tannhauser, Tristan* and *Lohengrin*, and from the lives of Hans Sachs and Walter von der Vogelweide.

A traveler says of these two castles, Hohenschwangau and Neuschwanstein, that they have the most romantic situation in the world, perched high on rocky crags in the midst of deep fir forests, with snowy peaks of the Bavarian Alps on the horizon and two lovely little lakes at their feet.

In was in the ornate music hall of Neuschwanstein that music-loving King Ludwig had Wagner's operas performed for himself alone. It must be remembered that in those days Wagnerian lovers came "singly" and not, as now, in "battalions." One of the very few who really appreciated the composer, not only to the point of hearing his masterly compositions but of coming forward with moral and material support that he might continue his work, was Ludwig. In the midst of almost universal disesteem, this wealthy and royal patron gave Wagner the aid he needed and was instrumental in having his operas performed in Munich.

Ludwig himself appears to have been more than a little of what the Scotch call "fey." At nineteen, when he came to the throne, he was like some prince of faerie, with his dreamy, poetic face and brilliant black eyes. Everyone found him charming and his people loved him. But as he drew more and more within himself he forfeited his popularity, and was at last forced to abdicate because of his extravagances which were bankrupting the kingdom. It is thought he committed suicide by drowning himself in the lake of Starnberg.

Mad—or merely madly extravagant—Ludwig may have been, yet the instincts of a people are seldom wholly wrong and Ludwig is still beloved of the Bavarian peasantry. They look for him to return to them one day. They say that sometimes on dark nights the sound of galloping horses echoes through the hills; then the lonely watcher may see approaching the flaring torches of outriders, and after them a coach drawn swiftly by fiery steeds. As the procession speeds by, an observer may catch a fleeting glimpse of a white and haunted face with burning black eyes before all is lost in the dimness and silence.

THE SWAN KNIGHT

In *Lohengrin* Wagner portrays the second Degree of the Christian Mysteries, which is only possible of attainment by one who has passed the first Degree, Purification—depicted in *Tannhauser*. By means of inner forces awakened through Purification, the brain mind becomes sufficiently sensitized to receive subtle impressions of the world of soul, and an individual then "remembers" the life of the soul as it is lived in inner worlds during hours when the body is asleep.

As pointed out in the preceding pages, the ego or spirit of man is able to construct a "soul body"—a body which resembles in appearance the physical body but is independent of it and so can be used as a vehicle of activity during hours of sleep. Because of this separation, persons still in the flesh may, especially in moments of stress or on passing, project their soul image so as to make it visible to those with whom they are in close attunement. There are many instances of this kind in the annals of the Society for Psychical Research. The candidate for Initiation, having passed through the first Degree, learns to create this soul-body consciously—a work symbolized in the homunculus of the alchemists. Thus he tremendously increases his opportunities for service, since henceforth it can be carried on with greater efficiency both on inner planes and in the outer physical world.

The First Degree of Purification has the twofold object of building a soul body and of awakening its organs—known in occult science as "centers" or "chakras"—which have a corresponding structure in the nervous system of the physical body. In this development music can be most helpful—as Wagner appears to have known, for he said that the purpose of all real music is to so lift man that he will find and commune with the Holy Grail (the divine godhood) within himself. Music, and in fact everything that is beautiful and true, acts upon the soul; but music such as Wagner's is, to an exceptional degree, initiatory in character and aim. With the preliminary work of the first Degree accomplished, the candidate enters upon the new life of service conferred by the attainment of the Second Degree.

In the person of Lohengrin we observe the fruit of the Great Work, its finished product, the Swan Knight, the perfected one, contrasted with a neophyte, Elsa. Elsa stands on a higher rung of the ladder than Tannhauser and so encounters temptations of a more subtle nature. She has passed the Degree of Purfication; her soul is innocent of base desire. It is her faithfulness and spiritual courage which are put to the crucial test. Apropos of this, Wagner writes: "The entire interest of *Lohengrin* rests upon a process in the heart of Elsa which touched all the secrets of her soul."

THE PRELUDE

The Prelude to *Lohengrin* is the Holy Grail set to soul-transporting music. "Out of the clear blue aether of the sky," writes Wagner in describing it, "there seems to condense a wonderful yet at first hardly perceptible vision; and out of this there gradually emerges, ever more and more clearly, an angel host bearing in its midst the sacred Grail. As it approaches earth it pours out exquisite odours like streams of gold, ravishing the senses of the beholder. The glory of the vision grows and grows until it seems as if the rapture must be shattered and dispersed by the very vehemence of its own expansion. The vision draws nearer and the climax is reached when at last the Grail is revealed in all its glorious reality, radiating fiery beams and shaking the soul with emotion. The beholder sinks on his knees in adoring self-annihilation. The Grail pours out its light like a benediction and consecrates him to its service; then the flames gradually die away and the angel host soars up again to the ethereal heights in tender joy, having made pure once more the heart of men by the sacred blessing of the Grail."

The *Tannhauser* music, as stated when discussing that opera, serves as an effective medium of communication between the living and the so-called dead. The *Lohengrin* music rises to a higher octave of experiences in which its identification with the powers of the Holy Grail make it an effective medium by which man may enter into communication with celestial Beings.

The Prelude begins with the Grail motif sounding in the highest heavens and gradually descending as Angels bear the Holy Cup down through the lower heavens, until they finally reach the physical realm where they deliver the Cup into the care of Montsalvat. This Cup, of pearly whiteness in the celestial realms, becomes tinged with a delicate pink glow as the atmosphere of earth is contacted. The Angels ascend once more, chorusing of man's divine destiny under the illumination of the Grail. The music becomes ever more ethereal until it is lost in the softness of muted violins, like Angel wings misted by rays of golden sunlight.

In his description of the Prelude motif, Wagner tells us of his own exalted experience, wherein he dedicated himself and all his powers to the dissemination, through music, of the holy Mysteries of Initiation. That he remained faithful to his heavenly vision is proved by the magnificence of his accomplishments, his immortal works.

Aloft in angelic realms where life and harmony are one, Wagner's transported senses caught the vision and the rhythm of the soul's innermost movements, and he later translated them into their true musical equivalents on the earth plane. He heard the highest notes of violins, most sensitive of musical instruments, convey the vibrant chorusing of angelic hosts. As Angels wafted earthward, wind instruments took up their divine melody in the mental realm. On the astral plane it was sounded by horns and bassoons.

When the golden glory finally reached the physical world, trumpets and trombones added their benediction as the illumined poet-musician was dedicated for all time to his unique work. Then the angelic hosts soared joyfully upward, their mission fulfilled.

In the white fire of his creative genius the powers of the ancient Esoteric Tradition have been fused with the power of music in a way never before attempted. The uniting of these two forces will, in time, produce a new and higher musical art hitherto unknown to the world, the "Art of the Future" of which Wagner so frequently spoke.

ACT I

The opening scene of the opera is laid in the province of Brabant, near the city of Antwerp. In a meadow all in flower and with a river running through it like a silver ribbon, stands a great and ancient tree known as the Oak of Justice. Seated upon a throne under the venerable oak is Henry the Fowler, King of Germany, with knights and nobles of Saxony and Thuringia assembled on one side of him and those of Brabant, led by Frederick of Telramund and his wife Ortrud, on the other.

During medieval times such assemblages were known as *Freigerichte*. Princes, counts, knights and citizens strove for the honor of taking part in them. During this period, when the Mysteries were entrusted to the knightly class, the king was not infrequently an Initiate, and as such was revered with more than the usual devotion accorded to earthly kings.

These Courts of Justice were usually held beneath great trees. Many of them were centuries old and had been planted with ceremonies remembered from the pre-Christian Mysteries which attuned them to the magnetic flow of earth forces. Also from ancient times came the tradition of divine justice administered under the ancient oak of the gods, such justice depending in no small measure upon the spiritual insight of the kingly judge. The opening of the Court was a sacred rite in which was evoked the guidance of angelic hosts.

Now the King, seated upon his throne, announces to the assemblage that he has come expecting to find the people united and ready to assist him to driving the Hungarians from the country, but instead he finds them disunited and divided into factions. He calls upon Frederick of Telramund to explain the meaning of these dissensions.

Frederick, a dark and sombre individual, replies that upon the recent death of the Duke of Brabant, he, Frederick, was appointed guardian of the Duke's children, Elsa and her brother Godfrey, with the understanding that he should marry Elsa. This, he says, he did not do for a reason which seemed good to him—for Elsa, he says, went one day for a walk with her brother and returned alone. On being questioned as to what had become of the boy, she made no reply. Frederick insists that in accordance with her father's request he had been betrothed to Elsa; but believing that she murdered her brother, he married Ortrud (a princess skilled in the dark arts), the daughter of the nearby Prince of Friesland. He now asks the King that Elsa be adjudged guilty and dispossessed of her kingdom, which should revert to him as nearest of kin.

Elsa of Brabant is a true mystic, possessing the extended powers of clairvoyance and clairaudience. "Rapt in strange dreams, a secret flame she surely nourishes in her heart." It is to assist her in the right use of these powers that Lohengrin has appeared to her in a vision, acting as her spiritual Teacher. Elsa enters upon the scene to the Grail motif, which represents the protective aura of her Teacher—such as always enfolds a worthy pupil.

King Henry asks Elsa what she can say in her defense. She makes no reply, but half sobs to herself, "Oh, my helpless brother!" Although she refuses to speak in her own behalf, she is so radiant in her innocence and purity that the King cannot believe her guilty; but wanting to arrive at the truth, he asks Elsa to choose a champion from among the assembled Knights to meet Frederick in combat, declaring that God will prove who is innocent and who is guilty in the trial by arms.

Elsa, to the exquisite accompaniment of soft chords sounded mostly in woodwinds and brasses, comes forward. Kneeling beneath the great tree she sings the beautiful aria *Elsa's Dream,* in which she describes certain happenings commonly called "visions" or "dreams," but which, to the developed mystic, are memories of actual soul experiences in the heaven world during physical sleep. Sings she: "Ofttimes when I am sad and the days are dark and lonely, I pray to heaven for help and protection. It is then that in my dreams I see a shining knight, clad in white and silver armor. I have never seen anyone on earth so pure and noble looking. He is surrounded with a great halo of radiance and when I see him I am filled with hope and confidence." The ethereal strains of the Grail and Lohengrin motifs are heard as she sings.

The King again calls upon her to choose her defender against Frederick, whereupon, in high spiritual exaltation, Elsa cries, "I choose my shining knight! Now heaven bear to him my weeping! Hasten to save me, my true knight! As a reward I offer to him sent from above this my ancestral kingdom, my hand, and heart's true love!"

The trumpets sound to the four points of the compass: "He who would fight under the judgment of God for Elsa of Brabant, let him appear!" At the first call there is no answer. Elsa says that her Knight dwells so far away he did not hear the call, and asks that it be given again. At the second call a boat drawn by a white swan is seen approaching. Within the boat stands a shining Knight clad in white and silver armor. Truly celestial in both melody and rhythm is the music as Lohengrin steps from the boat and blesses the swan, bidding it return to the happy land, the land of Dawn, whence they had come, while the tenuous music of the Grail emanates softly from flutes and violins. Lohengrin also says that duty has called him away from higher realms and that he must remain for a time in the world to serve in response to a disciple's call. He tells King Henry that he has come to defend an innocent maiden; then, turning to Elsa, asks her if she will keep her word and become his bride. When she replies in the affirmative he requests her promise never to ask whence he has come, his rank or his name.

Every high Initiate receives a new name that is fraught with power. None but an Initiate of similar degree may know and use that name. Elsa had not yet attained to that degree. Twice Lohengrin requires the pledge of Elsa: "If you would ever have me with you, a sacred oath you must keep to me. You must never ask me, nor tempt me to reveal whence I came to you, nor what my name is." And twice the Warning motif is heard in clear, powerful tones, as if admonishing the aspirant that she stands before the decision which can make or break her life.

All undaunted Elsa replies: "To you my soul is consecrated, of my self you are already lord." Unfaltering confidence in one's Teacher is always a prime essential on the Path.

Observe how the call was sent out for the champion *twice*, and Lohengrin *twice* repeats his warning to Elsa to the accompaniment of the Warning motif. From this we learn that Elsa has successfully passed through the First Degree on some previous occasion, and that her present trial belongs to the Second Degree.

As Lohengrin represents the White Brotherhood or the forces of Light, Ortrud represents the Black Brotherhood or the Forces of Darkness. Telramund is a pupil of the latter as Elsa is of the former.

Luminous with the power of faith and inner-plane guidance is the beautiful prayer of the King: "O great Heaven, fount of love, guide the arms of the two champions. Oh! let the just be the conqueror, let Truth triumph in the combat."

In the third round of combat Frederick is disarmed by the nameless Knight, who returns his sword to him saying, "God has given your life into my hands, now I give it back to you for repentance."

The Glory motif which aureoles Lohengrin is revealed to inner vision as white and silver light: white for his purity and silver for the love power of the heart which are always highly developed in a masculine Initiate—just as masculine attributes are developed in a feminine Initiate.

Elsa's motif is Doubt. This motif is dark in both color and tone. Fear is the great deterrent of spiritual progress and doubt is its offspring. In the beginning, intermingled with this Doubt motif, are brighter tones of Hope and Faith. The supreme testing of Elsa is to prove whether Faith (inspired by her First Degree experiences) or Doubt will become paramount in her life.

The purpose of a Teacher's admonition is that the neophyte may learn to live in a consciousness sufficiently elevated to respond to his high rhythms and thus be able to "tune in" with him at any time, regardless of the hour or distance. To do this ordinary personal love, which is so largely dependent on material factors, must be kept strictly in the background. The Teacher must be loved with a detachment which few, indeed, are able to achieve.

The motif of Ortrud, the Princess who declares that she "is not unskilled in the dark arts," is characteristic of her. It is deep and sinister music termed Dark Plots. Frederick has allied himself with evil, so his destiny must inevitably be destruction. His motif is the Judgment of God. The King's Call is high, noble and stately in measure. The Mystery of the Name is deep and filled with a portent of the inexplicable. The Swan is sweetness, harmony and benediction.

During the singing of her Dream, Elsa is surrounded

with a musical halo faintly reminiscent of the Glory motif of Lohengrin, which the Knight projects to her.

During the course of the combat between Frederick and Lohengrin, Frederick's motif, the Judgment of God, is loud and furious, indicative of Karmic Law. Lohengrin's Victory is announced by the Glory motif, high and clear.

The act closes with a triumphant chorusing of the assemblage over Elsa's vindication and victory. Always there are those on the visible and the invisible planes who chant in rejoicing for the spiritual triumph of an aspirant seeking Initiation. Of Lohengrin they sing:

Be eternal praise and glory
To the grave victorious warrior!
. . . . Never have we seen
So valiant a warrior on earth.

Again, high above the joyous chorusing, sounds the pure tones of the Glory motif, accompanied by the mystic notes of the Grail theme, signifying that the powerful influence of a great Initiate-Teacher dominates the entire proceedings.

ACT II

The opening scene of the second act is set to dark and sinister music. The Witchcraft motif of Ortrud and the Doubt motif of Elsa—a doubt which Ortrud means to intensify—are most prominent. Wagner has written that Ortrud is "a woman who does not know love. Politics are her essence. The only love she knows is of the past, of dead generations, the terribly insane love of an ancestral pride which finds its expression in the hatred of everything living, actually existing."

Ortrud and Frederick spend the night hours crouched

on the cathedral steps opposite Elsa's palace. No longer in gorgeous raiment, they are now garbed in black robes which accord well with their evil designs on Elsa and the strange Knight. They quarrel violently, each accusing the other for the lack of success so far attending their schemes. Frederick regrets that his sword has been taken from him so he cannot slay the "companion of his shame." Fortunately, evil can never become supreme in the world because its forces are disintegrating; it continues always to destroy itself. Two negatives will never make a positive, nor will two wrongs ever make a right.

In their duet, filled with a peculiarly sinister beauty, Ortrud and Frederick seal their dark and evil pact with a terrible imprecation in an appeal to the Powers of Darkness. In this music, as in *The Flying Dutchman,* Wagner introduces musical devices that are employed in the service of the Black Grail.

As Elsa appears upon her balcony and sings of her great happiness and joy, Ortrud sends Frederick away, telling him he may deal with the Knight but that Elsa is her prey. She then presents herself to Elsa, feigning humility and contrition and begging forgiveness.

It is significant that whenever Elsa contacts Ortrud the Doubt motif becomes louder while the Faith and Hope motifs are barely audible. Susceptibility to the poison of suspicion is already present in Elsa's soul, for she has yet to develop that subtle spiritual discrimination which is of all things the most important to the disciple. Without it even the greatest love and aspiration may fail to attain their goal. Lacking this discrimination, this spiritual insight, Elsa accepts in good faith the hypocritical protestations of Ortrud and invites her to attend the wedding festivities on the morrow.

In the duet sung by Elsa and Ortrud, the Doubt motif and the Mystery of the Name become increasingly prominent, showing the progress of Ortrud's dark plots. As Elsa disappears, Ortrud ascends the steps triumphantly singing: "Hallow my feigning and my lies: Grant me sweet vengeance!"

The stately measures of the King's Call announce the dawn. All is activity and happiness in preparation for the wedding festivities. With the coming of sunrise the consciousness of an aspirant touches a new and higher level. Here is heard a faint intimation of the Grail motif. Heralds announce that the heaven-sent stranger has refused the title of Duke, preferring to be known only as the "Guardian of Brabant."

Preceded by a magnificent procession but walking alone, Elsa approaches the Temple to the Grail music.

This is not to be interpreted as a marriage on the physical plane but as preparation for the mystic wedding of the lower nature with the higher in an indissoluble union. Along this Path the neophyte must always walk alone, else he would be a god-guided automation and not an emancipated spirit knowing the full and free development of his own innate God powers, the ideal extolled in every Christian Mystery School.

These beautiful spiritual truths are almost entirely lost to modern understanding. Wagner was always insistent that the singers be made to comprehend the "full import of the opera's action," and was deeply disappointed that the glory of the Lohengrin music caused both singers and audience to overlook the inner meaning of the story. He therefore requested that before each performance the stage director assemble the cast and read the story to them, without the music.

Ortrud bars Elsa's way, warning her that this strange Knight may be a magician instead of an Initiate, and that his powers may surround her with evil. "Whence," she asks, "did the river bear him? Whither will it take him back again some day?" She does not hesitate to reveal her true colors, demanding precedence over the bride-elect of a nameless Knight. The appearance of the King and Lohengrin silences her and the Knight assists the trembling and bewildered Elsa. As the procession moves forward, Telramund steps before them and fiercely accuses Lohengrin of being a sorcerer. This is proven, he declares, by the magical swan-drawn boat in which he had come. He then demands that the Knight reveal his name.

The King dismisses Telramund with contempt and he is driven away as the procession moves forward and enters the cathedral.

Subtle temptations accompany the aspirant to the very door of the Temple. *Twice* is Elsa tempted as she ascends the steps leading to the door opening upon the Mysteries.

Lohengrin is accompanied, as always, by the Glory motif with overtones of the Grail music. He asks Elsa if she still has faith in him. When she replies that she has, he says, "Then dry your tears amid the joys of that sacred place." He places his mantle tenderly about her and, together with the King, they enter the cathedral. The mantle represents the aura of spiritual protection with which a true Teacher always protects his pupils. During this action the Warning motif sounds above the festal music, suggesting that Elsa's supreme trial is yet to come.

By his great powers Lohengrin has for the moment disarmed Ortrud and Frederick. The song with which he sends them away is filled with tenderness, sorrow, and compassion for their weakness. So must the Illumined overcome evil with good.

During the highly dramatic and meaningful ascent of the cathedral steps the accompanying motifs reveal much that is overwise hidden, for if there are dramatic Mysteries which teach by sight, there are other Mysteries which reach the soul through the ear alone. Thus, as Elsa and Lohengrin approach the entry of the cathedral, the music rises in crescendoes of soul exaltation. The chorus of attendants, who typify fellow aspirants, add their song of rejoicing that one of their company is successfully passing through trials which give entrance into the sacred precincts—for there is no envy among those making the ascent to the Temple. The music takes on a higher and more ecstatic note when Elsa spurns the interference of Ortrud and Telramund.

Exquisite gentleness and understanding are expressed by Lohengrin, a Teacher who has won the conquest of self, for the difficulties and obstructions which always beset the path of one on the Quest of Light.

ACT III

The orchestral introduction to Scene I, Act III, is descriptive of the wedding festivities. In this epithalamium Prelude two themes are introduced, one graceful, tender and charming, which may be associated with the more gentle and sweeter feminine aspects of love; the other strong and joyously masculine. As the music grows softer, the curtain rises on the marriage chamber.

As previously stated, the marriage chamber has a spiritual significance relating to the union of the soul with God—or, as it is more commonly expressed, of the lower with the higher self. This is the only marriage which is made in heaven and the only marriage in which Temple Initiates can have any possible interest.

Elsa has gained entrance to the Temple. Now she must be tested further to prove her fitness for the sacred Rite of the Mystic Marriage. For this reason the lovely marriage music is heard here instead of being used as a processional as is commonly done today.

Elsa and the Knight are surrounded by eight pages bearing lighted torches. They form a circle of light about Elsa as she receives the blessing of the King and Lohengrin. Her maiden attendants, eighteen in number, bear wreaths of myrtle—the plant used in the Grecian Mysteries to crown a successful aspirant for Initiation. Eight is the number of the perfected life and nine, the digit of eighteen, the number of Initiation. The attendants sing as they leave Elsa: "We also bless as Heaven blessed you. We hope eternal this day's joy will be."

Elsa's entrance into the marriage chamber is accompanied by the motif of Doubt and the Mystery of the Name, both gaining in volume and insistence. Lohengrin realizes this and endeavors to save her, singing beautifully of the holy joys that are to come. "I come not out of the night and sorrow," he tells her, "but from a land of light and joy. Away with suspicion," he pleads, "let love be your surety." How strange that Elsa, who so quickly believed Ortrud, is so slow to accept the word of her Knight! She is not equal to the task of measuring good against evil, for she has no clearly defined ethical standard within herself.

In a panic of doubt and fearing that the swan boat will return for her beloved to take him from her forever, Elsa insists on knowing his name. At this crucial point there ensues a musical conflict between the Doubt motif of Elsa and the exquisite motif of the Swan, by means of which Wagner suggests the perpetual struggle between the higher and the lower nature of a neophyte even at a high place of attainment. The Mystery of the Name motif sounds furiously as Elsa asks the fatal question: "Thy name at once declare! Whence dost thou come? Where is thy home?"

Doubt has conquered Faith. Elsa has lost her place, for the time being, in the Great Light.

Just as she speaks the fatal words, Telramund rushes into the room with a sword and attacks Lohengrin. Elsa hands Lohengrin his sword, and with it he strikes Telramund dead. Lohengrin announces that on the morrow he will answer Elsa's question at the Oak of Justice, in the presence of Telramund's body, and then must leave her forever. He sums it all up sadly: "Ah, now forever our joy has fled." He departs to the strange motif of the Mystery of the Name. As he disappears the Grail music sounds, no longer triumphantly but in mournful cadences, as if the Angels themselves were weeping for Elsa's weakness. Frederick, representative of evil, could not have gained entrance into that Holy Place until Elsa, by her own weakness, opened the door. Man attracts his own upon all planes of being.

Wagner has given us a most beautiful and mysterious theme in connection with the unknown Knight. We have said that every Mystery School has its own characteristic keynote or key-theme. The Grail motif sounds the note of the Christian Mysteries as it is sung by Angels. Also, each full Initiate has an individual keynote which is the musical description of the "New Name" given him when he attained the Degree of Mastership. Aspirants of lesser Degrees do not know this name. Nor must they attempt its intonation, as its vibratory power is too high for their proper understanding and use. The wrong mode of rhythmic intonation can shatter the physical and mental vehicles of an unprepared neophyte. Elsa has presumed, and unworthily, because she has not earned the place in consciousness that gives her the privilege of tuning in at will upon her Teacher's time and attention.

The laws upon which Mystery Schools are based are unalterable and inexorable for the reason that they are centered in Truths which are universal and eternal.

Instead of *Lohengrin* being a romantic opera based on a fantastic legend, it is centered in the most profound of occult truths. Wagner reveals his esoteric wisdom by his expert handling of these truths. It was his ideal that singers of his opera should be students of the Ancient Wisdom as well as expert musicians. Their mission, as he visioned it, had a dual purpose: to instruct and illumine, and to heal physically and psychically. It was for this that he established the six-year apprenticeship at Bayreuth. Richard Wagner was the New Age emissary (like St. Paul, born out of his time) to revive musical initiatory Schools and to infuse them with Aquarian idealism, thus to produce power-music hitherto unknown to the world. In coming years, when Initiate Schools have been established in which this new "power-music" can be adequately demonstrated, Wagner will be accorded in earnest the title bestowed upon him in derision by the uncomprehending critics of his day: "Master of the Music of the Future."

Day dawns again. This mystic sunrise is not heralded with paeans of victory from watchers in the skies but with lamentations for one who has faltered upon the way.

The King and his court assemble beneath the great Oak of Justice. Elsa appears musically encircled by the motifs of Doubt and Mystery of the Name. She is pale and strangely altered in appearance. The King inquires as to the reason for this change but she refuses to answer. The white light of spiritual exaltation which animated her countenance in the previous act is gone—and there is nothing on the physical plane which can be substituted for lost soul radiance.

The motifs of Faith and Hope which belonged to Elsa in the beginning now appear in minor key, seeming to express the humiliation and sorrow which Elsa herself feels.

The body of Frederick is brought in and placed beneath the Oak of Justice to the accompaniment of his motif, the Judgment of God.

Lohengrin comes enveloped in the radiant Glory motif. His face luminious with vision and noble resolve, he describes the great Mystery Temple situated upon a loftly mountain where mortal foot has never trod. This, he tells the assemblage, is the Castle of the Grail, the initiatory Temple which man can enter only when clothed in his spiritual or soul-body. And to this Temple he had hoped to conduct Elsa.

"In her sacred oath she has failed," he states sorrowfully, "and faithless to heaven her fair gift forgot."

Elsa has permitted the evil forces of doubt, fear and

suspicion to thrust her from the Path leading to that Sanctuary. (With the ancients, palace, castle and temple were often identical, says Trumbul in his *Beginning of Religious Rites.*)

Lohengrin continues: In beauty and splendor this Castle far exceeds anything upon the earth. It is the home of an assembly of holy Knights, led by Parsifal and guarded by bands of Angels who have in their custody the Holy Grail. Each year, upon Good Friday of the sacred Easter season, the mystic power of the Grail is renewed by the descent of Holy Spirit in the form of a dove (the solar forces which inundate the earth at the vernal equinox). His beautiful song ends with the simple declaration: "I am a knight (Initiate) of this Castle and my name is Lohengrin." The ecstasy of the Grail motif intermingles with the radiance of the Glory music as he utters the name *Lohengrin.*

Elsa offers to expiate her failure in any way possible, but Lohengrin says that already he has been too long away from the Grail. When the neophyte has gone so far as to be admitted to the Temple and then falls he is rarely given a like opportunity until the doors of another earth life are opened.

It is here that Elsa sings the beautiful aria, "All is dark around me." Then we hear again the exquisite farewell song of Lohengrin in which he bids adieu to Elsa and the world. His is the lament of one who is in the world but not of it; one who came unto his own but his own received him not—which has happened to all spiritual Teachers since time began. Might still occupies high places while Truth is nailed to a cross.

Lohengrin bids Elsa give to her brother upon his return "these rare presents, this sword, this horn and this ring." The sword symbolizes comprehension of spiritual law; the horn, ability to control vibration; the ring, Truth and power to work therewith. These are rare gifts indeed and are found only in the possession of an Initiate—such as her brother has become.

Lohengrin adds:

He will conquer when the sword he raises;
The horn will aid him in an hour of need.
As for the ring, whene'er on it he gazes,
He'll think on one who thee from danger freed.

The swan reappears enhaloed with the harmony of its own motif. By such musical measures men and Angels may commune.

As Lohengrin enters the boat, Ortrud jeers that Elsa's brother will never return for he has been changed into a swan. Lohengrin kneels in prayer. The swan suddenly dives into the water and Godfrey, the young brother, appears clad in silver garments. "Behold," says Lohengrin, "the Duke of Brabant, your leader."

Elsa's brother, despite Ortrud's black arts, has achieved entry to the Grail Castle, whereas Elsa herself failed in this high accomplishment. It will be remembered that the Swan motif was heard in conflict with the Doubt motif at the very crisis of Elsa's testing within the Temple, to indicate that her Initiate brother is endeavoring to strengthen and fortify her.

The figure of a swan has always been symbolic of the Initiate because it moves with equal ease in the elements of earth, water and air. In like manner, an emanicipated spirit, freed from the trammel of a physical body, soars at will beyond the limitations of time and space. Lohengrin, at the call of Elsa, came to her aid in his swan-boat. In other words, by his powers of mastership he descended from higher planes in response to her summons.

As Lohengrin departs, Elsa falls lifeless in her brother's arms—that is, she dies to things of the outer world in a final supreme dedication to that shining Way which leads to the unbarred Gates.

Lohengrin disappears as he came, to the angelic music of the Grail, but his boat is now drawn by a white Dove.

The opera ends as it began, keyed to celestial harmony that leaves the hearer bathed in a soul radiance past all human defining.

SPIRITUAL ART WITH INITIATORY SIGNIFICANCE

No one can listen to this transcendental work of spiritual art and not experience an exaltation of feeling, a mental stimulation, some fresh measure of spiritual awareness. For those who hold the esoteric keys to its relation to the Great Work that leads to Initiation, this music is a means of conveying to their soul some of the most sublime intimations of Reality that mortal man can know.

Wagner once wrote to a friend concerning the "profound hypothesis of reincarnation which alone had been able to show the consoling point where all souls converge in the end to an equal height of redemption, after their diverse lives, running separately, though side by side in time, have met in full awareness beyond it. On that hypothesis the spotless purity of Lohengrin becomes easy to explain, in that he is a continuation of Parzival who had first to achieve his purity. In the same sense would Elsa also reach up to Lohengrin in (or through) rebirth."

Long after the score of *Lohengrin* had been completed, Wagner still despaired of ever having it produced. He would take up the sacred sheets and kiss them, with tears in his eyes as he laid them carefully away. When invited to conduct a series of concerts in London he carried with him the scores of both *Tannhauser and Lohengrin,* hoping for an opportunity to produce them, but was told that the English could not appreciate heavy German opera. He met with no better reception in Paris.

Through the help of Franz Liszt, *Lohengrin* was produced at length at Weimar, August 26, 1850, but by this time Wagner was in exile in Switzerland because of his activities in connection with the "May Revolution." That he became involved in social and political activities looking to a more democratic way of life is not strange, especially when we remember that Wagner was not an artist who lived just for art's sake, but to him the arts were for life's sake. He believed they could better fulfill their purpose in a more democratic society. Thus did this Aquarian pioneer set the seal of his genius on politics and economics as well as on music. It was during this period of exile, when unable to see productions of his operas but with sad longing in his heart, that he wrote a friend: "It seems as though I will be the last of my countrymen to see *Lohengrin*." Years after its first production his dream was realized and he witnessed the presentation of his glorious opera in Dresden.

Of all his works, the two Grail operas, *Lohengrin* and *Parsifal*, doubtless lived closest to the heart of hearts of this great master of the Music of the Future.

Tristan and Isolde

The Rite of the Mystic Marriage

PREFATORY NOTE

WAGNER had reached the age of forty-six when he completed the final orchestral score of *Tristan.* It is, therefore, the fruitage of his golden years of middle life when, after rich and varied experiences, he reached the summit of his genius which found its most perfect flowering in the incomparable *Parsifal.*

It is fitting that in the flood-tide of his vigor this great musical seer should employ the sublimest art to bring to the world that ancient mystic Rite, the highest of which man *as* man is capable, known in Christian esotericism as the Rite of the Mystic Marriage. Many saints of the church and many Initiates have experienced this Rite that lifted them to the threshold of angelic consciousness.

How nearly Wagner himself approached that threshold is shown in a letter he wrote: "When I bend brooding in formative stillness over the completion of my Tristan, who can imagine the wonder that fills me, and withdraws me so completely from the world that I have already overcome it? It is the desire of the inmost soul itself that brings about the affecting action of the drama, and it enters the light of day precisely as it was shaped beforehand in that inner shrine."

In statements such as these the profundity of Richard Wagner's occult knowledge, as well as his superlatively creative imagination, is fully evidenced. As he plunged with increasing ardor and intensity into the composition of his operas, each one exceeding its predecessor in deepened soul force and each a fuller revelation of great initiatory truths, his master dream of a School of Initiation motivated by music became more and more tangible. That Wagner was raised to fourth dimensional consciousness when writing *Tristan* is made clear by what he has related about the experience and by what the drama itself reveals to us.

In these words we find the thesis upon which all metaphysical and occult truth is based. St. Paul defined this same truth when he said: "Things seen are temporal, things unseen are eternal." In other words, the outer is but a reflection of the inner. Our own Ameican philosopher, Emerson, refers to this verity as he writes: "It is only the finite which has wrought and suffered, the Infinite lies stretched in smiling repose." It is this realm of repose, this high spiritual sphere, the land of Nirvana, toward which all the music of the opera tends and in which a large portion of the drama has its setting. As Laurence Gilman, the late eminent music critic, rightly observed, Wagner "conceived *Tristan* as a drama of the inner life of man and unless we realize that truth and are moved by that reality we get only the exterior of the work, overwhelming as that is."

The music of this opera is impregnated with the spiritual splendor of secret wisdom. It is the purest of initiatory music and is charged with the realization characteristic of illumined sages and mystics of all ages who have mastered the arts of Life and Death. It is the very apotheosis of human incarnation or, as expressed by Wagner, it is an achievement crowned by a "glimmering of the highest bliss of attainment."

In his *Mein Liben,* Wagner says that while the work on Tristan was one long ecstasy, it wielded over him a strange and uncanny influence. "It was made clear to me that I had embodied the most daring and most exotic conception in all my writings. While I was at work on the great scene of Tristan, I found myself often asking whether I was not mad to want to give such a work to a publisher. And yet I could not have parted with a single accent in that tale of pain, although the whole thing tortured me to the last degree."

THE MUSIC-DRAMA

Tristan and Isolde is much more than a romantic drama of a deep and fateful love. It is more than the greatest love music ever brought to earth. It is a mystery play dealing with the expansion, development and union of the two polarities of spirit as these manifest in masculine and feminine forms throughout all nature. "When I gave myself up to *Tristan,*" writes Wagner, "I immersed myself in the profoundest depths of spirit and fashioned the outer semblance of the work from the center of that inner world. Here in my music-drama, Life and Death, the whole meaning and existence of the outer world, depend entirely on the hidden mysteries of the spirit life."

Again Wagner writes to a friend: "There must be some indescribable inner sense which is altogether clear and active only when the outer senses are as in a dream. When I strictly neither hear nor see distinctly, this sense is at its keenest, and it functions as creative calm. I can call it by no other name, merely I know that this calm of mine works from within to without; with it I am at the spirit's center."

Certainly in no other of his works does Wagner give more convincing evidence of his profound grasp of occult knowledge and of spiritual power than he does in *Tristan and Isolde*. If he had done nothing else, the elevation of his creative genius as exhibited in this drama would earn for him from the spiritually understanding a recognition of his Musical Initiateship.

Ernest Neuman, the celebrated authority on Wagner's life and works, writing of the Prelude to *Tristan,* says that it "contains the spiritual essence of the drama in highly concentrated form. Hardly anything happens in the ordinary theatrical sense of the word." He continues, "The tragedy comes about, not because of what happens to the fated pair, but because of what they are. *Tristan and Isolde* is a drama of spiritual states, not of outward actions."

In this statement, Mr. Neuman touches upon the initiatory character of the opera which centers, not in external action, but in a metaphysical state of consciousness.

The Prelude to Act I of *Tristan and Isolde* contains the seven most important motifs which form the musical background of the opera. There are also seven important characters introduced into the action of the drama. In this connection it is significant to note that, occultly, man possesses a sevenfold body that is correlated to a cosmos which is basically septenary in structure and the evolution of which proceeds throughout seven aeons of time. Thus the drama, in its very numerical pattern, falls into harmony with the underlying rhythms of all nature.

It is also to be observed that the supreme significance of number seven for man lies in the fact that it is a combination of three and four, the former being linked to the trinity of spirit; the latter, to the quartenary of form—with man's present evolutionary task being to transmute the four lower principles into the three higher. The initiatory work portrayed in the drama bears directly on this transmutation process and gives a dramatic portrayal of the significance of the cryptic saying in mystic numerology that "When the Trine bends down to kiss the Square, then heaven and earth are conjoined."

The seven musical motifs of the Prelude outline the whole of the initiatory Path. The first motif, Confession of

Love, represents dedication to the Path. The Desire motif, mournful and repeated four times, describes the cleansing of man's four lower bodies: the physical, etheric, astral and lower mental. The Look motif is the beginning of work toward polarity in spirit, while the Magic Casket—which, according to Wagner, grows out of the Look motif—musically describes the soul body in which the aspirant must be clothed before he can take part in the exalted rites of the Mystic Marriage. This body cannot be fashioned until the two polarities of spirit, masculine and feminine, have been brought into balance.

The Death motif describes complete renunciation of things of the flesh for things of the spirit. The Love motif is filled with the mystic fire and beauty of transmutation from the lower into the higher. Together with the Look motif it forms the principal musical background of the opera. This glorious music reaches its culmination in the *Liebestod* or Love-Death which does not refer to physical death but to the soul's dying to all save divine love, and to the celestial bliss that comes with consummation of the Mystic Marriage.

Gertrude Atherton, in her *Towers of Ivory*, makes this vivid comment on the Act I Prelude: "Never has there been and never will there be so full an expression of unsatisfied longing. Surge upon surge from the opening phrase presaging a great yearning that is not all bliss and a torment that is not all pain, so long as mortals may die; surge upon surge of aching passion, sweet oblivion, mortal disappointment, infinite desire—a love that only the immortals can satisfy and only death can quench."

THE LEGEND

Of all medieval romance legends *Tristan* is, perhaps, the most popular. It is known and loved in the north as in the south. England, Germany and the Scandinavian lands rejoice in its beauty; so do Italy, France, Spain and other Mediterranean countries.

Tristan was the son of Blanche Fleur (White Flower), a Grail maiden, and the Knight of Kavelin. With the death of her husband, Blanche Fleur retired to her husband's estate in Brittany, attended by the faithful steward Kurvenal, and there Tristan spent the years of his boyhood. When he reached the age of fifteen he was sent to his uncle, the powerful King Mark of Cornwall, for knightly training according to the custom of the time. He accompanied King Mark in his wars against Ireland. When Mark was defeated and compelled to pay a heavy tribute, which was collected annually by the insolent giant Sir Morold, Tristan finally slew the latter and returned his head to Ireland in place of the tribute.

Now Sir Morold was the betrothed of the Irish Princess, Isolde. The Irish Knight had not died without in some measure avenging his own death, for he had inflicted upon Tristan a serious wound for which no aid could be found. Hearing of the magic arts and healing skill of the Irish Queen and her daughter, the Princess Isolde, Tristan disguised himself as a minstrel and repaired to their court. His wound was healed by the fair Princess, who in secret gave her heart into his keeping.

Upon Tristan's return to Cornwall, so loud did he praise the beauty and magic art of Princess Isolde that King Mark decided to offer her his hand in marriage, thereby to effect a truce between Cornwall and Ireland. He appointed Tristan his ambassador to convey his proposal to the Princess and, if it was favorably received, to conduct the Princess to Cornwall.

As previously stated, there are seven important characters in the opera. Tristan and Isolde, both royal souls, are far along on the Path of Attainment. Tristan's high development is revealed by the fact that Kurvenal, the faithful steward, typifies the personality which, from the beginning of the drama, is completely under the control of the spirit, as represented by Tristan.

Brangaene, Isolde's friend and attendant, represents the Law of Destiny or "ripe fate." Isolde describes her "as holding in her hands the threads of Life and Death, of Joy and Woe." Melot, King Mark's henchman who inflicts the fatal wound upon Tristan, is the lower nature which ever attempts to thwart the aspirations of spirit.

Sir Morold, the evil giant slain by Tristan, is the accumulated wrong doing of past lives which must be met and transmuted before the ego is free to pass into the wedding hall to celebrate the Rite of the Mystic Marriage. King Mark typifies the outer, objective consciousness which has no concept of the holy inner truths to which Tristan and Isolde are dedicated.

ACT I

The first act of the drama occurs on shipboard at sea, the ship representing the soul body and the sea, the uniiversal substance of the astral world in which the soul functions when out of the body during sleep or between earth lives.

In the musical motif of the Sea, Wagner has developed his theme in varied and unusual ways. The opera opens with sailors singing farewell love songs to Irish maidens as the ship slowly sails away from land. It is a scene designed to reflect normal conventional life that moves near the surface of things, with little thought for or interest in the deeper concerns of the spirit.

Isolde, piqued by the apparant neglect of Tristan, sends word for him to come to her. He replies that while his soul must always truly serve but her, the pearl of womanhood, he cannot now leave the helm of the ship, for they are passing through the treacherous waters of the Irish coast line.

Isolde then recounts to Brangaene her previous contacts with Tristan. This she does to the accompaniment of the Love motif, thus betraying her secret love for him whom she openly declares to be Destined for me, lost to me, head and heart forsworn." Thus does she give expression to the spirit's longing for the divine union of head and heart, of body and soul, of outer personality and inner being—prerequisite to the Mystic Marriage—for it is impossible to make any real spiritual progress so long as the head looks in one direction and the heart in another. Her song is climaxed with an appeal to the sea: "Give me air or I shall perish." In this aria, Isolde is passing through the Trial of Water, relating to the emotional life. As she successfully meets this test she aspires to the next Initiation, that of Air, which relates to the powers of the mind.

When the ship approaches the shore of Cornwall, Kurvenal comes to inform the ladies that they must now prepare to go ashore and greet the King. Isolde declares that she will never leave the ship nor be wedded to the King unless Tristan grants her an interview and makes atonement for the wrong he has done her.

The Irish Queen, having suspected the love her daughter bears for Tristan, has given her a magic love potion which she and King Mark are to drink on their marriage day to bind them together in bonds of an immortal love. She has also given Isolde a death potion to be used only if utter extremity calls for it.

As Kurvenal departs to carry Isolde's ultimatum to Tristan, the Princess commands that Brangaene prepare the death potion. After leaving a farewell message for her mother and friends, Isolde declares that she and Tristan will drink it together.

There is an ancient Temple maxim which says, "He that loseth life shall save it and he that saveth his life shall lose it."

Isolde and Tristan are now to renounce things of mundane life in order to attain the holy joys of Initiation. Because of this renunciation and under the guidance of Brangaene (Destiny or ripe fate), they find instead the ecstacy of love immortal and life eternal, for Brangaene substitutes the love cup for the cup of death.

Tristan comes eagerly to accept the cup of atonement offered him by Isolde. When he asks, "Where are we?" Isolde replies enigmatically, "Near our goal." Tristan drinks to "the end of a boundless mourning"—for he has divined her purpose and willingly assents to it. Unless one can interpret metaphysically the language in *Tristan* it is almost unintelligible.

Each step along the initiatory Path outlined in the Christian Mysteries is attuned to its own particular musical pattern. Wagner's transcendental genius recognized this and brought through for mortal hearing the keynotes of the several initiatory Degrees. At this point in the drama, he introduced the exquisite Look motif, music belonging to the Baptismal Rite of the Christian Mysteries. This Degree is referred to as the state of "bringing to sight" since those who participate in it obtain the power of extended vision.

As this music pours forth in dramatic intensity, Tristan and Isolde raise the love cup to their lips and drink the magic potion. Looking deeply into each other's eyes the while, they realize their destiny is to unitedly walk the path of spirit for all eternity. Still gazing, they sink into one another's arms while a great shout announces the ship's arrival at Cornwall.

As the boat reaches shore, King Mark comes aboard to greet his affianced bride. There is much rejoicing on both land and sea, but to all these outer demonstrations Tristan and Isolde remain insensible. They are centered in the inner life and their dedication in spirit. It is Brangaene (Destiny) who recalls them to their duties in the objective world. Royal robes are placed about them, to the accompaniment of the stirring love music, and they go forth to meet King Mark.

Unequal attainment between men and women in worldly affairs, and the many tragedies resulting therefrom, are the natural outpitcturing of an inner lack of equilibrium. The feminine principle is the love principle and the image building faculty that "fell" when Eve, the feminine polarity, ate of the forbidden fruit, with the result that in the exoteric life of humanity woman has been relegated to a position subordinate to that of man. A false balance has existed between the masculine and feminine polarities, with consequent inharmony resulting therefrom. Man can never properly respect and reverence woman until he awakens and develops the feminine principle within himself. It is for this reason that ancient seers declared that marriages are made in heaven, to which Jesus added that heaven (or the kingdom of heaven) is within. Marriages on earth achieve perfection only to the degree that they establish a harmonious inner balance between the two poles of the individual spirit.

Mary, the mother of Jesus, and the Lord Christ represent these principles in perfect equilibrium and, therefore, they both took part in the Mystic Marriage at Cana in Galilee, a union symbolically represented by the water and wine.

The Christ is the perfected masculine principle; the Blessed Virgin, the perfected feminine principle. This marriage feast is one of the rare instances in the Bible wherein activity of the Virgin is mentioned. This is because both the masculine and the feminine must take part in this divine Rite wherein the water of emotional life is transformed into the wine of spirit.

We observe throughout *Tristan and Isolde* how consistently Wagner develops this same esoteric theme, how logically and with what consummate art he portrays the two divine elements separately and then unitedly. In the first act the Tristan and Isolde motifs alternate, but it is the Isolde motif which is in the ascendancy. In the second act the Day and Night motifs are contrasted, with the Night or Feminine again preeminent. In the third act the Life and Death motifs are set against each other—death meaning new life through Initiation, which is achieved by means of the exalted feminine. Union is finally achieved in the glorious climax of the Love-Death.

Mention has already been made of the fact that each character in Wagner's operas is represented by its own individualistic musical motif. Tristan and Isolde are the exceptions to this rule. Both are identified by the same Love motif; but whereas Tristan is described in descending chromatics, Isolde is portrayed in ascending chromatics. These are always repeated three times and always conclude with the ascending chromatics of Isolde, the feminine in exaltation. Thus again Wagner demonstrates his profound wisdom as an occulist, for the chief purpose of Initiation is the lifting or liberation of the divine feminine.

This opera has often been criticised because it is so devoid of action. But this criticism—if it is a criticism—applies only on the objective plane. In the soul world the opera's activity is overpowering, and this is reflected in the intensity of the music. *Tristan* is a mystery play, dealing not with personalities but with the dual spiritual principles of man and the universe.

Every important experience in human existence is contributing directly to the strengthening of either the masculine or the feminine pole of spirit, depending upon the individual's reaction. When man becomes sufficiently wise to aspire to a realization of the Mystic Marriage, he works toward the development of the two aspects simultaneously. He then seeks to unite the strength and courage of the masculine with the gentleness and tender love of the feminine.

Wagner outlines the steps by which the soul moves toward this blending. In the second act of the opera, Isolde says, "I am in the light, but thou, Tristan, art in the dark." In the third act Tristan states, "I am now in the light, but Isolde remains in the sunlight of the day." The two are united for all time in the final scene of liberation.

Wagner states in an afterword that from the double grave of the lovers sprang two roses, one red and the other white, which grew out of their hearts and entwined above their heads. Herein we see the beautiful Rose-Garden symbol of transmutation of the Rosicrucians, the Jachin and Boaz of Masonry, the union of the Sun and Moon as taught by Paracelsus and medieval alchemical cults; also the water and wine of the Mystic Marriage in Cana of Galilee.

ACT II

The fervent orchestral introduction to Act II is based upon four themes that dominate the action of preceding and succeeding scenes. These are the Isolde Impatience and the Isolde Ardour which are heard during the course of events in Act I, and two new themes which set the mood of Act II. These latter are the Day motif, esoterically related to life of the outer objective world, and the Ecstasy or Night motif which belongs to the inner subjective realm. The Night theme, being related to the spiritual plane, is really a transcription of inner plane harmony—the "music of the spheres" whereof the universe is made.

The second act of *Tristan* is laid in the gardens surrounding King Mark's palace. The hour is near midnight and the garden is made luminous by a full moon. Isolde calls it her "Holy Night"— which Melot, significator of the lower nature, attempts to spoil. King Mark is absent on a hunt and we hear the sound of the hunting horns fading away in the distance. The faithful Brangaene suspects the treachery of Melot and tries to warn Isolde, but the maiden's exaltation of consciousness is beyond fear.

Arrayed in white, Isolde awaits the coming of Tristan. She is as luminous as the moon, radiant and joyful—a reference to the luminosity of the conscious Invisible Helper and to night-life activities of the ego when freed from its physical prisonhouse.

Isolde signals Tristan with a light—reminding us of the esoteric maxim given to every neophyte when he first begins to achieve inner-plane consciousness: "Beware of any being who does not shine."

In this scene of the opera is heard the greatest love music that has ever been given to the world.

Brangaene enters to watch over and guard the two, still fearing treachery. The Night Watch sung by her is music not of this earth. It is the voices of the night harmonized with the song of angels: "Realms where the air we breathe is love."

Both the music and the words of the entire drama have an inner and an outer meaning. With profound metaphysical understanding, Wagner interwove the musical patterns of day and night, day symbolizing the outer world with its objective knowing; night, the joyous freedom of spiritual realms. Tristan and Isolde sing of the night as their friend and of the day as their enemy, for day can neither comprehend nor sanction their union. Tristan says: "Eyes hallowed by the night mock at the boastful splendors of the day, whose dusty sunbeams are woven in vain for one who knows the raptures of the night wherein the secrets of love lie forever hidden."

As Isolde awaits his coming she commends herself into the keeping of the Goddess of Love, and we hear the exquisite Love motif merging into that of the Ecstasy as Tristan approaches, and culminating in the high Transport motif as the two are again united.

In all the annals of music there is nothing to compare with the ecstasy of the duet "Descend on us, Oh Night of Love." Tonal waves climb from height to height in great swells of harmony until they mount to the very heavens. Tristan sings, "I am no longer Tristan, I am Isolde." Isolde replies, "I am no longer Isolde, I am Tristan." Herein the aspirant knows the pure spiritual bliss of balance, and for its musical description Wagner brought down to earth celestial strains of the Transfiguration Rite as heard in the Christian Mysteries. The heavenly Love music continues until the stars pale and the softly glowing dawn begins to brighten the sky. Brangaene's song of warning is now heard, prophetic of tragedy approaching with the dawn, but the lovers pay no heed.

"Must I awaken?" sings Tristan, and Isolde pleads, "Let me die here."

In these words is voiced the queery of the Mystic who, conscious and awake in his soul-body, does not desire to exchange his freedom and rapture for the cramping confines of a physical body and the limitations of everyday activities. However, no one has earned complete liberation until the duties of mortal life are finished. Even the supreme Master came down from the Mountain of Transfiguration to share its inspiration with those who remained in the valley below. So Tristan and Isolde must descend to assume responsibilities belonging to day or mundane existence.

Now the faithful Kurvenal rushes in, calling upon Tristan to save himself for the King has returned.

King Mark appears to the accompaniment of the Day motif, which is his musical keynote or aura. He lives wholly in the world and cannot understand the ardor of those who have found the central mysteries of life and being. He speaks a different language and lives in a different world from the heaven-embraced Tristan and Isolde. Nonetheless, King Mark is noble and kind. He expresses nothing of anger or revenge, only a profound and sorrowful amazement. "Who can understand the deep and mysterious cause of it all?" he exclaims as he pronounces banishment upon Tristan and Isolde.

Tristan replies: "Banish the false vision of the day!" and adds, "I cannot tell you, O King, for you would never understand." He then asks Isolde if she is willing to follow him into that land of eternal darkness from which he came and to which he must now return. Isolde answers that she had no fear in following Tristan to this foreign shore, so why should she fear to follow him into that land which encompasses the entire world with love.

As Tristan bends to press a reverent kiss upon her brow, Melot, inflamed with jealousy by Isolde's beauty, rushes forward and inflicts a grievous wound in the side of Tristan, who falls into the arms of his faithful attendant, Kurvenal. It is the untransmuted power of the lower nature (Melot) that obstructs the culmination of this holy Mystic Marriage Rite. As Isolde bends anxiously above Tristan, holding him close to her heart, the second act of the opera closes to the soft, tender strains of the Night motif.

ACT III

Upon the opening of the third act we find that Kurvenal has brought the fatally wounded Tristan to Brittany and his ancestral estate situated on high rocky cliffs overlooking the sea.

The orchestral Prelude to this act has been described as the saddest music ever written. In it Wagner transcribes the musical patterns of the Gethsemane and Crucifixion Rites of the Christian Mysteries. In its mournful cadences is a heartfelt desolation and a sense of impending calamity. Its somber measures echo the tragedy which has overtaken the lovers. Even the Love motif sounds a somber note, but an upward ascent of the violins gives an effect of great spaces of sea and sky. A sad phrase by horns and cellos expresses the spirit of solitude prevading all.

In the opening scene, Tristan, in a coma, lies on a couch beneath an ancient spreading lime tree in his garden. As he regains consciousness (returns to his physical body), his words well describe the spirit of the music which Wagner termed a "wishful thinking toward Nirvana." Says he, "I was there where I have ever been, wither forever I go, in the wide realm of the world-night, where there is but one knowledge, divine, utter oblivion."

The ego of Tristan—that is, the real man—has been wandering, free and illuminated, in that high realm known as the great Hall of Silence because its spiritual activities are so intense that to physical knowing they appear inert. (So does matter appear to the eye of flesh which sees not the atomic forces of which it is in reality composed.) Wagner's music now describes this divine realm of stillness, which is stillness only to the physical senses but not to the spirit. Wagner wrote of his inner experiences while working on *Tristan*: "Everything here is foreign to me and I often turn with longing toward the land of Nirvana. But Nirvana quickly changes into Tristan."

And so Tristan speaks to the faithful Kurvenal who bends above him, "Where I awoke I stayed not, but where I stayed I can indeed not tell thee; . . . what I saw I cannot tell thee. This terrible yearning that consumes me, could I but name it! couldst thou but know it!" But Kurvenal, the personality, can neither follow nor comprehend flights of the illumined spirit into higher realms.

Kurvenal has sent for Isolde to come and again work her magic spell for the healing of Tristan. All the land, all the sea, all the air are luminous with the mystic power and purpose of her coming. A shepherd lad perched high upon a cliff changes his plaintive melody to one of rhapsodic joy as he sights her ship, typifying the Initiate consciousness in joyous realization of the approaching Mystic Marriage Rite soon to be consummated.

Tristan exultantly describes the Love Cup and its mysterious contents. "It is brewed," says he, "of fathers' pains and of mothers' fears. Of past and present, lovers' tears. Of joy and gladness, of tears and sadness. Thus I have brewed this cup of madness." A true account, indeed, of the experiences of an advanced spirit at this stage of Illumination. Tristan is recapitulating experiences of past lives when he lived upon earth as father, mother, lover. Only as one is able to read the scroll of past lives can he extract pabulum from both joyful and unhappy experiences to nourish his soul body, the golden wedding garment in which he is arrayed when worthy to celebrate the Rite of the Mystic Marriage.

After a momentary awareness, Tristan slips into seeming delirium. To the accompaniment of ethereal music—sounded first in the oboe section, then by the clarinets and finally, the violins—he describes a vision of Isolde floating to him over the sea. His ecstatic burst of song, "O Isolde, how fair thou art!" has no rival for tenderness and poignancy of expression.

Now Isolde's voice is heard, calling, "Tristan! Beloved!" And Tristan cries, "I hear the Light! To her! To her!" Leaping from his couch he staggers forward to meet her, tearing the bandage from his wound as he goes. In the flowing of his life's blood he experiences the full agony of the Crucifixion Rite, (which occurs at that point of consciousness where pain is sublimated into bliss) and cries, "Now fade, O world, in my jubilant haste!"

An important part of the Crucifixion Rite is the sublimation of pleasure and pain. At this stage the disciple cannot permit himself to be swayed by either pain or pleasure as an emotion. He must be able to accept them both imperturbably as an essential part of his life experience that is to be incorporated as part of his soul growth.

The flowing of blood always has a deep esoteric significance, for it is inseparable from mystic fulfillment and always tends toward purification. There is a lovely legend which comes to us from the early Christian Mysteries illustrating this point. A disciple brought to St. John a figure of the Crucified One, in which the five sacred wounds had become eyes. As St. John looked at the figure, he said, "Only a Wise One could have done this work, for are not wounds always avenues of light?"

Isolde enters and Tristan sinks into her arms, crying "Isolde!" Isolde promises him she will heal his wounds, and when she sinks beside him her physical senses ebb as her spiritual perceptions are intensified. King Mark now arrives, accompanied by his retinue and Brangaene, who has confessed her responsibility in the matter of the love potion.

Kurvenal rushes upon Melot and slays him, receiving a death wound in return. Tottering toward his master, Kurvenal cries, "Chide me not, O Tristan, if I follow thee!" Thus the faithful servitor, the personality, like the regenerate Kundry in *Parsifal*, becomes one with spirit at the summit of attainment. The final preparation for the culmination of the Mystic Marriage Rite is the entire subjugation of the lower nature (death of Melot) and the complete dedication of the personality as a channel for the spirit (death of Kurvenal).

Altogether unconscious of what is taking place about her, Isolde gazes upon Tristan. Gradually her face becomes illuminated with an ethereal radiance and a rapt, far-away expression shines in her eyes. Tristan's whispered words to her are, "May we twain become one in the realms of Light Eternal!" Isolde is now engulfed by the sweeping harmonies of the incomparable Love-Death: "Hear ye not . . . round me flowing . . . the wondrous melody?"

Do I only hear this chanting
Which so wondrously and haunting

From his winging, soft is ringing,
Clearer growing, round me flowing?
Are these winds sweet rapture shedding?
Shall I breathe then? Shall I listen?
Shall I live without resistance?
Breathe out joyful mine existence
In the sway and the swell,
In the harmony?

Thus the death song yields to the Ecstasy, culminating in a burst of glory before the music melts away into a divinely spiritual calm as Isolde breathes forth the words: "In the billowy waves, in the resonant harmony, in the life-breath of creation, drink deep and drown in dreamless sleep, in purest bliss."

The transcendant music of the Ecstasy, which is drawn from highest heaven itself, relates to the Rites of Resurrection and Ascension in the Christian Mysteries. Wagner describes musically the final transmutation of all human desire into the divine oneness of spiritual Being. The Love-Death is the "utter and divine oblivion" of the senses, wherein love is no longer personal and finite but becomes universal and eternal.

Tristan and Isolde have found not death, but life immortal. All the holy joys of the Mystic Marriage Rite are theirs at last. The divine bliss of this state is such that by comparison the most perfect union this earth can offer seems but a shadow or an illusion. They have exchanged personal consciousness for God consciousness. They are now in that high realization wherein All is One and One is All. The finite and personal have been merged into the Infinite and Universal. The two have become one with each other and with the vast heart-beat of the world.

The glory of the *Liebestod* or Love-Death music is a transcription of the sound pattern which accompanies the Mystic Marriage Rite. As this Rite represents man's highest human attainment, so is this glory music the highest ever brought to earth. In great tides of ecstasy it lifts and swirls, ever rising, ever mounting, ascending in great waves of melody that seem to storm the very gates of heaven and to echo and re-echo the infinite harmonies of the music of the spheres. No other composer has ever brought such a maze of melodic harmony, nor has the world ever before been privileged to hear such magic music. No one can listen to it without becoming spiritually aroused and stimulated, while a sensitive and understanding hearer is conscious of a downpouring blessing that remains long after the heavenly melody has wafted back to its celestial home.

When an aspirant dedicates himself to the Path through holy and aspirational living, he awakens within himself the sacred essence of the spinal spirit-fire and it begins to ascend toward the head. Along the passageway of the spine are located seven important spiritual centers. As the spinal force ascends, its emanations enfold and permeate these centers, arousing their latent activities. This force gains in power, momentum and beauty with every ascending spiral. When it reaches the last of these seven centers of force, located in the top of the head, the disciple comes to know the holy joy of the Mystic Marriage. Each stage of spiritual progression has its parallel in the body-temple, which is truly the abode of the indwelling God.

The Love-Death music accurately describes the ecstasy cycles of the ascending spinal spirit-fire, for both increase in volume, intensity and beauty with each ascending cycle. Isolde describes this inner process in her words: "How he beameth, ever brighter, How he riseth, ever radiant." And as the culuminating point is reached, she sings in ecstatic transport: "Now I behold him—all steeped in starlight."

The Mystic Marriage is the Rite of Light. When we have learned to walk with Him in that Light, we, too, shall know the Oneness of All and the Allness of One.

This music will be used in coming days to aid disciples

in learning to walk the path of first-hand knowledge. It was conceived by its composer to serve such a purpose and in the New Age now dawning that purpose will be fully realized.

Those divinely inspired are always channels for deeper truths than they themselves are aware of transmitting. "Tristan is and remains a marvel to me," wrote Wagner. "I am more and more unable to understand how I could produce such a thing."

A Wagner devotee sums up the magnificance of this immortal work when he says: "Wagner in this parable of body and soul bent his transfiguring gaze upon the prisoning flesh until it became as fire and air and he beheld, instead, immortal, incandescent shapes, immortal vestures—'holy garments' for glory and for beauty."

Tristan and Isolde is a work which, in the words of the late Laurence Gilman, "stands alone among the musical masterpieces of the world."

"Years ago," he wrote, ". . . I defied the peril of superlatives and recklessly declared that this was the most wonderful music that had ever sprung from the creative mind of man. That was doubtless a foolish thing to say; and yet I still believe it to be true. I still believe that to Wagner some mystical glimpse of the fountain of all loveliness must have been vouchsafed, some vision of a supreme and beatific peace, and that the music preserves those revelations for the enduring solace of the minds of men.

"From its opening notes—the sigh of the cellos and that mysterious chord of the woodwind—the terrible magic of this music seizes and possesses you, enters your mind and your blood, overwhelms and shatters you. There is no escape from it—until the Enchanter is done with you, and you are restored to the familiar realities of the outer world, dazed and stumbling and half blind, as a man might be after gazing too long into the heart of the sun."

Parsial

The Degree of Mastership

PREFATORY NOTES

PARSIFAL is the crowning work of Wagner's mature musical genius. For approximately forty years he carried about with him in the recesses of his soul the secret inspiration for this divine drama. He writes in his autobiography that on Good Friday of 1857, in an "hour of deep poetic revery" on the Parsifal legend, he conceived the idea of this soul drama. Twenty years later he set it to transcendent and immortal music. The score was finished as a birthday-Christmas present for Cosima Wagner, December 25, 1881, and was given its initial public performance at Bayreuth during the summer of 1882.

Wagner's heart of hearts lay in the resurrection of the ancient Grecian Mystery Temple drama. In keeping with this ideal he always referred to *Parsifal* as a "sacred festival play." "History," said he, "supplied me with a model for the ideal relation between the theatre and its public of which I had dreamt. I found it in the theatre of ancient Athens, where its walls were thrown open on none but special sacred feast days; where the taste for art was coupled with the celebration of a religious rite in which the most illustrious members of the State themselves took part as poets and performers, to appear like priests before a public filled with such exalted expectations of the sublimity of the conceptions to be set before them that a Sophocles, an Aeschylus could express the deepest meaning of all poems, assured of their understanding by the populace."

Edouard Schure, the late eminent occulist and author of *The Great Initiates,* wrote with unerring penetration: "The theater as Wagner conceived it was a Temple, whereas the theatre of his day was a booth or a fair. He spoke the language of priests, yet shopkeepers were expected to understand him."

In keeping with Mystery Temple tradition, *Parsifal* is divided into three steps or Degrees: The Coming, The Temptation and The Crowning. These three steps may be correlated with the three Masonic Degrees of Apprentice, Fellowcraft and Master, and also with the Student, Probationer and Disciple of modern esoteric schools.

The *Parsifal* music describes the path of self-abnegation, of loneliness, of misunderstanding and persecution, which leads to high spiritual attainment. Its purpose is not to soothe and satisfy the senses but to awaken the spirit. Its rhythms play directly upon certain centers of force belonging to the inner or soul nature of man, revivifying them and accelerating their activity, thereby awakening and developing spiritual faculities, or soul senses, of angelic Man. Such is the mission of this sacramental music.

An astute French author, Charles Tardieu, has observed a correlation between the mystic beauty and design of the paintings of celebrated Flemish and Italian masters with the music of *Parsifal.* In the anointing of Parsifal's feet by Kundry, for example, he sees the loveliness and sanctity of a Magdalene by Mabuse. "For the musician," says he, "takes upon his palette of sound the tones that the painter would have drawn from his color box." The music of *Parsifal* is indeed some rare and fragrant light which has been transformed into sound.

Wagner has been called the Apostle of Music; and rightly so, for his was a truly divine mission. He served the highest purpose to which music can be applied—the liberation of spirit from the limitations of its mortal house so that it may soar at will into timeless realms of the soul. Thus it becomes "infinite music," a term which well describes the incomparable Wagnerian scores.

PRELUDE TO ACT I

In the Prelude to Act I of *Parsifal* we first hear the keynote of *Initiation by Music* (into the sacred Christian Mysteries) which constitutes its distinctive theme and reason for being. It opens with the ethereal motif of the Eucharist. This motif owes its quality of ineffable sweetness to the fact that it is music transcribed direct from higher realms. At the same time it is calm and majestic, articulated first in A Flat and later repeated in the minor, thus suggesting the shadow of sorrow which contact with the earth always casts over heaven-born beauty.

The Prelude consists largely of the intermingling of the four dominant themes of the opera: first and foremost, the Eucharist; then Faith, the Grail and the Lance. The last is formed by an expansion of four notes of the Eucharist together with the Faith theme. These four motifs continue to appear and disappear throughout Acts I and III—like varied soul experiences of a mystic and his continually shifting perception of the Infinite.

The opening measures of the Prelude sound the music of the Eucharist, penetrating and sublime. The Grail motif is also angelic in content and depicts musically both the Cup and the holy Temple in which it abides. The Faith and Grail motifs interweave in divine melodic rhythm like no music ever heard on earth before, with the Eucharist music finally expanding into the new harmonies of the Lance.

As the Prelude begins with the mystic Eucharist, so does it end, maintaining from first to last the ineffable joy of angelic chorusers such as glorify the ceremonial of the Last Supper when it is observed by Initiates in the great Temple of the Christian Mysteries.

Wagner explained the fundamental ideas of this Prelude in notes prepared for its private performance, in Munich in 1880, for his patron, King Ludwig II. The Eucharist theme, which embodies Love, Faith and Hope, he describes as follows.

First Theme: Love

"Take ye my body, take my blood, in token of our love." (Repeated in faint whispers by angel voices.) "Take ye my blood, my body take, in memory of me." (Again repeated in angelic whispers.)

Second and Third Themes: Faith and Hope

Promise of redemption through faith. Firmly and stoutly faith declares itself, exalted, willing even in suffering. To the Promise renewed Faith answers from the dimmest heights, as on the pinions of the snow-white dove, hovering downwards, usurping more and more the hearts of men, filling the world, the whole of nature with the mightiest force, then glancing up again to heaven's vault as if appeased.

But once more from out the awe of solitude throbs forth the cry of loving pity, the agony, the holy sweat of Olivet, the divine death throes of Golgotha, the body pales, the blood flows forth and glows now in the chalice with the heavenly glow of blessing, shedding on all that lives and languishes the grace of ransom won by love.

For him who—fearful rue for sin at heart—must quail before the godlike visions of the Grail, for Amfortas, sinful keeper of the halidom, we are made ready, will redemption heal the gnawing torments of his soul? Once more we hear the Promise—we hope.

From this passage alone it will be seen how profound a significance faith and hope possessed for Richard Wagner. Regarding them as soul attributes he wrote: "Only Love rooted in sympathy and expressed in action to the point of a complete destruction of self-will is Christian Love. In it Faith and Hope are of themselves included; Faith as the infallibly sure consciousness confirmed by the Divinest Prototype of the moral significance of the world; and Hope as the blissful assurance of the impossibility of any deception in the consciousness of Faith."

Both faith and hope are living powers, and Wagner has brought to earth the musical keynotes of these great spiritual forces in the surpassingly lovely Temple themes of *Parsifal.*

THE COMING OF PARSIFAL

Wagner, seeking a higher type of musical drama, explored both myth and philosophy to their inmost depths, and discovered beneath and above all, as sole foundation for a true humanitarianism, the Logos, the Christ, the Son of the Living God.

—Albert Ross Parsons in
Parsifal or The Finding of Christ through Art

Parsifal is the story of human aspiration and spiritual attainment set to the world's most glorious music. Although its beauty and pathos have universal appeal, one who does not accept or understand the truths of esoteric Christianity can never adequately interpret this sublime work. Only the mystic recognizes it for what it is—a spiritual myth dealing profoundly with the mystery of Initiation and the pathway leading thereto.

In the School of Christian Initiation we are told that we are all Christs in the making. In *Parsifal* we behold all the elements of the Christ process blended with a mystical structure of sound patterns so that both the mental eye and the mental ear are nourished to the edification of the soul. The unseen world speaks to us in the sound patterns of *Parsifal* and lives for us in its glowing imagery. Paradise itself is set before us as the Mount of the Holy Grail.

In the ancient Christian Mysteries there were three steps or Degrees—Preparation, Purification and Perfection—

corresponding to the three steps or Degrees previously enumerated as (1) The Coming of Parsifal, (2) The Temptation of Parsifal, (3) The Crowning of Parsifal. The name Parsifal has been interpreted to mean "The pure Fool." An ego comes into this world pure and innocent but without experience; therefore, it is unable to distinguish between good and evil. The knowledge of good and evil, or the power of discrimination, is acquired through temptation, by means of which man learns to differentiate between the real and unreal, the important and the unimportant, the temporal and the eternal. By always choosing true and noble values he ultimately achieves the crown of liberation.

Legend tells us that the holy Castle which housed the Grail was situated on a high mountain called Montsalvat, the Mount of Salvation. It was guarded by Angels because it was the repository of the two most sacred relics of Christendom—the Cup or Grail used by Christ and His Disciples at the Last Supper and which also held His blood when it flowed on Calvary, and the sacred Spear which pierced His side and loosed His redemptive blood.

There were bands of holy Knights who dwelt on this mount, guarding with their lives the Mystery sheltered within the Temple's shining walls. Here they abided perpetually except when the Grail itself sent them out into the world to right wrongs, uphold justice, protect and succor the weak. When there was a knightly deed to be done in the great world that lay beyond the sheltering walls, the name of the Knight who could best accomplish it shone in letters of flame round about the Cup, whereupon he rode forth on high adventure.

In the Castle were holy maidens, chaste and free of evil, whose special task it was to care for the Cup in the seclusion of its sanctuary. When a Savior was to appear in the world, one of these maidens was chosen to bring him immaculately to birth. Her name would then appear in letters of fire around the holy Cup, whereupon she, in obedience to the divine command, would go forth, bearing within herself the fragrance and holiness of the Grail Mystery.

The mother of Parsifal was such a maiden. His father was Gamuret, a great Knight who had fallen in warfare against evil. After his father's death, his mother—by name Herzeleide, meaning heart's sorrow—retired with the infant Parsifal to the depths of a great forest, far from the tumult of cities. There, midst the peace of ancient trees, he learned wisdom from the lips of his blessed mother. He learned to live with the wild, shy creatures of the wood, for he himself was a child of nature with the clear, fresh mind which is the heritage of childhood when encompassed by simplicity and beauty.

Thus Parsifal spent his boyhood, growing strong and upright in body and, all unknowingly, undergoing simple but stern disciplines in preparation for undertaking the exacting tasks of Grail service.

One day his attention was attracted by a group of Knight's riding through the forest, their armor gleaming where the sun smote it. Among them was Sir Launcelot who, according to one legend, was attracted by this strangely innocent youth of manly bearing whose face was beautiful with the courage of innate goodness. In response to Parsifal's eager questioning, Sir Launcelot told him that they were Knights from the court of King Arthur, riding on adventure of the Holy Grail. Instantly Parsifal's own life's purpose flamed up in his youthful heart and he exclaimed, "Give me too a horse and I will ride forth with you to King Arthur's court and win knighthood."

The Knights departed, leaving Parsifal behind. But with Launcelot's encouragement still burning in his heart, he vowed to become a knight. Despite his mother's tears and entreaties, he went forth from the peaceful glades of the forest to seek the Grail. In these wanderings he was led by Angels unaware—as is every soul that truly seeks the face of destiny—and came in due course to Montsalvat, for to this end had he been born into the world.

At this point of the story Wagner begins his music-drama.

ACT I

The first act of the drama as Wagner has interpreted it opens at dawn in a forest, shadowy but not gloomy. This is depicted musically by exquisite strains of the Dawn motif. The ground is rock-strewn, as are also rising slopes that lead to a Castle on near-by heights. But there is a sunny, open glade which melts into a low-lying forest lake in the background. In this glade is the aged Knight, Sir Gurnemanz, and two esquires asleep under a tree. They are guardians of the approach to the Temple. As Gurnemanz is awakened by the sound of trumpets in the distance, he immediately rouses the two youths beside him. Together they fall upon their knees as the Faith theme sounds the call to prayer.

They have no sooner completed their orisons than two Knights approach them. These are emissaries from the Castle, announcing that King Amfortas craves his bath earlier than usual, for the remedy brought him by Sir Gawaine has conferred but momentary relief and his pain has returned keener than before. "Sleepless from pain past bearing," says one of the knightly messengers, "he bade us quick prepare the bath." The mention of Amfortas introduces the Suffering motif which always accompanies the wounded King.

Sorrowfully Gurnemanz exclaims with drooping head,

Fools are we, alleviation seeking,
When but one salve relieves him;
For every simple, every herb we search
And hunt wide through the world,
when helps but one thing—
And but one Man.

The first Knight asks him to explain his meaning but Gurnemanz evades the question, turning away toward the lake with his two esquires. At that same moment there is an outcry from one of the youths: "Behold yon frenzied horsewoman!"

To the wild, uneven dissonance of her characteristic motif, the Gallop, Kundry enters on her magic steed, riding through the air. She springs down and, approaching Gurnemanz, thrusts into his hand a small crystal flask which contains a healing balm for Amfortas. In response to his query as to whence it came, she replies, "From farther hence than thy thought can fly. If this balsam fails, Arabia bears nought else to give him ease."

Kundry's long, flowing robe is bound by a cord made of snake skins—symbol of rebirth, whereby the soul takes on repeated embodiments. Her hair, black as ebony, falls wildly about her shoulders and her skin is dark from the sun. Her eyes are one moment black and piercing; the next, fixed and glassy.

The early morning hour is the time when the stricken King bathes in the soothing waters of Swan Lake, to find some alleviation from his suffering, if only momentary. The hour immediately preceding dawn is well known to mystics as one when joy cometh after sorrow.

There now enters upon the scene a train of esquires and Knights, bearing and attending the litter in which Amfortas lies. Gurnemanz turns toward his two youths and sternly bids them be heedful of their duties. The bearers set down the litter and Amfortas, raising himself, inquires for Gawaine. He is bitterly disappointed to learn that Gawaine is gone again to seek a new medicine for his wound. He commands:

Let none my feelings harry;
For him, the promised one, I tarry:
By pity enlightened—was it not so?
. . . . The guileless Fool . . . .
To me he doth unveil him.
Might I as Death but hail him!

Gurnemanz moans in sorrowful lament as he looks upon the piteous spectacle of the fallen King: "The proudest flower of manhood faded, the master of the conquering race to his own sickness bound, a slave." From the orchestra sounds the motif of the Knights of the Grail.

Throughout the drama the temptation and weakness of Amfortas always elicit from the orchestra the melancholy Suffering motif; but mention of the Redeemer, that One who is to come, calls forth the clear, pure sound of the Promise motif, Parsifal's own soul note.

Gurnemanz now urges Amfortas to try the new balsam Kundry has brought. "But first accord to this a trial," he pleads. Amfortas, regarding the crystal vial, asks, "From whence this wondrous looking flask?" To which Gurnemanz replies, "Twas brought for thee from Araby afar." Kundry, in no mood to appreciate the gratitude Amfortas expresses for her service, laughs bitterly at the thought that her proffered remedy will be of no avail.

At this point the procession moves on toward the lake, leaving Kundry still writhing uneasily on the ground where she has flung herself. Gurnemanz and several young esquires resume their conversation. As one of them looks toward Kundry lying on the ground, repulsive in appearance and behavior, he addresses her contemptuously, "Why liest thou like a savage beast?" Insolently Kundry replies: "Are not beasts here safe and sacred?"

One of the company ventures the opinion that Kundry's drugs, far from helping Amfortas, are likely one day to slay him. Gurnemanz, feeling this suspicion to be unjustified, comes to her defense, reminding the others how she serves in time of danger, asking nothing in return, having nothing in common with the Knights yet encouraging them by her courage: "If only thus she harm ye, it need not much alarm ye!"

Nevertheless, the young neophytes are uneasy. "She hates us!" exclaims one, "See there, how hellishly she looks at us!" Another declares her to be a pagan or a sorceress. To which Gurnemanz observes that she is indeed under a curse, but that she seeks to wash out past sins by service to the Grail. This is a new thought to the attending esquires, drawing from one the question "Then it is not her fault so much distress hath come on us?" Gurnemanz replies that, on the contrary, when she is with them all goes well. It is only in her absence that misfortune breaks upon them. "I long have known her now," says he, "but Titurel knew her yet longer; when he yon castle consecrated, he found her sleeping in his wood, all stiff, rigid, like death. Thus I myself did find her lately."

Gurnemanz turns to Kundry to ask where she was when their King lost the sacred Spear. Why did she not help then? Kundry makes no reply but maintains a sullen silence. Indeed, she cannot answer this riddle for it is the riddle of her own changeable nature.

Finally Gurnemanz relates to the youths the story of the missing Spear: how Klingsor, a wicked Knight rejected by Titurel because of his evil heart, raised up magic gardens all about the holy Mount; how he peopled them with maidens more lovely than flowers; how the Knights of the Grail must travel through these gardens on their journeys to and from the Castle; how these gardens are filled with noxious beauty. Then he tells how Amfortas himself, their great and holy King, son of Titurel who built and consecrated the Castle of the Grail at the behest of Angels, was overcome by "a maid of fearful beauty," and as he lay in her arms, he let fall the holy Spear. Says Gurnemanz, "There was a deathly cry; I rushed near, but too late; already Klingsor had the spear, and he fled, I pursuing in vain, and at last I returned to our king, and there I found that in his side a fatal wound was burning; and that wound has never healed, it is still open and pains Amfortas day and night. And," he concludes,

The spear is now in Klingsor's hold:
Even the holy it can cleave asunder:
The Grail already he counts as his plunder.

Then
Before the plundered sanctuary
In prayer impassioned knelt Amfortas,
Imploring for a sign of safety:
A heavenly radiance from the grail then floated;
A sacred phantom face
From lips divine did chase
These words, whose purport clearly could be noted:—
By pity enlightened
A guileless Fool - -
Wait for him
My chosen tool.

This narration is accompanied by a contrasting of the glory of the Grail music against the dark and sinister foreboding of the Klingsor motif.

In the characters presented thus far we have Amfortas, who represents humanity, suffering from an ever open wound inflicted by Klingsor, representative of the spirit of evil, who perverts all that is good to sinister ends. His ministers are spirits of sensuousness, lovely maidens serving as temptresses to stimulate and awaken animal impulses in those Knights of the Grail who fall into their hands. Chief of these is Kundry, the "maid of fearful beauty." Evil that is ugly has little potency; but evil that appears in beauty's guise is powerful. Even the high-minded may mistake its nature and embrace it, believing it to be good.

Like Amfortas, all are tempted, though not all to a like degree. Even the Christ was tempted. It is only through temptation that the soul may be brought to perfection, for what physical law is to our physical world moral law is to the soul world. None come to Montsalvat without first passing through the gardens of temptation. The true Montsalvat is of the inner world, not the outer. It is a Mystery Temple located in etheric realms where it is as substantial in relation to its own environment as a physical temple is to this physical world. To and from this inner-plane Temple servants of Christ come and go, as do also angelic Beings on their redemptive ministry, celestial and terrestrial.

Kundry is the personality which alternately serves Knights of the Grail and the evil Klingsor. Thus does it function in the life of unperfected humantiy, now responding to the call of the higher self and then yielding to the lure of the lower sense life. In the life of Kundry sleep is the gate from one condition to the other. Whoever finds Kundry in a sleeping state may call her to his service. It was in trance that Gurnemanz found her in the wilderness; it is from trance that Klingsor calls her to evil practices in the Garden of Pleasure.

In Klingsor and Kundry we have two types of that evil entity, the shadow self, which dwells on the threshold of the soul world. Klingsor, the opposite of Amfortas and Parsifal, is king of evil. He symbolizes the One Evil of the world, which uses various impulses and desires of human nature as channels for conquest. Kundry is the most subtle of these human impulses, not intrinsically evil but evil when directed by Klingsor. In the Garden of Pleasure she appears to be dangerously beautiful; in the pure atmosphere of the Mount she is ugly and repellant. Even so, in the lowest regions of the astral world, where souls of the earthbound dwell, evil has the appearance of great beauty. But to the angelic eye of the illumined this beauty of the underworld is noisome. The work of Initiation consists in transforming the nature of Kundry, the personality, so it will no longer be subject to alternate impulses of the base and the noble; but will, instead, become an instrument for consistent expression of the divine only.

Gurnemanz is the Teacher who instructs young neophytes—that is, the young in experience in relaton to the soul world.

Gurnemanz' discourse is interrupted by a loud commotion down by the lake. Cries are heard as a great white swan flutters to the ground, dying. A youth is brought before Gurnemanz, and this youth is Parsifal. Parsifal admits it was he who killed the swan. Gurnemanz rebukes him, saying, "Didst thou not know that all life is sacred and that pain and fear and death are unknown on this holy mount?" Then, with a view to awakening in Parsifal a feeling of compassion, he observes ruefully that this swan had been their joy. "But now," says he, "behold where thy arrow struck; there stiffens his blood; hang powerless the pinions, the snowy plumage darkly besplashed, extinguished his eye—markst thou its look? Art thou now conscious of thy trespass?"

These words of Gurnemanz go straight to the heart of the youth, who recognizes his guilt and instantly resolves to kill no more. Breaking his bow in two, he flings it and his arrows aside, saying as he does so that he knew not the wrong he had committed.

Parsifal is here taking a definite step forward on the path that leads to the holy Temple on the Mount and all it represents. It is a step every aspirant takes at one time or another as he treads the Path of Initiation. So is every other advance Parsifal makes on his journey toward becoming King of the Grail, for Parsifal is the type of pattern for every one who seeks to achieve mastership.

When Parsifal discards his bow and arrow it is to lead a

harmless life. Henceforth he will never again wittingly inflict suffering upon any living creature. This marks the beginning of a compassionate life, out of which flows the spirit of selfless service to all that lives. Until this becomes a natural and joyful expression of man's every impulse there can be no entrance into the kingdom of the Grail.

The appearance of Parsifal is accompanied by his own motif, the Promise, together with ethereal harmonies of the Swan motif taken from the Lohengrin score. This is pure initiatory music as sounded forth from sacred Temples. In this scene it surrounds Parsifal in a glory of arpeggios on harps and violins, proclaiming musically the spiritual status and attainment of the unknown youth who has found his way into the environs of the Grail Temple.

A curious conversaton between Gurnemanz and the youthful newcomer indicates why Parsifal is called a Fool. To Gurnemanz' question concerning his name Parsifal answers: "I do not know." A colloquy follows:

Gurnemanz: Who is thy father?
Parsifal: I do not know.
Gurnemanz: Who bade thee wander this way?
Parsifal: I know not.
Gurnemanz: Thy name then?
Parsifal: I once had many, but now I know not one of them.
Gurnemanz: Thou knowst not anything!
(aside) A dolt so dull I never found, save in Kundry here.

Gurnemanz sends his esquires away with the dead swan and directs the others to finish their ministrations to Amfortas. He turns again to Parsifal and asks that he tell him something about himself: "Of something thou must have knowledge!" says he. Parsifal replies simply, "I have a mother; Heart's Affliction is her name; the woods and the waste of moorlands were our home." Then he goes on to explain that he had made his bow and arrow to drive away fierce eagles of the forest.

Kundry, who has been crouching near, interrupts in hoarse tones to supplement this information by saying that his father, Gamuret, perished in battle, and that his mother reared him alone in a forest. Parsifal, again picks up the story of his life and relates how he saw "men all a-glitter" pass by one day, riding on great horses. Laughingly they galloped away, pursued by him whose instant wish was to become like them. Day and night, he says, he wandered, lost in deserts and over hill and dale, using his bow and arrows to defend himself against wolves and from people whom he feared might destroy him "The fierce-striking boy," says Kundry, "brings fear on spirits."

Asks Parsifal innocently, "Who feareth me, say?"

Kundry: The wicked.
Parsifal: Those who attacked me, were they then bad?
Gurnemanz laughs.
Parsifal: Who is good?
Gurnemanz: Thy dear mother, whom thou forsookest, and who for thee must now mourn and grieve.

Kundry, with her witch-like knowledge, again interrupts: "She grieves no more; his mother is dead."

This staggers Parsifal. "Dead?" he demands, "My mother? Who says so?"

Replies Kundry: "I rode along and saw her dying. Poor Fool, she sent thee her blessing."

In unreasoning grief, Parsifal leaps wildly at Kundry and seizes her by the throat. Gurnemanz holds him back, rebuking him: "She speaks the truth, for Kundry lies not, and much has seen."

Parsifal turns deathly white and stands trembling, while Kundry hastens to obtain water for him from the brook. Gurnemanz commends her action but Kundry replies sadly, "I do no good thing; but rest I long for." She crawls to a thicket: "But rest—but rest—alas, I'm weary!—Slumber, O, would that none might wake me!" Then, with a timid start, she exclaims, "No, I'll sleep not! . . . . Terror grips me! . . . . Vain, vain to resist." She sighs: "The time has come . . . . slumber . . . slumber . . . slumber . . . ," and sinks out of sight in the thicket.

The procession returns from the lake. Amfortas, refreshed by his bath, is borne again on the litter. Gurnemanz leads Parsifal slowly along, saying, "From bathing comes the King again; high stands the sun; let me conduct thee to the Holy Feast; for, an thou art pure, surely the Grail will feed and refresh thee."

Parsifal asks: "What is the Grail?"

Gurnemanz replies:

I may not say: but if to serve it thou be bidden
Knowledge of it will not be hidden.
And lo, methinks I know thee now indeed,
No earthly road to it doth lead,
By no one can it be detected
Who by Itself is not elected,–

He means that the heights of soul exaltation must be found by an aspirant individually. The music here is typical of the straight and narrow path that leads to Illumination.

Together they ascend the path and, in company with others, enter a door which leads into the mountain itself. As the procession ascends through passageways tunnelled in the living rock, Parsifal observes wonderingly, "I scarcely move, yet swiftly seem to run. What is the meaning of this strange, new thing?" Gurnemanz replies, "My son, thou seest that here space and time are one and all is God."

The procession moves onward as bells peal in slow and majestic rhythm. At last they arrive in a great hall that loses itself overhead in a mighty vaulted dome from which light streams into the hall. The sound of the bells seems to fall from infinite space above. Gurnemanz turns to Parsifal, saying, "Now give good heed, and let me see if thou art a Fool, and pure, what wisdom thou presently canst secure."

"My son, thou seest here that Space and Time are one." If we had nothing else to show us that the Grail mountain is the world of spirit, this would reveal it to us. Those who have been even partially conscious out of the body—as in sleep, for example—know that when in the astral body on inner planes it is not necessary to walk in the slow, laborious meaures of earth, that it is possible to glide effortlessly through space. The subtler body is not subject to the gravitational pull of the physical and so can rise and fall and move at will. But doubt and fear act upon the soul as does gravity upon the fleshly body. Hence, the frequently experienced dream of being immovably rooted to a given spot by the fixation of some grave fear, however great the urge to flee from threatened danger. Where there is no fear, only confidence and joy born of knowledge, movement is as swift as light, for on that level space and time are one.

In the Bell theme Wagner has interpreted magnificently the transposition of time into space. They are astral bells that are heard faintly in the distance but become increasingly audible on approach to the Temple, until they sound forth in a deep and powerful rhythm.

A new theme is now introduced. It is the Savior's Lament, presaging the agony of Amfortas and echoing the anguish of the Christ over the weakness and frailty of humankind. This profound theme is interpreted musically in vivid and drastic dissonances, the very quintessence of suffering and sorrow.

As we have previously noted, Wagner's music is set to the rhythms of the Christian Mysteries. Gurnemanz is conducting Parsifal to the inner-plane Temple where these Mysteries are celebrated to the joyous pealing of astral bells and the triumphant strains of celestial music. The glorious processional of Knights entering the Temple, singing their praise of the Love Feast that is about to be commemorated, is set to the rhythms of the sacred bells.

The distinguishing mark of Wagner's musical dramas is the manner in which motifs surround each character like a musical halo, an aura of sound. These motifs reveal the essential nature of each character. According as their emotions and thoughts change and the plot develops, so do the motifs undergo continual transformation. The Promise motif which enhaloes Parsifal is a delicate harmony that lifts one's vision to higher and wider vistas of what may be. It is not meant to be Parsifal's promise only. It is every man's promise—the promise of glories awaiting everyone upon the conquest of self. So also, the Suffering motif of Amfortas is humanity's motif. Amfortas typifies man in his all-encircling sorrow and pain. The incurable wound in his side is humanity's suffering caused by its fall into the sense life—which brought in its train want, disease, discord, death and all the great sorrows that burden dwellers of earth. This wound can be healed only by redemption through purification of the lower sense nature and transmutation of its powers into faculties of the soul. This work is accomplished by Parsifal who becomes thereby the agent for bringing healing to pain-racked Amfortas. The suffering motif is characterized by a strange, irregular rhythm, like blood throbbing in an open wound as life ebbs away.

The musical aura of Gurnemanz is the spiritual Faith motif. Kundry, as previously noted, represents the personality that alternates in its allegiance between the lower and the higher self, serving Klingsor and the Grail in turn. Under Klingsor's domination she seduces the Grail Knights. But when she comes into the atmosphere of Montsalvat, she strives ardently to serve them and the Grail. The galloping rhythm of her motif is a dramatic expression of the plunge of spirit into materiality, for the steed she rides through the air is symbolic of the desire force which drives the personality to action.

Today personal desire is the mainspring of activity. In the distant future, however, it will be replaced by love, the love of God which is *the love of Good for its own sake*. Thereby our personal wills will be so harmonized with the Will of God that we act with Him to a single purpose. The Will of God will be our will. No longer will there be two wills striving against each other, but His one Will only.

The Gallop expresses perfectly the restless, surging currents of an unbridled desire nature. With Kundry's final redemption this strange wild motif is transformed into a wondrously beautiful and soothing cadence, termed the Healing Balm. The early Kundry motif makes a descent of the stringed instruments through four octaves, symbolic of the ego's submergence in currents of desire.

From two doors in the background a procession of Knights of the Holy Grail solemnly enter the hall and range themselves by Degrees at two long, covered tables. The Knights chant:

The Holy Supper duly
Prepare we day by day,
As on that last time truly
The soul it still may stay.
Who lives to do good deeds
This meal forever feeds;
The Cup his hand may lift,
And claim the purest gift.

Voices of younger men come from mid-height of the hall:

As anguished and lowly
His life stream's spilling
For sinners He did offer,
For the Savior holy
With heart free and willing
My blood I now will proffer.
His body, given our sins to shrive,
Through death becomes in us alive.

Boys' voices fall in sweet, clear accents from near the summit of the dome:

His love endures,
The dove upsoars,
The Savior's sacred token.
Take the wine red,
For you 'twas shed;
Let Bread of Life be broken.

Parsifal now beholds maidens entering to the stately rhythms of a Temple dance, some bearing lighted torches and others delicately carved silver cups and plates to be used for the Supper—a Rite which always accompanies the unveiling of the Cup.

The lights and colors, the perfume and music, together with the radiance illumining the faces of these maidens and youths, make an unforgettable picture which engraves itself upon the heart of Parsifal.

Amfortas is brought into the hall on his litter. Before him march boys bearing a shrine draped in purple-red cloth. A raised couch occupies the center of the hall in the background and is overhung by a canopy. Upon this couch the brethren tenderly lay Amfortas; and on a marble table before the couch the boys place the veiled shrine.

When the song is ended and the Knights are all in their places, there is silence. Then, from an arched niche at the back, is heard the sepulchral voice of Titurel coming as from the grave and asking of his son Amfortas if he is at his post. Once more there is silence. Titurel queries: "Shall I again look on the Grail and quicken?" Still no reply. A third time the aged keeper of the Grail cries out in agony, "Must I perish, unguided by my Savior?"

Amfortas, who followed Titurel as guardian of the Grail but has failed in his holy office, cries out in pain and terror, pleading that his superannuated father again perform the sacred Rite of the Unveiling. "Assume the office, thou!" he entreats. "Live on! Live, and let me perish!"

Titurel pleads inability: "Entombed, I live still, by the

Grace of God," says he, "too feeble am I now to serve Him; in works for Him thy guilt efface!" He then commands Amfortas to unveil the Grail.

As attendants come to the assistance of Amfortas he cries out for deliverance by death rather than endure the pain he suffers whenever his eyes fall upon the unveiled Cup, which opens anew his unhealed wound. Yet he must perform the service since it is the very source from which the company of Knights draw that spiritual sustenance by which they live and carry out their tasks. Except their inner strength be replenished from that Cup of living wine, their Brotherhood will perish.

Again Amfortas begs for relief· "Have mercy, have mercy! God of pity, O have mercy! Take all I cherish, give me but healing that pure I may perish, holiness feeling!" He sinks into half consciousness as the voices of the youths float down from the high vault above:

By pity enlightened,
The guileless Fool—
Wait for him,
My chosen tool.

Here the Suffering motif of Amfortas reaches its greatest height of musical eloquence while the Grail, Lance and Eucharist motifs, tremulous and soft, are challenged by the dark and sinister theme of the evil Klingsor.

As the Knights plead to see the Grail once more, Titurel again commands Amfortas to unveil the Cup. Finally resigning himself to the inevitable, the stricken King of the Grail prays silently before the sacred object as a mysterious dusk spreads throughout the hall. All present kneel. When a chant from the lofty dome again falls on the assembly, a blinding ray of light streams down from above and shines upon the Cup, making its veil glow with increasing purple luster. The face of Amfortas momentarily brightens with spiritual courage as he raises the Grail aloft and waves it gently from side to side. Titurel cries out in rapture. "How light now the looks of the Lord!" As the Cup is uncovered, its flaming glory fills the hall and the Knights and maidens sink to their knees in ecstasy.

Wagner set this scene to the transcendent beauty of the Grail motif which shimmers in celestial glory throughout the great hall. As part of this magnificant ensemble, the Promise, Parsifal's soul note, is softly chanted by Angels.

Amfortas sets down the Grail which grows paler as the room lightens. The attending youths cover it as before and place it within the shrine. When full light returns to the hall, it is seen that the cups on the table are filled with wine and that beside each cup is a piece of bread. The assembly partakes of the repast. With a gesture Gurnemanz invites Parsifal to sit beside him but Parsifal makes no response, standing as though dazed and dumb while chants echo once more from the dome in celebration of the Eucharist.

Knights on one side of the Eucharist board sing the Song of the Wine; those on the other sing the Song of the Bread. Angelic voices chant: "Take this my blood and drink in bond no death can sever. Take this my body and eat in love to live forever."

This is the Feast of the Fellowship of Spirit. Bread and Wine symbolize the polarities of heart and head, love and reason, which become a unity in Christ. The profoundest teaching given by the Master to His most advanced Disciples was this one on polarity between a purified heart and a spiritualized mind—a teaching He revealed in its fullness at the Last Supper From the Christ Fountainhead the spiritual wine has flowed century after century, a "Stream of Knowledge" or sacred tradition that brings joy and healing to all who drink of it. Like the cup which the Angel gave to Esdras in the Field of Ardath, it is filled with the fire of immortality. And the bread, that manna descended from heaven, is the Truth whereby men live when they come to know they cannot live by physical food alone but must be nourished by every Word proceeding from the mouth of God.

Again we hear the glorious chorusing of the Faith theme, then the Grail motif sung by the choir of youthful voices midway up, and by a choir of children's voices in the topmost spaces of the lofty dome. The chorus immediately above the Knights represents the Invisible Brotherhood that stands between humanity and the higher worlds; the uppermost chorus symbolizes the angelic Hierarchy that guards the Grail and the powers that flow therefrom.

As the Grail motif dies into silence, the lower chorus sings the motif of Contrition while from the higher chorus comes the ethereal Faith theme to an orchestral accompaniment which reverberates through the vast hall like echoes of some cosmic harmony from interstellar space.

As previously stated, Wagner surrounded all his characters and every object of special significance, such as the Grail and the Lance, with appropriate musical themes by which they may be identified. For example, in *Parsifal* the Lance motif is usually heard with the Grail motif, appearing to emerge from it, true to the powers they represent. The Grail signifies soul wisdom of an Initiate; the Lance, the spiritual force awakened in one who aspires to live the life leading to Initiation. The Eucharist motif is luminous with the sacrificial light of the Christ. It has been described as gleaming with arpeggios that hover over and around it as angel forms encircle the Virgin and the Christ on canvasses of early masters. The Faith motif is exquisitely modulated, conveying a sense of that great peace gained through Initiation, the peace that passeth understanding.

At last the Holy Rite is finished. For Amfortas the ecstasy is gone. The light vanishes from his face; he bows his head and presses his hand to the wound which is bleeding afresh. Attendants approach, assist him onto his litter and carry him away, the shrine preceding him. To the solemn strains of the majestic Processional, with its suggestion of ringing bells and an intermingling of the Grail motif, the Knights march out of the Temple.

Eagerly and earnestly Gurnemanz questions Parsifal as to what he has observed during the sacred ceremonial. The music alone replies by the Promise and the Swan motifs, thus proclaiming future Initiateship for Parsifal. Parsifal himself speaks not. The heart of the lad is over-full with wonder. He can find no words for what he feels. Gurnemanz is disappointed. Impatiently he closes the Temple door upon the mute and wondering youth, saying, "Guileless thou mayest be; but mystic Fool thou art."

Parsifal is one of the few chosen from the many who are called. With that choice comes a commission that necessitates a preparation not common to the average tyro. It is a preparation that sets him apart in some ways from other men, thereby earning for him the epithet of Fool. And so he is, in the sense that "the wisdom of God is the foolishness of men." Parsifal is in the world but not of it. He is a bearer of the light, the light that shines in darkness but the darkness comprehends it not.

Alone in the great pillared hall, Gurnemanz hears high in the dome an Angel softly singing: "The guileless one whom I have ordained, await his return until my will is done." That voice is accompanied by joyous strains of the Promise, while high above floats celestial echoes of the Grail and the Lance.

Gurnemanz has shut the door on the Promised One because the time of fulfillment is not yet come. Parsifal is gold, but gold not yet purified in the fiery furnace. And so angelic voices proclaim his triumphant return. From this the wise Teacher, Gurnemanz now understands that Parsifal is, in deed and in truth, that Promised One who should some day return and liberate the Grail Castle from the evil spell of Klingsor. For that day he is content to wait in prayerful patience.

ACT II

THE TEMPTATION OF PARSIFAL

The dominant theme of the second act of *Parsifal* is the battle between the dark and sinister forces of Klingsor and the simple purity of Parsifal. The orchestra conveys this in the heavy, menacing motif of Klingsor's sorcery which sounds forth in marked contrast to the high clear notes of the Promise, the musical motif characterizing Parsifal.

Deep in caverns of earth where no ray of light can penetrate, Klingsor plies himself to his evil work. Surrounded with tools of sorcery, he prepares to ensnare Parsifal—who, as he knows by his secret arts, is on his way thither.

"The guileless lad comes! and I must command the presence of the maiden who sleeps beneath my spell," cries Klingsor exultantly. Then looking into his magic mirror he calls, "Kundry, come forth! Thy master calls thee."

Here the music depicts a conflict between higher and lower natures; Klingsor's menacing motif is followed by the strange uneven measures of the Kundry motif. The Savior's Lament is also heard. Then, in clear, pure tones, Parsifal's Promise theme mingles with the Suffering motif of Amfortas, the wounded King.

A blue vapor rises and fills the air—a stage device true to the etheric state it aims to represent since the densest of the four ethers, the ethers which compose the ectoplasm of materialization phenomena, is of a bluish hue when seen by etheric vision.

Klingsor has power over Kundry by reason of her evil past, for she is the embodiment of the fallen feminine. She confesses to having been Herodias, for whose sins she has ever since been under the curse of being an unwilling slave to black forces despite her aspirations spiritward.

Now, in response to Klingsor's conjuration, in a sleeping condition she rises from the abyss of darkness. But as she rises she awakens. Her sudden scream of terror dies away to a whimper of helplessness as she hoarsely cries for sleep, for death in loathing of the role Klingsor compels her to play—for he purposes to possess, not only the Spear which he took from Amfortas, but the Grail also, that as the possessor of both he may achieve absolute sway over the earth and man.

Klingsor reminds Kundry that she cannot gain her freedom until some Knight of the Grail proves strong enough to withstand all the temptations she puts before him. "Try the lad who is now coming here," he urges, whereupon Kundry prepares to obey, though not without anguish of heart at the thought of the probable outcome.

As this colloquy proceeds, the orchestra sobs half in anguish and half in joy, but at the mention of the one who is to be victor, it pours forth the pure tones of Parsifal's Promise. Kundry's hopes are in that promise as she prepares to play the role of temptress once more.

Meanwhile Parsifal has approached the garden walls, sword in hand, and has routed warriors of the Black Grail. His features rosy and gay with laughter, he stands proudly on the ramparts, surveying the garden with childlike amazement. Klingsor and his castle have sunk into the earth and nothing appears to his view but magic gardens with their palaces and the luxuriant beauty of tropical flowers. As he stands there his own theme, the Promise, enfolds him in its aura of protection. "Never," he cries, "have I seen anything so lovely. This scene reminds me of my happy childhood days."

From every side, from garden and palace, beautiful maidens rush to greet him—at first a few, then more and still more, all clad in veils of delicate hues which float like careless mist about their lovely forms. These are the Flower Maidens. One moment they are maidens; next they are flowers. Exuberant and beguiling, they press ever closer to Parsifal who looks upon them with a growing sense of wonder and delight: "What fragrance . . . . Are you real flowers?" he asks. (Wagner here introduces the sensuous and subtle sweetness of the Flower Maiden music.) Because of his innocence, Parsifal is immune to their witchery. There are a variety of themes conveying their subtle temptings—gay and brilliant with a succession of chromatics, beautiful with the spirit of youth and of capricious vivacity. They beg him to join them in their gaiety: "We do not play for gold, but only for love," they tell him, in the dulcet tones of the Caressing motif.

Gently Parsifal pushes them away, saying, "My little sisters, I like you better in your flowery dances." When they again seek to embrace him he repulses them sternly: "False Flowers, you cannot snare my heart!" The Promise motif, high and clear, proclaims the strength of Parsifal in withstanding temptation. As he hastily turns to leave the garden he hears his name spoken in soft, enticing tones. Turning, he beholds the fairest of visions. Upon a flower-decked couch lies Kundry, draped in silvery tissue resembling shimmering moonlight mist kissing midnight flowers.

As Kundry softly calls Parsifal, the music seems to grow heavy with the perfume of roses—that deep, cloying fragrance which, according to the legend, had lured so many Knights away from their quest of the Grail.

At sound of his name Parsifal stops. "Who called? Who called the name that, dreaming, my mother once murmured!"

When Kundry speaks the other maidens vanish, reluctantly and with backward glancess toward Parsifal. Though they have been repulsed, they respect the virtue that turns them away, singing, "Farewell, you winsome gallant, sweet fool!"

Through her diaphanous garment Kundry's body gleams lustrous as a pearl. Lovely as a houri, she waits for

Parsifal upon her flowery couch. But she knows this pure Knight cannot be won by mere physical glamor. Subtly she appeals to his love for his mother and works upon his sympathy, telling him of her death and how, in sorrow and anguish, she had called for him alone.

Parsifal falls at the siren's feet weeping, blaming himself for his mother's death. "My mother! My mother! How could I forget her?" he moans. And Kundry, bending over him tenderly, caresses his forehead and lays her arm gently about his neck, murmuring, "Take from me thy mother's blessing and farewell, both greeting thee in love's first kiss." Whereupon she kisses him upon his lips, long and ardently.

In that moment it is as though heaven and earth hang in the balance, that the turn of the scales depends upon his decision. It is an instant with eternity in it. The very heartbeat of the earth seems stilled. Only the throb and beat of Amfortas' Suffering motif is heard through the heavy stillness.

To every neophyte, as to Parsifal, a moment arrives when the same momentous decision must be made. In the garden of pleasure, under the allurement of the most exquisite temptation, each soul must make its decision to serve only the highest that it knows. Certain of the fallen Angels of Bible legend, known as tempters, appear to the neophyte when he first awakens in the Desire World. Their appearance is strikingly beautiful, their subtlety beyond anything mortal man has ever known. If they tempt the neophyte it is not because they desire his destruction. Like Kundry, they work under the law of necessity in their own being. Their office of tempter is like that of a tester of gold in a laboratory. They try the soul again and again until, like Parsifal, it is pure enough to resist; then they become servants of the soul—as Kundry finally surrenders her very life at the feet of Parsifal.

In this fateful moment when Parsifal must make the choice upon which his whole future hangs, the Promise motif is heard again, together with the heavenly strains of the Eucharist. The Grail and the Lance foretell musically what his decision will be.

Mystics know that the astral plane is a realm of emotion, and that therein souls feel merged with one another; one who achieves consciousness on that plane actually feels the pain and anguish of all the world as if it were his own. Parsifal, with the intuition of love which we know as compassion, feels within himself the pain of Amfortas and knows it for what it is. He starts up with a gesture of utter terror, pressing his hand against his heart in anguish and crying, "Amfortas! Amfortas! the wound! Thy wound my heart is searing! I see thy blood outpouring, but now in me the wound, here, here! . . . Now I know why all the world is storm-tossed and wrecked by the terrific passions of the heart!" The Grail music sounds out in its unearthly glory, and Parsifal suddenly understands the full meaning of Amfortas' sin and knows how it can be healed.

During these tense moments Kundry watches the object of her feminine wiles with astonishment that becomes admiration as she realizes that here at last stands one who is proof against her charms. Seeing in him her redeemer, she sings:

O noble knight, throw off this spell,
Behold, I love and wish thee well.

But Parsifal, seeing through his own experience that of Amfortas, thrusts her away: "Ha, that dread kiss! Thou sorceress, out of my sight!"

Wildly Kundry pleads for mercy, describing her remorse as she remembers again how she laughed at the Christ when He staggered under the weight of the cross; and how His look penetrated to her very soul, laying upon her the curse of unending remorse: "Many lives I have lived upon the earth," she declares. "Once I walked the fair streets of Galilee, and the day the Master bore His cross up Calvary I looked at Him and lightly laughed in scorn." She pleads:

Have pity, and bring me salvation!
Through ages eternal
For thee have I waited,
For the Savior long have yearned
Whom once I rashly spurned.
Oh, if thou knewest the curse
Which haunts me, sleeping, waking,
Me ne'er forsaking,
No respite giving,
Which day by day doth breed anew
Endless torture, endless woe!
I saw Him - - Him - -
With laughter mocked Him;
Upon me fell His glance!
Since then I seek through all the world,
And hope that again I may meet Him!
In night's dark woe,
My frenzied mind feels Him to be near.
Again His glance I see;—
Then comes on the fit of cursed laughter!
A sinner yields to my embraces,
Hell's laughter mocks me—for weep I cannot.
With shouting, shrieking, storming,
I plunge again into the mental night
From which, repentant, scarcely I've been waked.

This seduction scene employs all of the amorous and sensual themes previously used and introduces another theme of powerful magnetic appeal called Kundry's Supplication. The temptress' recital of her meeting with the Christ is accompanied by a throbbing, heart-rending cry carried by flutes and piccolos as the music descends rapidly from high B to middle C sharp.

It is a fact known to spiritual science that the evil of past incarnations will continue to reappear from life to life until it has been fully transmuted. This transmutation process is accomplished by consistently directing one's soul energy into channels serving only the good and the true. When the desire for atonement is awakened there can be no more contentment in allurements of mere sensual pleasures.

In initiatory work, Kundry signifies the Dweller on the Threshold. This being is a composite entity, ensouled by the collective evil of past incarnations upon earth. It may act as Conscience, as Temptation, or as Fear; but with its overcoming an ego earns the right to know the Angel that leads him through the portals of Initiation.

The neophyte is then at the point where Parsifal stands when he rebukes Kundry. He is fully aware of his mission. He knows that "Damnation endless wouldst thou share with me if but one moment in my mission I should falter to yield to thy embraces."

The contest for supremacy between the inner spirit (Parsifal) and the outer personality (Kundry) is given magnificent musical expression. The Promise, the Grail and the Eucharist themes are pitted against the Kundry, the Sorcery and the Flower Maiden motifs.

Driven by the curse upon herself, Kundry continues to tempt Parsifal in every conceivable way. But Parsifal is proof against them all, and when she flings herself amorously upon him he repulses her violently. In fury she calls for help and lays upon him the curse of Wandering: "Wander! Wander! Thou whom I love, take this curse for thy guide!"

Parsifal does indeed become a wanderer for a season. This is not his curse, however, but his blessing. It is the period in which he makes further preparation for the high Temple office he is one day to assume.

Kundry summons Klingsor, who instantly appears with

the Spear and to the musical accompaniment of the pure Lance motif, thus showing that his evil powers have become as naught before the Christed One. Hurling the sacred weapon at Parsifal, he cries out, "The Fool I win now with the Master's spear!" But he has no such easy victory. He finds himself confronted with a power he knows not of. A spiritual aura of protection surrounds Parsifal so the shafts of evil cannot reach him. The Spear that is hurled to kill remains suspended above the head of the pure Knight, leaving him untouched and unharmed.

To the pure all things are pure. The Spear represents that divine force which animates creation. This selfsame force is used both in black and white magic. A candidate for Initiation who has withstood all temptations knows that this universal force should be used for purely spiritual ends only. Having gained this understanding, he is proof against the onslaughts of evil, which finds nothing in him to use as a nucleus for futher operations.

Parsifal seizes the Spear and makes with it the sign of the cross, saying, "By this sacred sign I banish the evil magic of Klingsor and his castle forever." Instantly Klingsor's power is vanquished and his palace falls in complete collapse.

A profound mystery is hidden in the sign of the cross. Early Christians knew that the lines of magnetic force upon which the material world is built intersect at right angles. This is one of the first facts discernible to etheric vision. These lines of force are responsive to thought. Evil influences traveling through them may be utterly cut off if the neophyte makes the sign of the cross, by means of which he cuts through the network of force and causes the thoughtforms enmeshed therein to return to their source. This knowledge was also possssed by pre-Christian Gnostics. But later Jews suppressed it because of popular association of the cross with Christianity. Among a few Jewish kabbalists of our own time, however, the power of the cross is known and used even though the Christ is denied.

In ancient Greece it was customary to make a cruciform gesture at every crossroads because they were sacred to the dread Hecate, Goddess of Death and the Underworld. If this gesture were omitted, sickness, ill luck, even death were thought to result. In Herbrew Mysteries it is the Spirit of Elijah who stands at the crossroads, with no threat of evil but, on the contrary, to aid the souls of men in their journeying; for Elijah is the great Hierophant of the Hebrew Mysteries, harbinger of the Messiah and every man's unfailing Helper in trial and tribulation. In the Christian Mysteries he is known as John the Baptist, according to the Master's own word.

When the Christ hung upon the cross on Golgotha, His blood flowed into the earth, not as blood but as etheric and astral force, to spread throughout the globe in the twinkling of an eye, dissolving ancient evil and providing man with new substance drawn from the interplanetary world of pure solar ether so that thenceforth he might build his bodies of purer materials. Thus, the path of evolution was immeasurably shortened for the whole human race.

Parsifal repeats the story of the cross in his own person. As he makes the sign of the cross with the sacred Spear, Klingsor's castle sinks from view and his gardens become a desert strewn with withered flowers. Kundry falls senseless at the feet of the Knight.

This sequence depicts allegorically the first of the three most important steps in the processes of Initiation—submergence of the personality to the power of spirit. The music realistically portrays the transitory nature of things material and the permanence of the things of spirit. The Lament of the Flower Maidens sounds faintly as from a distance, only to be completely drowned in the glorious music of the Grail.

Parsifal turns to depart, but from the top of the ruined wall he calls back to Kundry: "Thou knowest where thou and I can meet again! At the place of Mercy and Redemption." As Parsifal disappears, Kundry raises her head and gazes after him.

PRELUDE TO ACT III

The Prelude to the third act of *Parsifal* recapitulates many of the principal motifs of the opera, suggesting by a musical picture the experiences encountered by Parsifal from the beginning of his quest until its consummation upon his return to the Grail Temple.

The sorrow and sadness which envelop the Knights of the Grail because of Amfortas' failure and his inability to lead them in the sacred ceremonial of the Grail, are depicted in a new motif called the Desolation theme.

The celestial Grail music is broken and distorted. Kundry's motif is also irregular and uneven and is climaxed by a rapid descent intermingled with subdued tones of the Flower Maiden and Sorcery motifs.

Throughout this musical description of his wanderings in search of Illumination Parsifal's motif, the Promise, his own soul signature as it were, sounds insistently high, clear and triumphant, signifying that the spirit of the hero is unconquerable and that he has the innate strength and courage to surmount all obstacles. Parsifal has turned his face toward the Light Eternal, the pivotal theme of Act III.

ACT III

THE CROWNING OF PARSIFAL

The scene of Parsifal's return is laid amid the beauties of nature on a bright spring morning. It is Good Friday, and a benediction of peace lies over all the landscape.

There is a strange contradiction between the ecstasy of nature in the springtime and the Lenten ceremonials observed at this season by the orthodox church. Places of worship are swathed in somber black while penitents kneel in tears and contrition, meditating on the Passion of Christ. Nature, on the contrary, is arrayed in her most beautiful robes of the year and everywhere are heard songs of gladness and rejoicing. Parsifal describes the one as "the day of darkest agony divine;" of the other he says, "How beauteous the morning meadows are, they speak of the infinite love of God!"

When man fell—that is, lost perfect attunement with his spiritual consciousness—he also lost equilibrium between the two poles of spirit within himself, the masculine and feminine or balance between head and heart. This want of equilibrium brought sorrow, poverty, disease and death into the world. The cross on which the Christ permitted Himself to be crucified is the great cosmic symbol of this loss of equality between the two polarities in nature, humanly represented by man and woman. The cross is found in all lands and has been used by all peoples because the whole human race suffered this loss of equilibrium in its early days of evolutionary progress.

As Christ hung upon this cross—which, according to esoteric Christian tradition, was both literal and symbolical, an historical event and a spiritual dramatization—He opened the Way of Initiation whereby all mankind might again find completeness within; and by means of that completeness or integration, rediscover the Edenic state of abundant well-being and immortal life.

Nature already manifests the "boundless love of God" as polarity. Each year with the crossing (crucifixion) of the sun at the vernal equinox from south to north, northern latitudes enter upon their resurrection season and all nature demonstrates the beauty and joy of a perfect alchemical blending of life forces. Parsifal refers to this, the great Easter Mystery, when he baptizes the repentant Kundry with the words, "Rejoice with all nature harmoniously redeemed."

Kundry represents the Divine Feminine which fell

through emotional instability, as typified by the horizontal bar of the cross. Later, accompanied by the triumphant Parsifal, she enters the Temple to the joyous pealing of Temple bells. Together they pass between the two upright columns which have replaced the cross and which are symbolic of Initiation through Polarity. These two columns will replace the cross as universal symbols of religion in the Aquarian Age now dawning.

At dawn on this Good Friday morning in the environs of Montsalvat, Gurnemanz is before a hut deep in the forest, where he has retired for silence and meditation during the holy days of the Resurrection Season. The Easter meditation of this wise Teacher is attuned to the motifs of Kundry, the Promise (of the Liberator) and of Klingsor and his sorcery. He appears greatly aged and is clad as a hermit, but wears the tunic of a Knight of the Grail.

A horse cry is heard in a nearby thicket. Gurnemanz investigates, to find Kundry wrapped in cataleptic sleep from which she is beginning to awaken. He rubs her hands and temples and at last she opens her eyes and utters a cry. Once more Kundry is in her penitent's coarse garb as first we beheld her, but a gentleness has come upon her so she is no longer wild. She rises, arranges her clothing and hair, and pleads brokenly, "Service! Service! Only let me serve thee and the Holy Grail." Here is introduced a new motif, Expiation, which presages the transformation of Kundry.

Sadly Gurnemanz tells her there is no further need of messengers for the society of the Grail is all but vanished, due to Amfortas' refusal to conduct the Grail service which formerly supplied Knights with divine sustenance. So greatly altered is Kundry's conduct that the ancient Teacher cannot fail to observe it. She obtains water from the spring and, seeing a Knight approach, asks,

Who yonder nears the holy spring
With sombre arms and harness?
A stranger knight, for certain.

Parsifal's motif sounds in minors descriptive of the sorrow and travail of his long questing.

Kundry disappears into the hut with a pitcher of water as Parsifal, clad in black armor, enters. Gurnemanz approachs and greets him: "All hail, Sir Knight! Hast lost thy way? May I not direct thee?" Parsifal shakes his head. "Hast thou no greeting on thy lips?" Parsifal lowers his head. "What, no word? . . . Dost thou know what holy day this is?" Parsifal again shakes his head. "Speak, where hast thou been, not to know that this is the dawn of thrice-holy Good Friday morn?" Parsifal's head droops lower. In some impatience, as before on a like occasion, Gurnemanz commands: "Quick, doff thy weapons. It is not meet, sir, that thou shouldst come into these holy grounds in warrior's garb. . . Grieve not the Lord who bared his body on this day, and for a sinful world His atoning blood did shed."

After a long silence Parsifal rises, thrusts the sacred Spear into the ground, lays shield beside it, raises his visor, removes his helmet to place it with the other articles, then kneels in silent prayer before the Spear, eyes up-raised. In all this he is watched by Gurnemanz who has begun to suspect the Knight's identity. He beckons to Kundry who has reappeared from the hut, and asks softly, "Do you know him? . . ." Kundry nods. "'Tis he, indeed, the Fool whom I thrust away. The Spear, I know it well! O holy day, whose advent is again vouchsafed to me!" he exclaims in deep joy.

Parsifal's return to the Mount is described musically in shimmering arpeggios, suggestive of intense spiritual rapture.

Parsifal, rising from his knees, recognizes Gurnemanz and gently offers his hand in greeting. "What joy, that again I have found thee!"

Gurnemanz questions, "Thou knowest me still? . . . How camest thou here, and whence?"

Replies Parsifal:

Through error and through devious wanderings
Came I; and am I suffered now to think them ended
Since I am blest with sounds
Of this sweet forest's murmurs,
And thou, good sage, hast given me greeting?
Or doth error still pursue me?

He tells of his long wandering under Kundry's curse, suffering hunger and pain; how he has borne many wounds but never used the holy Spear in battle or to inflict pain, but only to heal "that safe I might restore it. It was only by receiving wounds and never by giving them that I have kept the sacred Spear inviolate, and now I bring it to be dedicated to its work, the healing of him whose lament I once heard in foolish wonder, but for whose healing I now deem myself appointed."

The Spear represents power which the ego has acquired through all of its life cycles. This spiritualized power knows no shadow of turning and may be used in the mortal world to heal and bless all whom its illumined possessor contacts. It can be kept only as Parsifal kept it, by willingness to receive wounds and not to inflict them. It is fulfilling the injunction of Christ to "love thy neighbor."

Behold it gleaming clean and clear,
The Grail's most sacred Spear . . .

the Spear which Parsifal now brings, pure and undefiled, to be rededicated to the work of healing.

Gurnemanz joyously informs him that the curse is no longer effective as he is in the Grail's domain, and that his coming is awaited by the other Knights. "Ah, they have need of succor!" he exclaims sorrowfully:

Since thy sojourn in the Grail's domain
The affliction which thou camest to know,

The apprehension, has grown to direful woe!
Amfortas, by his torments driven,
By his soul's great torture maddened,
In defiant agony raving longs for death,
No prayer, no pleading of his knights
Prevails on him to perform his sacred function.
The shrine, unopened, long has hid the Grail;
Its guardian, sore his sin repenting,
Knowing he needs must live if on the cup he looks,
Thus seeks his dissolution
And with life's end he hopes for torture's ending.
The heavenly manna we are now denied;
With vulgar food must we content us;
Our old puissance thus has oozed away;
No messengers come now,
No summons more they bring to holy warfare;
Wan and wretched, filled with dread,
The knights of leader, courage, and of hope bereft!
Here in this forest I seclusion sought,
For death in patience waiting;
For Titurel, my pious Lord,
No more sustained by sight of the holy vessel,
Expired - - a man no more.

Hearing of Titurel's death, Parsifal springs up in deep grief, crying, "And I am he who all this woe have wrought! . . . To me a saving work was given, but I, through false endeavor, the grace have forfeited . . . ."

Meanwhile, Kundry has returned. Kneeling before Parsifal, she bathes his feet in the sacred waters and dries them with her long, flowing hair. This represents the final purification of the vital or etheric body and is a familiar allegory of the emancipation of the feminine, as described biblically in the story of one of the foremost women disciples of Christ Jesus, Mary of Bethany. The act of the Footwashing is performed to the accompaniment of a solemn and beautiful motif, the Benediction.

Gurnemanz unbinds the armor from about the *heart* of Parsifal and sprinkles sacred waters upon his *head,* anointing him to his kingship of the Grail. Says the officiating Knight.

Thus was it all appointed!
My blessing then receive,
Thou king today anointed,–
Thou pure one,
Pity-inspired one,
Help-bringing knowing one!

When first he appeared, Parsifal was the "Fool," but through experience he has acquired knowledge he formerly lacked. He is now the "help-bringing *knowing* one!" Without knowledge his compassion proved inadequate. Possessing knowledge gives purpose and design to that compassion.

Unbinding the armor enclosing Parsifal's heart and anointing his head with water is again an allegory of the blending of masculine and feminine polarities, showing that the Knight has attained equilibrium in spirit. He is, therefore, the victorious disciple prepared to enter consciously into the initiatory Temple and to become King of the Grail. Parsifal sings the lovely aria "This day a king I shall become."

His *final* act of preparation and *first* act of kingship (the two are one) is the Baptismal Rite administered to the newly awakened Kundry–which is accomplished to the gentle and lovely Expiation and Faith motifs. The baptism of Kundry represents the second important step in the process of Initiation: complete absorption of personality in spiritual purpose.

Taking water from the spring in his two hands, Parsifal bends over Kundry who kneels before him, and pours it upon her head, saying,

The primal task I thus perform:
Be thou baptized,
Believe in the Redeemer!

Sinking to the ground Kundry weeps passionately, while Parsifal gazes in silent revery upon the woodland scene bathed in morning light. He comments on the beauty of the scene:

True, I did meet some marvelous flowers
Which sought around my neck to twine their tendrils;
And yet so fresh never seemed before
The grasses, frondage and blossoms;
Nor did their fragrance seem so sweet,
Or speak with such appeal to me!

"That is Good Friday's Spell, my Lord!" says Gurnemanz.

"How can that be?" asks Parsifal. "Surely instead of joy and blossoms nature should mourn and sorrow for that day of agony?"

Gurnemanz explains that the great glory of the Eastertide is due to the tears of sinners, wept in contrition and falling like holy dew upon the earth to bring it to flowery fruition. "Hence it is they flourish. All living things rejoice, they hear the Savior's voice, and Him they cherish!"

The groves and fields, he goes on to say, cannot look to Christ upon the Cross, but they look to man redeemed. In the blossoming of flowers may be observed the counterpart in nature of the process of Transmutation as it takes place in the lives of individuals.

Gurnemanz continues to expound the inner mystery of this sacred season:

Each blade of grass, each twig and tiny blossom,
Knows that on this day can come no harm,
But that as God, with mercies manifold,
Remembered man, and for him died,

So man this day will be less bold
And walk with careful stride.
Now grateful all things animate
Which live a moment and go hence,
That all-absolved they may await
And greet this Day of Innocence.

As Parsifal reminisces about the Flower Maidens, Kundry weeps tears of joy. He presses a holy kiss upon her now pure forehead—where the divine flower of spiritual vision unfolds—thus sealing her salvation.

In the exquisite soul enchantment which Wagner wove into the Good Friday music he blended all the sadness and sorrow of the exoteric religionist with the ecstasy manifest throughout nature in the spring season. It is music that typifies the culmination of the great transmutative process whereby the personality (Kundry) is raised into atonement (at-one-ment) with the spirit (Parsifal). It is this alchemical blending which raises the aspirant to the third or Master's Degree, described in the opera as the Crowning of Parsifal. The Crowning is accompanied by that most ethereal of earthly music, the combined Eucharist and Grail motifs.

The descent of the Dove on Good Friday to replenish and bless the Grail and to nourish and sustain the Knights for another year, has reference to exalted occurrences belonging to the Degree of Mastership as observed upon this day in inner plane Mystery Temples. According to ancient legend, it is on this holiest of days that nature puts forth her loveliest tribute of blossoms. Also, the animal kingdom responds to the accelerated life rhythms of the planet by drawing closer to one another and to man. Thus, all nature contributes to the holiness of Good Friday. The mystic knows that it is pre-eminent among the holy days of the year because it is the time when Temple doors open wide to permit "the qualified and worthy" to pass through the portals of glory.

All this Wagner incorporated in his Good Friday's Spell which, like the alchemy of nature herself, reveals life where there seems to be naught but death. This music, drawn from the fount of the Mysteries, shows us the human lifted to the divine, to that world beyond our world which is the sole Reality. Even upon the unillumined this "other world" casts its magic spell with indescribable loveliness.

Temple bells begin to chime in heavenly melody, calling the devout to Temple service.

At the hours of midnight and high noon astral bells sound for this same purpose. This once known but long forgotten fact accounts for the chiming of bells in our great world cathedrals at noon and midnight. Wagner has transcribed the harmony and rhythm of astral chimes in his Bells of Montsalvat.

Gurnemanz places about Parsifal the white robe of Mastership. To the glorious strains of Temple music and the triumphant pealing of bells at the hour of high noon, Parsifal prepares to return with Gurnemanz to the Temple. The bell-like rhythm of the procession of the Grail echoes through rocky vaults in the interior of the holy mountain. Wearing Gurnemanz' mantle—for Parsifal is now the sage—and carrying the holy Spear, they go forward, Kundry with them.

The scene changes to the great hall, but the refection tables are missing. In faint illumination a procession of Knights enter, bearing the coffin of the saintly Titurel. Another procession accompanies Amfortas, borne on his litter and preceded as before by the Grail in its covered shrine. Titurel, the holy one, is dead, and Amfortas has promised he will unveil the Cup for the sacred Death Rite, but that never again will he take part in the holy Mystery. From the orchestra comes the sombre strains of the Desolation theme.

Even now Amfortas can scarce bring himself to endure

the sight of the Grail. Chants echo through the hall, reminding him of Titurel's death and its cause, and commanding him to perform his office for the last time. Comes the call:

Guardian of the Grail,
Do thou thy office fulfill!

Amfortas again prays for forgivness and for the promised Redeemer, while the Knights chant their command to uncover the Grail: "Thy father commands! Thou must!"

But Amfortas, maddened with pain, rushes into their midst, crying out that he feels the approach of death. Baring to them his gaping, bleeding wound, he beseeches them to slay him forthwith. "Here am I, and here my bleeding wound," he cries. "Out with your weapons! Bury them deeply, here, here, up to the hilt!"

But the Knights fall back, leaving Amfortas in indescribable pain and death desire. Meanwhile Parsifal has approached unnoticed. He now steps forward and touches Amfortas' wound with the Spear, saying,

Only one weapon can staunch thy pain,
The one that struck must heal again.

In this couplet is given one of the most important teachings in the great soul drama of *Parsifal;* it tells us that the power within man which, when uncontrolled, leads to degeneration will, when lifted and transmuted, carry him to the heights of regeneration.

The face of Amfortas becomes radiant with rapture. His wound is healed because the sin which occasioned it is removed. He arises, redeemed and reconsecrated to a new life of Temple service. Titurel also arises from his couch of death to take part in the general rejoicing. The Suffering motif of Amfortas is silenced as Parsifal's Promise encircles Amfortas in a halo of glory.

As previously mentioned, death, disease and lack on any plane are transmuted through Initiation into general well-being, harmony and enduring life.

The healing of Amfortas is accompanied by the luminous beauty of the Spear and Grail themes. Amfortas' motif is in minors until his healing occurs, when it changes into triumphant majors expressive of the great peace which passeth understanding.

Gurnemanz supports Amfortas, weakened by emotion, while Parsifal pronounces the formula of forgiveness:

Be whole, forgiven and absolved!
Thy office henceforth be my charge;
And blest be all thy suffering
Which gave compassion's power
And wisdom's mighty dower
To him, the timorous Fool!

These words refer to the Law of Unity, whereby all mankind suffers as one and is redeemed as one. The failure and suffering of Amfortas was felt by Parsifal who, as a result thereof, came into knowledge that would not otherwise have been his. It is for this reason that Parsifal can say to Amfortas: "Blest be thy sufferings which gave compassion's power to the Fool!"

When a truly enlightened one stands within the shining light of the Soul World, he may, like the Christ, know the pain and sorrow of the world-in-darkness without being in the dark himself. He has acquired all the wisdom that comes from corrected error without ever having committed error. A lesson too often overlooked by those who have acquired virtues is that they have been helped in many ways by those who have yielded to vice and suffered the consequences thereof. Truly the sage owes something of his own wisdom to those who have not themselves become wise.

Holding the Spear high before him, Parsifal walks solemnly to the center of the great hall, announcing its presence of the assembled Knights:

The sacred Spear, behold; I bring it back.
O crowning marvel of great joy!
The Spear which healed the bleeding body
Itself now drips a current ruddy,
  In conscious kinship with the pulsing wave
  Which throbs within the holy vessel.
Never again be it hid from sight!
  Uncover the Grail! Open the shrine!

Parsifal ascends the steps to the altar, takes the Grail out of its shrine which has been opened by the youths, and kneels in silent prayer before it. The Grail motif is heard as a golden radiance emanating from the Cup flames throughout the great hall. A white dove descends from above and hovers above Parsifal's head, while again the angelic chorus in the dome's height and the chorus of the Brotherhood in mid-dome chant in unison with the Knights below the majestic initiatory theme of Faith (heart) blended with the theme of Hope (head) thus repeating the idea of polarized masculine and feminine powers, the achievement of Parsifal.

O highest Holy marvel
Salvation to the Savior!

Parsifal waves the Grail in blessing over the assembled Knights while Gurnemanz and Amfortas, deposed sage and king, kneel before him who is King-Sage after the Order of Melchizedek, Lord of the Ages!

Kundry is kneeling before Parsifal and gazing raptly into his face as he elevates the Grail. Her countenance illumined by the glory emanating from the Cup; and to the uneven dissonances of her Gallop motif changing into the soothing and peaceful modulations of the Healing Balm, she dies before the altar. The death of Kundry represents complete and final dedication of the personality to the service of the spirit. The third step of the transmutative process is now complete.

In joyous adoration the Knights kneel before the holy Cup (typifying celestial wisdom gained through Initiation) rejoicing that peace and harmony have returned to the Temple of the Holy Grail.

The white dove descending upon the Grail symbolizes the spiritual force that is released throughout the earth at the Spring Equinox and reaches its culmination on Good Friday. If one learns to place himself in attunement therewith, it nourishes and sustains him both physically and spiritually during the following year. This is the bread of life about which the Master spoke to His Disciples. When they learned to partake thereof, they were never again in want.

To the strains of the Eucharist or Love Feast motif, Parsifal holds aloft the sacred Spear, its tip alight as if with celestial fire. He remains long in profound contemplation as though beholding in a vision the very countenance of the Christ. Throughout this action the Faith, Eucharist and Grail motifs sparkle in a radiant shower of translucent golden notes from the harps.

Surrounded by his rejoicing brother Knights, Parsifal is crowned King to the accompaniment of a triumphant, upsweeping Alleluia: "Salvation to Parsifal the savior." Again the choruses at all three levels are united as the holy Eucharist theme concludes this most sublime of musical masterpieces.

Thus, the cycle of Illumination is brought to a close. The music dies away in the haunting beauty of the Grail motif, growing ever more ethereal as Angels wing their way through translucent golden mists and are lost to human sight and hearing. Man will eventually come to understand that out of this Temple music of Parsifal he can build a golden bridge of sound whereby he may commune with angelic and archangelic hosts.

• • • • •

Richard Wagner, the grand Musician-Initiate of our age and the prophet of Aquaria, has brought to us an ancient Christian Mystery drama.

The orthodox Church still retains much knowledge regarding the occult powers of music despite its almost complete silence on the subject—as shown by the fact that in the last century a mass was composed and sung in St. Peter's for the cessation of a plague in Rome. The score contained twenty-four different parts, and was sung by a choir of two hundred singers arranged in six groups occupying circles in the dome. The sixth choir was placed near the summit of the cupola. This is the plan, as we have seen, which Wagner used to such glorious effect in *Parsifal*.

That the Grail Mount theme is ancient and also indigenous to Christianity is shown in the words of Clemens of Alexandria, who might almost have been writing of *Parsifal* when he said: "This is the chosen mountain of the Lord, it is dedicated to Truth. A mountain of great purity, overspread with chaste shades. It is inhabited by the daughters of God, the fair Lambs who celebrate together the venerable orgies, collecting the chosen Choir. The singers are holy men, their song is the hymn of the Almighty King. Virgins chant, Angels glorify, Prophets discourse, while music sweetly sounding is heard."

• • • • •

"The kingdom of heaven is within you," said the Christ. Even so in *Parsifal* we behold many occult elements at work, all of them to be found in man himself. The sacred Spear is for all to possess if they will but live the requisite life of purity and selfless service whereby the sacred creative fire is raised from the sacral plexus to the pineal gland in the head, a *spiritual* organ of regeneration or re-creation. This fire may be seen rising upward like the gleaming stem of a flower. When it reaches the throat a flower uncurls, its petals rising upward to the head where the pituitary body, another flowery chalice, unfolds to receive the water of life. The light which now bursts forth and radiates from these two organs of regeneration in the head forms the mystic Bread and Wine. This is the sublime attainment of holy ones who partook of the Last Supper with Christ. They achieved immortality and took their place with the Masters, laboring from inner worlds for the salvation of humankind; and there they remain to this day. Any one who attains to this state is numbered among the Elect who sit with Christ at the eternal Feast of the Grail, and that seat is theirs for all time.

In the score of *Parsifal,* Wagner's swan song, the crown and culmination of his life's work, he revealed as much of inner Temple activities belonging to the Christian Mystery School as can now be given openly. For this reason he held *Parsifal* a veritable sacrament of the soul, to be performed only amid the silence and beauty of nature and solely for the benefiit of those willing to make a pilgrimage to his sacred Theater-Temple at Bayreuth. "Never," he wrote to King Ludwig, "shall Parsifal be produced in any other theater for the amusement of the public. How can an action into which the most sublime mysteries of the Christian faith," he asks, "be presented in theaters like ours, be closely associated with the customary operatic repertoire and be given before such a public as assembles there? I should not blame our church committees if they took a firm stand against the presentation of the most consecrated mysteries on the stage upon which yesterday and tomorrow frivolity comfortably disports itself and before a public attracted solely by such frivolity.

"Imbued by the spirit, I called my Parsifal 'a Festival Play for the Consecration of the Stage.' I must therefore endeavor to consecrate a stage to this work and this can only be my isolated stage Festival House in Bayreuth. There the Parsifal is to be given for all time and there only; never is the Parsifal to be presented in any other theater nor offered to any audience as a mere diversion."

This decree of Wagner's, while respected in spirit, was not adhered to in letter. Parsifal is being played outside of Bayreuth. But whenever it is presented it is listened to by audiences that recognize they are witnessing a sublime Temple ceremonial whether or not they accept or understand its true spiritual import.

The first performance of *Parsifal* to be given outside of Bayreuth was in New York City in 1903. Certain religionists at that time greeted it with exactly the reactions Wagner had anticipated. There were denunciations from pulpits and cartoons in the city's leading newspapers lampooning the sacred music-drama as unsuitable to a stage devoted primarily to mere entertainment.

Parsifal won its way to universal respect and reverence both on the New York stage and elsewhere, as everyone knows who has witnessed its sublime rendering. To thousands upon thousands the annual presentation of *Parsifal* on Good Friday in the Metropolitan Opera House of New York is a spiritual experience of such exaltation that it will live forever as a most cherished memory. We have evidence in our own lifetime of a rapidly changing world outlook as the Aquarian Age approaches and its messengers receive some small part of the honor due them.

Upon the performances of *Parsifal* at the Bayreuth Theatre in July-August, 1882, for the first time the financial success of the undertaking was assured, and Wagner saw the realization of his dearest dream in the performance of his sacred initiatory drama whose soul note, in his own words, is "Strong is the power of desire, but stronger yet is the soul-power gained through resistance."

Wagner began preparation for work on *Parsifal* in 1845

with his study of the *Parsifal* epic of the medieval minnesinger, Wolfram von Eschenbach. This preparatory period, which was not wholly subjective, extended over thirty-seven shadowed and tumultuous years that included efforts toward the creation of a dramatic work on the life of Jesus of Nazareth and also a Buddhist play, *Die Sieger* (*The Victors*), in which the dominant theme, as in *Parsifal,* was the renunciation of sense life necessary to attain union with the Highest.

The literary part of Parsifal was completed in 1877. The following five years were devoted to composition of the music. It is significant to note in this connection that Wagner commenced this part of the work on a Good Friday, the day fraught with the spirit that the composer incorporated into his sacred music-drama.

Franz Liszt once wrote: "The sketch of *Parsifal* which Wagner read to us recently is filled and permeated with the essence of Christianity . . . I am willing to confess that most of our poets who are regarded as Christian-Catholic stand far behind Wagner in their religious sentiments."

Realizing the deep esoteric values that were being imparted to *Parsifal* and the important role it was to play in the future spiritual development of mankind, Wagner spent long hours in meditation upon each theme and in working out corresponding instrumentation. He was fully conscious of the purpose of his life work and determined that barriers of superstition and envy set up by the uncomprehending should not defeat this purpose.

Perhaps some inner intimation that his days were drawing to a close prompted Wagner to take the baton and direct the latter part of *Parsifal* on the occasion of its last performance at Bayreuth in the season of its initial production, 1882. At the conclusion of that performance a group of the master musician's close friends gathered together, too much moved for words. Finally one of them said, "Wagner is not long for this world." To anxious queries came the response, "When one can bring through a thing like that, his work is finished."

And so it proved to be. A few months after the white dove had hovered above the head of *Parsifal,* another messenger, this time one in sable, entered the Palazzo Vendramine in Venice. On February 13, 1883, news was flashed round the world that "Richard Wagner is dead!"

Greatly appreciated as they are, Wagner's works are not yet valued at their real worth; nor can they be until the initiatory truths embodied therein are generally recognized. Nor is there yet an adequate understanding of those deeper purposes in relation to man's spiritual development and racial evolution that Wagner's compositions are designed to further. But decade by decade this understanding and appreciation increases. There are already great numbers who, even if they have not accepted intellectually the spiritual message of a sacred drama like *Parsifal,* are nevertheless influenced by its subtle musical powers which play upon the soul-senses and awaken them to activity. Thus the music-lover's spiritual progress is accelerated though he be unaware of his own gains.

We have seen only the smallest beginning of a great spiritual revelation destined to come to people of the Aquarian Age through the agency of music. As Wagner himself said, "Music preaches repentance and amendment of life in the profoundest sense of a divine revelation. As Christianity arose under the Roman universal civilization, so much bursts forth from the chaos of a heartless, materialistic, modern civilization; in music's engimatically entwined lines and wonderfully intricate characters stand written the eternal symbols of a new and different world. The spirit of both Christianity and music is Love, and both affirm 'Our kingdom is not of this world.'"

BRUNNHILDE SLUMBERING, GUARDED BY MAGIC FIRE

From the painting by Herman Hendrich

PART III

Cosmic Evolution

I. The Rhinegold
The Water Path

II. The Valkyrie
The Air Path

III. Siegfried
The Earth Path

IV. Gotterdammerung
Twilight of the Gods
The Fire Path

THE RING CYCLE
(*Der Ring des Nibelungen*)

Four Steps in Racial Evolution

INTRODUCTION

THE RING OF THE NIBELUNGS—a cycle of four operas adjudged by the world's ablest critics to be unparalleled for grandeur, breadth and composition—was the object of Wagner's attention for more than twenty-six years, beginning with the period when he held the post of conductor at the Dresden Opera. At that time he first became deeply interested in ancient sagas of the North, the rich mythology of which he blended with masterly skill into this fourfold drama allegorizing the rise and fall of Aryan civilization.

The title of the Cycle is derived from a medieval epic known as the German Iliad—the *Nibelungenlied*, authorship of which medieval writers attributed to Tannhauser, but this has been refuted. It has been pointed out that the *Nibelungenlied* is the only great national epic produced by European writers since antiquity and that it belongs to every country peopled by German tribes. The myths woven into this early masterpiece are drawn from the hero traditions of the Franks, Burgundians and Goths; in addition, there are remnants of myths carried over from Asia. King Nibelung was a chieftain of a mythical Burgundian tribe, who, according to the legend, bequeathed to his two sons a hoard of treasure beyond all price and incapable of diminution. This treasure was won by Siegfried, who warred upon and conquered the Nibelungs.

Much of Wagner's time and activity were devoted to an attempt to reshape the political and economic thought of his day. Freedom, liberty and equality were keywords of the new life about which he dreamed and for which he wrote and labored. He brilliantly satirized obsolete religious practices that had lost the life of the spirit. Nothing escaped his critical attention. He declared that only a new and free humanity could produce the new music he could hear.

His last letter, written January 31, 1883, just thirteen days before his passing, reveals his inspired vision and the sorrow of his tortured heart for the blindness of mind and soul that prevented others from recognizing the dangerous trend of civilization as he portrayed it in his Ring Cycle. He wrote: "To see, to see, to really see! Here is where they all fail! *Have you eyes?* is a question that may be forever addressed to this eternally chattering and listening world in which gaping takes the place of seeing. Whoever has really seen knows how he stands."

Few people realize how wide was the span between Wagner's thought and works and the era in which he lived. Even the full century that has elapsed since he disturbed a smug and complacent society with his musical compositions and advanced social thinking has been insufficient for the world to grow up to truths he uttered and ideals he projected.

Concerning the social question he wrote in his autobiography that "The task must be to cultivate mankind and to bring about the greatest well-being of all . . . when as many active human beings as the earth can support would unite in well-organized societies to enrich and bless one another by the interchange of their various, multifold activities. God will enlighten us so that we may find the right law by which this principle may be introduced into actual life. The demonic idea of money, with all its hideous attendant evils of public and secret usury, swindling with the currency, interest, and the speculation of bankers, will vanish like a bad nightmare."

In 1848, the year he was exiled from Germany for his revolutionary activities, he was saying things that could well be spoken this very day. On June 15, 1848, and "to the dismay of the radical, practical men of politics and to the horror of all worthy Philistines," he indignantly reported in his own record, *My Life*:

> Or do you perhaps see or smell in this the doctrine of Communism? Are you so foolish or so wicked as to declare that the necessary redemption of the race of man from the grossest, most immoral enslavement to base materialism is the same as putting into practice that most absurd and senseless doctrine, Communism? Will you not see that in this doctrine of a mathematically equal division of property and earnings an unthinking attempt has been made to solve the problem? But will you therefore also decry the problem itself as absurd and nonsensical? Beware! The result of thirty-three years of peace shows you human society today in such a state of ruin and pauperism that by the end of this year you will see around you the ghastly figures of pale famine! Take care before it is too late! Do not give alms, but recognize the right, the human right bestowed by God, or you may live to see the day when nature, violated and mocked, will rise in brutal vengeance. Then her wild cry of victory might well herald that Communism; and if it last for only the briefest time, because it is impossible that its principles should prevail, yet this brief rule would suffice to destroy perhaps for a long time all the achievements of a civilization two thousand years old. Do you think I am threatening you? No, I am warning you!

The racial background of the *Nibelungenlied* readily accounts for the ease with which Wagner makes ancient myths tell the story of the fate of civilization in the Aryan Epoch. He carries us back to the beginning of our present evolutionary cycle in ancient Atlantis, where the Aryan race first sprang into being. This state is represented in *The Rhinegold*, the beauty and joyousness of the Rhine maidens in their watery home reminding us of the blissful civilization known to Atlantis before her degradation and submergence. Following this preliminary stage, he introduces us to our immediate order of civilization—represented by Wotan—and we witness its disruption and fall in the *Twilight of the Gods*. But Wagner is not a nihilist. He sees the Old Order disappear only to give way to a New and better Order; and, as we shall see later, on that note of promise the magnificent Ring Cycle is concluded.

Unlike Wagner's other operas that relate specifically to individual initiatory work, *The Ring* deals with the evolutionary processes of the race as a whole. Even so, the dramas carry a spiritual significance applicable to individual development, since the race is a collective organism corresponding to the individual units of which it is composed. Consequently, forces operative in a civilization will be active in its individual members although they are only discernible in their big broad outlines when viewed in the life of the race as a whole and over a long period of historic or evolutionary time. It is that broad view that Wagner gives us in his cosmo-conception of music-dramas, *The Ring*.

The four Paths of Initiation, usually spoken of in terms of the four primary elements in nature—Fire, Air, Water and Earth—are allegorized in the four operas comprising the Ring Cycle, each with a keynote corresponding to a spiritual principle. The four elements are not to be understood as referring to physical matter out of which our material world is composed, but to four types of cosmic energy corresponding to the physical substances whose names they bear, and the manner in which they operate in the life of man.

It is the primary task of every neophyte to learn to know himself as the "I Am," as an ego divine in essence, and thus to separate himself from the four "elements" which constitute the mortal personality with its animal soul. These four elements are sometimes called "sheaths" in which the ego is swathed, the densest of the "sheaths" being the physical body. This body corresponds to the element Earth.

Immortalization of body is the work of the Earth Initiation and is accomplished by "conquest of the Dragon." Its keynote is heard in Siegfried as the Song of the Bird.

Emotions represent another "sheath" in which the pure self is enwrapped and thereby shut off from the great world of divinity. They correspond to water. The transmutation of emotion is the work of Initiation by Water—correlated with the Rhinegold theme, its keynote being given in the Water Music of *The Rhinegold.*

Air corresponds to mind. The transformation of the mind is shown in *The Valkyrie* and its keynote is heard in the Ride of the Valkyries.

The fiery "passions of the heart," the desire "sheath," correspond to Initiation by Fire—for Divine Fire alone can burn out the sensual fires of the lower or animal soul, fire fighting fire. In this Initiation passion is transmuted into compassion. Its keynote occurs in the glorious Fire motif heard in this colossal work. Amalgamation of this fourfold labor is sounded in that sublime Redemption by Love theme heard in *The Twilight of the Gods.*

Unfortunately, our civilization has shown itself largely incapable of receiving or acting upon these cosmic principles. Siegfried renounces the open portal of wisdom upon the heights in favor of the world and its treasures. Wotan (mass mind) puts Truth to sleep that selfish and predatory interests may be served. Consequently the Fates (Past, Present and Future) pronounce sentence: "Twilight must come, bringing to an end the day of selfishness and war." Yet the Spirit of Truth, Brunnhilde, continues to hover above the world and its pilgrims, as she did above Sieglinde and Siegmund. Although her words are all too often unheeded even by leaders of the race (Siegfried), a new and better humanity will ultimately usher in a brighter day wherein the Rhinegold (the All-Good) shall again repose in the oceans of universal consciousness to sustain and benefit mankind.

The Rhinegold

(Das Rheingold)

PREFATORY NOTE

"In music the idea [archetype] of the world manifests itself."

SINCE the days of his racial infancy man has stood at the crossroads of decision with two divergent paths before him. One is the way of self-giving that leads to God; the other, the way of selfseeking that leads to gold. That the masses have chosen to follow the second path is evidenced by the chaos and devastation engulfing the world today.

There is a close connection between the words *God* and *gold.* Remove the 'l' from gold and the word God remains. "L" in Hebrew is Lamed, the letter denoting pain and sacrifice. It is represented by a camel, the burden bearer, servant of all. The loss of this principle of sacrifice impels men to seek for gold rather than for God.

In his great world-drama of *The Ring,* Wagner gives a prevision of the conflict which is rending the twentieth century, its origin in economic insecurity and the loss of spiritual values, and its ultimate conclusion in a new world order that will supersede present chaos.

Wagner moved in the vanguard of his time. He left many letters excoriating the inhuman practice of vivisection. He also issued many pleas for the harmless life, for the welfare and protection of the animal kingdom. One so thoughtful and tender in his care for his little brothers of the animal world naturally concerned himself seriously with the fate of his fellow man. In his efforts to bring about a better standard of living for all men, he suffered many hardships: the loss of friends, position and prestige, and was compelled to spend years in exile and dire poverty.

Keenly conscious of the unjust inequalities and unfair discriminations then existing, he wrote, when only a lad attending school at Liepzig, a "Political Overature" and endeavored to have it produced at one of the Leipzig Garden concerts. He later described the introduction to this work as representing a mood of gloomy oppression from which emerges a theme called *Peace and Freedom.* This theme was intended to develop in increasing magnificence and splendor until it soared to complete triumph—a concept he developed later in the glory and wonder of his Ring Cycle. Human freedom is earth's noblest theme, and Wagner revealed the way to this freedom by his sublime Ring music-dramas.

Laurence Gilman, who always wrote with rare poetic insight, stated that "With the writing of *Das Rhinegold* a new master was born. Wagner had attempted no such range of evocation in his earlier works." He goes on to say "Nor had the art of music before his time dared to conceive so vast a canvas. With *Das Rheingold* had been born not only a new master and a new imaginative world, but a new art of tones, magic, Promethean, sustained by a divine effrontery. In *Das Rheingold* he discloses a new heaven and a new earth, breathes a new air, and we who are privileged to accompany him, share in his exhilaration."

ACT I

The opening scene of the introductory opera, *The Rhinegold,* represents the river Rhine with the lovely Rhine maidens, wise daughters of its waters, floating gracefully through its undulating currents and singing joyously as they guard the Rhinegold, a glittering treasure which rests in its depths.

These graceful beings chant of the wondrous powers of "the sleeping gold" as they dive and float and swim in the softly flowing river. The orchestral accompaniment portrays the quiet, picturesque and altogether innocent beauty of this scene.

Wagner wrote that his first inspiration for *The Rhinegold* music came to him as he lay ill and half asleep on a hotel bed in Spezia. To quote:

> Returning in the late afternoon from a long walk I stretched myself dead tired upon a hard couch awaiting the long desired hour of sleep. It did not come but I fell into a kind of somnolent state in which I felt as though I were sinking in swiftly flowing water. The rushing sound formed itself in my brain into a musical sound, the chord of E flat major, which continually reechoed in broken forms; these broken chords seemed to be melodic passages of increasing motion yet the pure triad of E flat major never changed, but seemed by its continuance to impart infinite significance to the element in which I was sinking.
>
> I awoke from my sleep in terror, feeling as though the waves were rushing high above my head. I at once recognized that the orchestral prelude of *Das Rheingold,* which I had long carried, but had never been definitely able to fix, had at last come to being in me and I quickly understood the very essence of my own nature—the stream of life was not to flow to me from without, but from within.

Esotericists are well aware that every stream, waterfall or mountain range possesses its own keynote which is audible to spiritual hearing above the noise and confusion of the earth. Upon the Rhine's keynote, long sustained as though drawn from the river's nether-most depth, the Prelude to *The Rhinegold* begins. Soft, smooth, rhythmically singing, a golden shower of tones simulate the gentle undulations of the water, high-lighted by the sparkling shimmer of the Rhinegold.

Seated upon the river bank is the ugly dwarf Alberich. the Nibelung, enthralled by the beauty and grace of the Rhine maidens. They laugh and tease him, their laughter wafting back in the music, while he, pursuing them, draws ever closer. Suffering humiliation as they scorn his affectionate advances, he finally begins to heed the words of their song. The maidens are chanting about the magic powers of the Rhinegold—"This great golden Eye that wakes and sleeps in the depths and fills the waves with its light"—which, if forged into a ring, confers upon its possessor unlimited wealth and power over gods and men. But the ring can be forged only if love is foresworn. Alberich, smarting under the gay laughter of the Rhine maidens who have refused him their love, is willing to pay this price. Before the maidens are fully aware of what is happening, he snatches the mass of gold from its river bed, crying out exultantly as he does so, "See, I take it! And hear me, ye floods! I foreswear love forever."

With his treasure he disappears, while the music depicts the wild lashing and confusion of the waters and, in minor key, the lament of the Rhine maidens who are comfortless over the loss of the Rhinegold.

The story thus far is accompanied by some of the more important themes of the opera. The Water Music, illustrative of the Rhine maidens and their lovely water setting, typifies the spirit of universal brotherhood and peace—which was symbolized in early Atlantis by the Garden of Eden, wherein human consciousness was as yet undivorced from angelic realms. The dwarf Alberich, the Nibelung—like Mime and the Giants who are clothed in animal skins—represents later Atlantean races, in which the curse of separativeness first was known. He alone has no motif of his own; but whenever he appears he brings dissonance into the other motifs, indicative of the discord which self-centeredness always generates.

The Rhinegold symbolizes cosmic wisdom, the All-Good. Alberich's act in forming the gold into a ring is a symbol of the selfishness that appropriates to itself alone the good which is properly the heritage of all. The Rhinegold motif ascends an entire octave, its concluding notes sounding an infinitude of blessing. All motifs relevant to the

Rhinegold sing in high trebles of its all-encompassing good.

The Ring motif begins and concludes on the same note, aptly expressing the confinement and limitation created by transforming the free-flowing Rhinegold into the Ring—that is, cosmic welfare being sacrificed to a lesser good which begins and ends in self.

The Renunciation of Love is a poignantly sorrowful theme, but not because of Alberich's misdeed alone. It suggests human travail down through the centuries as *things* increasingly relegate *spirit* to a place of secondary importance.

These motifs are supplemented by the Adoration of Gold, Bondage and, later, by the Curse of the Ring when Alberich is forced to yield it up to the Giants. Through these motifs Wagner portrays man's fall under the delusive spell of separativeness. The pain, sorrow, death and destruction which follow upon separativeness make up the epic story of the Ring Cycle.

The wild downward rush of the music as Alberich disappears with the treasure indicates that the waters are left swirling in darkness when bereft of their shining gold. But soon this darkness gives way to a light mist which gradually clears. As it vanishes a high mountain peak, flower-covered and brilliant with sunlight, merges into view. This is Valhalla, homeland of the gods. Its appearance is announced in the orchestra by the majestic Valhalla motif.

In the distance rises a magnificent Gothic castle with towering pinnacles, home of Wotan, father of the gods, and of Fricka, his consort. As these two typify the Old Order, so does the great castle stand for the power of our age which is directed toward material rather than spiritual objectives. This castle is doomed to ultimate destruction at the end of the Cycle, being incapable of accommodating itself to more free, expansive and spiritual concepts belonging to the New Day. Wotan represents the Old Order whose powers are waning because of misuse; Fricka typifies the rigid rules and regulations by which the Old Order is sustained. Wotan is *authority;* Fricka is *tradition.*

The Old Order can conceive of nothing superior to itself. It confidently looks forward to an eternal existence, and so one hears Wotan hailing with pride this "everlasting work, the stately fortress, peerless and proud." Stately and majestic indeed is the musical motif descriptive of Valhalla, perhaps the most majestic in the entire Ring Cycle.

The great castle was built for Wotan by the Giants, to whom in payment he promised Freia, sister of Fricka and Goddess of Love and Beauty. The Compact motif tells of this bargain between Wotan and the Giants, by which beauty and idealism are bartered for power and glory. Valhalla is the stronghold of the Old Order. It is significant that this compact so weakened Wotan's spear that Siegfried (the New Order) is able to break it. Equally significant is it that all the gods of the old era are assembled together in Valhalla when Brunnhilde (Truth) with a burning brand destroys the Old Order to make way for the New.

The two Giants to whom the lovely young Goddess has been promised are Fafner and Fasolt. Both the Giants and the Dwarfs (Niblungs) portray the lower nature, which always follows the paths of self-seeking. Their motifs reverberate in the deep basses, heavy and somber with evil and destruction.

Wotan (mass consciousness of the Aryan Race) was known in legend as the Wanderer who possessed but one eye—because he had forgotten the spiritual world. That is, he lived primarily in material consciousness—as does the vast majority of our day, with the result that mankind is actually falling behind in its evolutionary program. Under the Divine Plan man should now be victorious over selfishness and all the evils springing therefrom. His world should be attuned to the Golden Rule, with peace, plenty, happiness and health the birthright of a united race.

In the opera it is not until Siegfried comes that the victory is achieved, and then only after much bloodshed and tribulation.

In a letter to Rockel, the celebrated German insurrectionist, Wagner wrote: "After his parting from Brunnhilde, Wotan truly is nothing but a departed spirit; his highest aim can only be to let things *take their course*, go their own gait, no longer to definitely interfere; for that reason, too, has he become the 'Wanderer.' Take a good look at him! He resembles *us* to a hair, he is the sum of the intellect of the present, whilst Siegfried is the man of the future, the man we wish, the man we will, but cannot make and the man who must create himself through *our* annihilation."

Wotan and Fricka are discussing the compact. Fricka expresses her concern for Freia, her beloved young sister and the victim of Wotan's heedless bargain. As Wotan gives Fricka his promise that he will not permit Freia to be taken away from Valhalla, Freia herself rushes in, beseeching protection from the Giants who are pursuing her. The Giants, clothed in animal skins, appear and demand that Wotan yield Freia to them according to his bargain. Wotan pretends he has no knowledge of such an agreement.

The orchestra sounds the menacing notes of the Compact as Wotan tells Fricka that he depends on Loge, the crafty fire god, to extricate him from his dilemma. He has no intention of yielding up Freia to the Giants, for Freia is guardian of the Tree of Golden Apples, its fruit enabling gods and goddesses to remain forever young, but without which they suffer old age and death. The celestial food of the gods is that spiritual ideality that alone confers immortality—the good, the beautiful, the true which man loses sight of to the degree that he descends into materialism.

Wotan has sent Loge to discover some precious thing acceptable to the Giants as a substitute for Freia. While awaiting his return, Wotan continues his altercation with the two. Loge, the fire god, symbolizes the fiery desire nature, "the passions of the heart."

The Giants solemnly declare that a curse will come upon Wotan and take peace from the earth if he fails to honor his pact with them. The gloomy Compact motif is heard repeatedly during this altercation but gives way to the elusive, darting Fire music with Loge's entrance upon the scene.

When Wotan demands to know where Loge has tarried thus long, the latter replies that he has wandered over the world seeking a ransom for Freia, but in the "whole wide world nought is so rich that man will value it more than woman's wondrous delight." One only has foresworn love for gold—the Nibelung Alberich, and this in revenge because he could not win love from the beautiful Rhine maidens. Having stolen the Rhinegold, he has forged it into a ring and by its power is amassing a great hoard of gold in the nether world.

The thought of this gold subtly influences each of them in turn. Wotan thinks of it in terms of immeasurable power; Fricka, as a means of feminine adornment; the Giants, as an acceptable ransom for Freia.

But how procure the Ring from Alberich? Wotan inquires of Loge. By theft, Loge replies. "What a thief stole, steal thou from the thief—could aught be more simply acquired?" This subtle sophistry Wotan accepts.

The Giants, now eager for the gold, quarrel with Wotan, who declares angrily that he cannot give them what he does not posses. They drag the shrieking Freia away, saying they will return with her at nightfall and that if Wotan does not produce the gold at that time there will be no more parleying; the lovely Freia will become forfeit and have to dwell with them forever.

Wotan bids Loge lead him to the abode of Alberich that he may endeavor, with the fire god's aid, to secure for himself the gold and thus gain mastery over the world.

In his Fire music Wagner has given the most spectacular evidence of his superlative genius and occult knowledge.

Fire is symbolic of desire force which runs the gaunt from the depths of degeneration when uncontrolled to the heights of spiritual regeneration and illumination when properly directed by mind and spirit. Wagner demonstrates all this in his Fire music. Variable and mysterious in its hissing, sparkling chromatics, the Fire theme emerges now as the low flame of sensuous desire, and again as the leaping and pinnacled splendor of spiritual ardor.

ACT II

Wotan follows Loge down into the dark caverns of the earth. In a red glow of light and to the sound of hammering which dominates the orchestral accompaniment, the Nibelung Forge motif, they find Alberich forcing his fellow Nibelungs, tiny dwarf people, to toil ceaselessly day and night under the whiplash of cruel necessity in order to amass for him vast fortunes in golden treasure.

Kissing the Ring, Alberich calls to his enslaved people: "Tremble in terror, downtrodden hosts! Obey the Ring's great lord!" From the orchestra is heard again the Renunciation of Love.

The Nibelungs represent the great masses of mankind—the "little people" to whom Abraham Lincoln referred when he said that God must love them well because he made so many of them.

In this scene we have an analogy to the dark and unsightly slums of our great cities, to the cruelty of child labor and to injustices of the economic system as a whole, all belonging to the Old Order so soon to disappear. Its orchestral illustration is the Rising Hoard motif, heavy and foreboding, charged with a sense of the inevitability of cosmic reckoning, the hatred of the Nibelungs for their enslaver, the restless, surging discontent of the working masses, having its roots in economic inequalities.

As Wotan and Loge enter the cave, Alberich is engaged in a violent quarrel with his brother, Mime, who has been making the Tarnhelm, a magic cap which enables the wearer to assume any form or condition he desires. Alberich snatches the cap from Mime and, becoming invisible, begins to flog his brother most unmercifully.

The Tarnhelm motif is replete with mystery. It accompanies Alberich's transformations under the spell of the magic helmet. The helmet, being associated with the head, suggests powers that are mental in nature—the transforming powers of thought.

When Wotan explains to Alberich that he has heard of his wonderful magic and has come to see if the reports are true, Alberich boasts of his powers. Tempted by Loge's artful suggestion, he demonstrates them by taking upon himself the form of a huge dragon, frightful to behold. This apparition symbolizes the collective evil of the human race, evil which inhabits the dense ethers of the earth just beyond the range of physical sight. It is frequently seen by clairvoyants and takes several forms that are curiously similar among all the peoples of the earth, the dragon and the hound of hell being the most common.

Loge next suggests that Alberich assume a small shape. This he does, taking upon himself the appearanc of a toad—another figure symbolic of evil, the favorite familiar of witches.

Alberich has no sooner changed himself into a toad than Wotan puts his foot upon him. Thus he is captured and dragged up from his underworld to the light of day where the gods reign. There he is compelled to yield up the Ring, the magic Tarnhelm and the heap of gold.

In this is the just action of cosmic law. Alberich has acquired the gold by dishonesty and evil. In so doing he has incurred the envy and hatred of his companions. Now, through his own egotism, he himself becomes a prisoner to illusion and deception.

Freed at last, Alberich lingers for a moment to place a curse upon the Ring: "Death shall be the portion of whoever owns it. He shall never know either happiness or mirth, but shall be consumed by care and anxiety, while he who does not possess it shall be torn with envy. He who is master of the Ring shall become its slave until the day when it is restored to the waters of the river Rhine." From the orchestra comes the direful motif of the Annihilation of the Gods, with the Curse motif rising to a height of frenzy and held in long sustained tones, suggesting that it bides the time of its terrible fruition.

While it is yet sounding the Giants return with the lovely Freia. They have agreed to accept gold as a substitute for the goddess, but it must be enough to conceal her completely. All of the hoard taken from Alberich is not enough to accomplish this. Freia is still visible behind the heap of gold. The Tarnhelm is added, but even this is not enough. Wotan must yield up the Ring to complete the pile. This he at first refuses to do, for he has set his heart upon possessing the Ring. Here again is a deeper descent into this materialistic age; the quest for gold is paramount, idealistic concepts relatively unimportant and obscure.

As Wotan hesitates before sacrificing his personal ambition, a misty light arises from the earth. In it is seen the awesome form of the Earth Goddess. Erda, Spirit of Mystery, wise with the wisdom of the ages, possessing all inner knowledge and clairvoyance. Her motif expresses the power and sublimity of the Ancient Wisdom. Erda is the mother of the three Fates—Past, Present and Future—who are contiually weaving the destiny of man. She represents the immutable and inescapable Law of Causation govering our planet, by which man must reap even as he sows.

"Fly from the accursed Ring," Erda admonishes Wotan. "There is endless ruin for you in its possession. What everything was, I know. What everything will in time become I also know. Erda, the everlasting one, summons you. Everything that exists will come to an end. Night will fall on the Gods. I warn you, give up the Ring!" Having so spoken, she sinks into the earth.

Wotan throws the Ring upon the heap of gold. At last Freia is concealed behind the treasure so the Giants take their gold and prepare to depart. But almost at once they begin to quarrel for possession of the Ring. Fasolt seizes it, whereupon Fafner slays him and leaves with the treasure. Already the curse of Alberich has begun its work. A trail of devastation will be left across the entire Cycle. During this action the motifs of Bondage and the Curse of the Ring sound with prolonged intensity.

ACT III

Murky clouds veil the heights of Valhalla as Donner, God of Thunder, summons the gods home. The storm passes away and Valhalla is again visible in the light of a setting sun, while across the Valley of the Rhine arcs a gorgeous rainbow, the bridge over which the gods may enter Valhalla. Esoterically, this is the bridge whereby heaven meets earth, for in a brighter Edenic day the disembodied in heaven and the embodied on earth were as one. Death held no terror, no pain. Transition from one world to the next was peaceful and beautiful. The rainbow is a reminder of that ancient, happy time.

To interpret adequately the sheer radiance of the Rainbow music, sixteen additional harps are required in the orchestra. They paint in shimmering arpeggios the exquisite beauty of a tonal rainbow against a musical sky.

The gods move in solemn procession across the rainbow bridge leading to the glistening and turreted castle of Valhalla. Loge remains behind. In deep meditation he gazes upon their passing, saying: "They are hastening toward their end though they deem themselves strong and enduring." The return of the gods to Valhalla signifies the choice of the masses centering in the objective might and power of the Old Order rather than in the idealism and truth of the New

At last Loge ascends the iridescent bridge as the lament of the Rhine maidens rises from the valley, imploring the gods for their lost gold. But the gods, laughing and heedless, pass on into Valhalla. Then the Rhine maidens sing mournfully: "Rhinegold! Guileless gold! Oh would that again in the waters thy gleam might shine! Tender and true it is only in the waters. False and base are those who revel above."

Alone, Wotan halts for a moment in thought, as the motif of the Sword is heard thunderously in the orchestra—for by means of that sword he plans to win salvation for his Order from the destruction which threatens it so long as the Ring, with its power over gods as well as men, exists.

Wagner has woven into the stately measures of the solemn Valhalla procession all the themes of temptation and renunciation known to a soul on the Path of Initiation. A flourish of brasses sounds the menace of the Ring and its curse; and together with ominous drum beats so typical of the Fate motif, it sounds the unholy theme of the Adoration of Gold. These move side by side with the undulations of the Water motif and the minor Lament of the Rhine Maidens until all are lost in the glow of the Rainbow—the merging of that which has been and is into that which is yet to be.

The Valkyrie

(Die Walkure)

PREFATORY NOTE

WAGNER wrote Franz Liszt on New Year's Day, 1855, announcing the completion of the composition drafts of *The Valkyrie* in the following words: "Brunnhilde sleeps! I, alas, am still awake."

He had written during the previous year: "You are to have the *Rheingold* but you shall not set eyes on it until it is in a form worthy to contemplate . . . I cannot delay over it now, I must set to work on *Die Walkure* which I am gloriously full of."

That he was indeed on fire and alight with the full glory of this "wonder music" is attested by the fact that the first act was done in approximately nine weeks, the second act in less than eleven weeks, the third and final act in about five weeks–surely a feat possible only with superhuman aid and direction!

Wagner completed the scoring of *The Rhinegold* on May 28, 1854, and a month later, on June 28th, he began work on the second of the great epic operas, *The Valkyrie.* It has been estimated that the score of this work in its completed form contains one million notes.

During the following July he again wrote to Liszt: "The Walkure music is started! My! how the thing begins to hum."

In the magnificence of this colossal work, the sublime creative genius of the great musical seer appears to have attained its full maturity. He traces, easily and deftly, the lines of both personal and cosmic demarcations as they are to be read in the Eternal Records of Nature. He traces beginnings of the decline of Aryan civilization and follows its progressive disintegration–through greed, avarice, selfishness and the strife which they bring in their train—to its inevitable destruction. These racial traits and historic events, together with their underlying cosmic processes, are set forth by Wagner in musical language such as no other composer has ever produced.

In *The Rhinegold* the cosmic principles underlying our present civilization are portrayed and the roots of its misery laid bare. In *The Valkyrie* Wagner carries the drama further on the course of its fruition, sounding archetypal music belonging to the Aquarian Age in the motifs of Siegmund and Sieglinde, Wotan's chosen people as progenitors of a race of heroes and pioneers of the New Day. The archetype of a race or a nation is a musical pattern in the Soul World. The genesis and evolution of a race or people proceeds in attunement with its archetypal keynote, that sounds continuously so long as either endures. In the Siegmund-Sieglinde motif an Aquarian pattern is revealed in deeply tender and compassionate strains.

Laurence Gilman, with rare understanding, expressed something of this when he commented: "The tenderness that speaks from the music of Die Walkure is peculiar to that work. There is deep and impassioned tenderness in the passages between Siegmund and Sieglinde . . . Repeatedly in Die Walkure this peculiar quality comes over the music and gives it an inestimable beauty and nobility.

"We come from a performance of Die Walkure with a sense of dazed and shaken incredulity, the conviction that we have experienced some capturing of essences, some projection of reality that transcends art."

Through the magic evocation of this supreme master, it has indeed been a privilege to stand for a brief moment on the threshold of the Eternal. He causes time to stand still, permitting the beholder to glimpse the past, present and future as attuned to the golden measures of his divine harmonies. He sometimes gave to friends an autographed notation that has reference to his glorious gifts. It reads:

"Things impossible to conceal, yet impossible of utterance! By this I felt I had conveyed, though with happy vagueness, some idea of the secret knowledge which was my sole inspiration."

THE PRELUDE

The Prelude to The Valkyrie is one of the most magnificent of all symphonic compositions. It is filled with the wild tumult of a storm. The voice of mighty winds echoes the wailing cry of great tree spirits. One seems to hear the lashing rhythm of pouring rain from a sky overcast with heavy clouds and rent by lurid flashes of lighting. In the midst of all this storm music is heard the rapid beat of footsteps, as of a solitary traveler fleeing for his life through forest and downpour. High and clear above the riotous din of nature sounds the eerie song of the Valkyries as though, mounted on their glistening steeds, they were dashing from crag to crag among the lofty peaks. Their voices echo in the song of the winds and fill every crevice and abyss with unearthly music

When working on this portion of the drama, Wagner lived in seclusion among the fastnesses of lofty Alps. There he opened his Initiate consciousness to observe and study the life and activities of sylphs, spirits of the air, and their song is the motif for the Valkyries' theme.

The Valkyries are feminine spirits. They belong to the element Air. It is by means of the higher feminine (intuition or soul knowledge) that many of the marvelous secrets of the new air age will be revealed. Brunnhilde, the spirit of Truth, is a woman; so is Sieglinde, pioneer of the New Day. When Brunhilde admonishes Sieglinde to have courage, there sounds an echo of the glorious Redemption motif which heralds the destruction of the Old and the birth of the New as given in the finale of the Ring Cycle.

With prophetic vision Wagner knew the important role that the "Woman of the Future," to whom he so often referred, will assume in the redemption of humankind. He frequently alluded to her as the "Divine Woman" and as such she is associated throughout the Ring Cycle with its noblest musical motif—a motif which forms the keynote of the whole work, namely, Redemption through Love.

ACT I

As the storm of the Prelude subsides, the curtain rises on the interior of Hunding's forest dwelling, a hut made of hides and hewn timbers and built around a mighty ash tree into which a sword has been thrust.

To comprehend what now occurs in Hunding's dwelling one must understand something of what Wotan has done since the closing action of *The Rhinegold.* He alone of the gods knows the danger threatening them all, so he conceives a plan of salvation by means of which the Ring—the Ring that carries with it the curse of separateness—can be regained and the Old Order preserved forever.

The Rhinegold concludes with the solemn procession of the gods into Valhalla The accursed Ring had been transferred by Wotan to Fafner. Alberich, bitter with thoughts of revenge, schemes for possession of the treasure. Wotan knew that if it came again into the Nibelung's hands he would use it to bring destruction upon both the race and the gods.

Wotan realized that confusion and terror followed his forgetfulness of the runes engraven upon his spear. These runes are symbolic of cosmic principles that are the basis of all evolution, both of worlds and of men. A people or nation progresses or retrogresses in proportion as it lives or fails to live according to these principles, chief of which is the principle of love—the Golden Rule. Already Wotan's forgetfulness of these principles has resulted in the theft of the Rhine treasure and an unethical compact with the Giants, a compact he as a god had to repudiate. Having been compelled to fulfill his compact by surrendering the Ring, he proposes to retrieve it by means of a human instrument. To this end he has fathered in the earth realm two beautiful children, Siegmund and Sieglinde, their mother a mortal woman.

This youth and maid portray pioneers of a new and better race, a race of heroes. Half human and half divine, their aspiration of mind and soul is incomprehensible to Old Order servitors among whom they live. Hence, these pioneer Volsungs (Walsungs), as they are called, are hated and persecuted. Speaking of his lonely fate, Siegmund sighs pathetically: "Whate'er I did, where'er I fared, if friend I sought or woman wooed, still was I held in suspicion. Ill fate lay on me. Whate'er to me seemed right, others reckoned it ill. What I held to be foul, others counted as fair. In feuds I fell where'er I dwell, wrath ever against me I roused. Sought I for gladness, found I but grief; so must I woeful call me, for woe still walks in my wake."

Having brought forth these two fair children as the executors of his plan, Wotan loves them beyond all humankind, even as he loves Brunnhilde (Truth) best of all his daughters. The principle of law, though enmeshed in tradition and enslaved by selfishness, must, by the truth inherent within itself, endeavor to promote futurity.

Wotan has lived for a time in a forest home with Siegmund and Sieglinde; but on a day when he is absent, the home is broken into by an enemy tribe and Sieglinde is carried away to become the unwilling bride of the enemy chieftain, Hunding. At this point the first act of *The Valkyrie* opens.

A man, storm-drenched, pale and distraught, appears at the door of the hut. He holds his hand on the latch while he gazes about the room. Seeing no one, he closes the door behind him and staggers to the hearth, where he casts himself down upon a bearskin rug. Exhausted, he says, "Whoever owns this hearth here must I rest me."

Sieglinde enters the room and beholds with astonishment the recumbent stranger, for it is her husband, Hunding, whom she expects to see. So still does the stranger lie that Sieglinde thinks he may be ill. She bends over him to listen to his breathing. "I hear still his breathing, it is sleep that has seized him," she murmurs. "Valiant is he, me seems, though so worn he lies."

Siegmund awakens and calls for water, which Sieglinde gives him. Revived, he is able to speak and explain his presence. He has been attacked and wounded by enemies and his sword broken, he says. Weaponless he comes into this house, claiming hospitality according to ancient law. His name is Misfortune and his presence here, he thinks, is likely to bring sorrow to the house. To this, Sieglinde sighs that he cannot add more sorrow than is there already. Soft music by the cellos here denotes the awakening of mutual soul recognition.

Hunding, a dark, surly and suspicious man, enters shortly, characteristically accompanied by a heavy and sinister motif played by the tubas. Grimly he accosts the stranger. Learning that this is the enemy sought by his own kinsmen, he challenges him to combat the following morning; he says that for the night Siegmund is safe, having taken advantage of the laws of hospitality, but when he quits the hut in the morning they must meet in battle. "No longer life will follow you, but the toll of murder will I take," he avows harshly. Hunding and Sieglinde retire for the night leaving Siegmund alone in the room, now visible only by the flickering light of the hearth fire.

As he thinks of beautiful Sieglinde who has had compassion upon him, from the orchestra comes their love motif. Then, in despair of his situation, he cries, "Walse, Walse, where is the sword?" remembering that his father has promised that he can have a sword when his need is greatest. As if in response to his cry, the firelight gleams for a moment on the hilt of the sword in the tree; but Siegmund, not realizing what it is, lies down to sleep.

Shortly thereafter Sieglinde steals in and says she has put an opiate into her husband's drink. She urges the stranger to flee, telling him of a wonderful sword she can give him. This sword, she explains, was plunged into the tree on the night of her wedding to Hunding by a stranger—an old man with one eye hidden by his hat, who decreed that only a great hero could draw it forth, and that her bondage would be at an end when that hero comes.

Siegmund embraces her tenderly as he replies, "The man for whom the sword and the wife were decreed holds you in his arms."

Suddenly the door swings wide upon the night. The storm has passed and a full moon glimmers in the heavens. Startled, Sieglinde tears herself away, crying, "Who went? Who entered here?" In the bright moonlight they see one another clearly, and Siegmund murmurs in gentle ecstasy: "No one went, but one has come. Laughing, the Spring enters!" He draws her to a couch and in the pale glory of the moonlight sings of their love to the accompaniment of th Spring motif: "Winter snows have given way to the lovely month of May. . . . Sieglinde, you are my May. . . . Twas Love that lured the Spring; deep within our bosoms was she hid; now gladly she laughs to the Light. The bride and sister is freed by the brother; in ruin lies what held them apart. Joyfully greet now the loving pair. . . . Made one are Love and Spring!"

To the Love motif Sieglinde replies, "Thou are the Spring I have longed for in Winter's ice-bound days. My heart greeted thee with the holiest fear when thy look at first on me lightened. All things seemed strange to me, friendless all was around me; like things I never had known all that ever came near. But thy soul lay bare at once to me; when my eyes fell on thee, knew I my own one. What lay hid in my heart, what I am, clear as the day dawned on my sight, in resonant tones rang on my ear, when in Winter's dreary desert there came my first friend to me."

Gazing upon one another in their new-found love, they experience the sublime ecstasy of soul recognition and soul communion—which the orchestra interprets in the inexpressibly beautiful motif of Delight.

Siegmund sings in transport: "O wondrous vision! O woman divine!" Sieglinde: "A memory masters my spirit. Though but today we met first, I deem not strange thy face."

Thus it may happen that soul recognizes soul, spanning barriers of time, distance and differing embodiments; knowing in a single instant that destiny has brought them together in a common cause and for a common good.

"Was Walse thy father? Art thou Walsung?" Sieglinde cries. "Struck then for thee was this sword! No longer art thou Misfortune! Siegmund I name thee, the Victorious One!"

Siegmund springs to his feet, runs to the tree and takes the hilt of the sword in his hand, exclaiming, "Nothung, Needful, I name thee, sword. Come from scabbord to me!" With one powerful effort he draws it forth from the wood. Branishing it exultantly, he proclaims, "Siegmund of the Walsungs stands before thee! As bridal gift he brings this sword. Let us fly from this house into the laughing world of Spring!"

Their faces illumined with a rare shining, the youth and maiden step into the moonlit forest, to a triumphant and pulsating rush of music that engulfs the scene.

The human characters in this action are all representative of social forces found in *The Rhinegold* in the similitude of gods. Behind the mortal scene the drama of the gods continues to be enacted, the root and cause of all that eventuates on the stage of the world. Hunding stands for convention, which always holds to the Old Order. Siegmund and Sieglinde are progressives, pioneers of a new day and a new way of life.

As we can see from observation, convention always seeks to shackle the New and bind it with the ordinances of the Old—as Sieglinde was held in bondage by Hunding. When the revolutionary New, figured in Siegmund, becomes too strong, too courageous, too free, convention ordains that it must be slain.

The motifs accompanying these characters reveal their essential difference of soul and mind. Hunding's motif is oppressive and menacing. The Siegmund and Sieglinde motifs, although sad and subdued at first, are rich with love and compassion and are sustained by a noble, majestic strain expressing their divine origin and destiny. The sword symbolizes Truth at its original source of purity—that can be recognized and fully used only by those with the illumined understanding of the New Order. Its motif is glittering and ecstatic, opening vistas of far distant horizons.

The most beautiful music of this act of the opera is the Song of Love and Spring, in which Siegmund and Sieglinde recognize their love for one another and the exalted destiny awaiting that love. It is with this music that the storm ceases, the moon shines forth in splendor, and the door of opportunity swings wide upon the vistas of a larger life.

ACT II

Act II opens with an orchestral Prelude suggesting the flight of the Walsungs through forest and over mountain. This is followed by a motif not heard before, the popular Valkyrie theme, its pure cadence sounded in the basses.

The Valkyries, of whom Brunnhilde is the leader, are

love-daughters of Wotan. Their work is to fly over the world and carry to Valhalla the spirits of all who have died a hero's death. Their motif is the Song of the Valkyries wherein, as previously described, the voice of the winds is mysteriously interwoven with suggested infinitudes of space.

The curtain rises upon a mountainous scene. Brunnhilde, in full panoply and with her steed Grane, stands on a cliff overlooking a rock-strewn pass. Wotan, also armed, comes up the pass and commands her to defend Siegmund in his coming battle with Hunding .

Brunnhilde springs lightly up the cliff, her shout echoing along the mountain passes. From the heights she sees Fricka approaching in a rage and calls down a warning to Wotan. Then, to her wild cry, she disappears from view beyond the summit.

Fricka comes on the scene to the Bondage motif and demands that Brunnhilde's assistance be given to Hunding. As the goddess of marriage she cannot condone the lawless love of Siegmund and Sieglinde, so she insists that they be punished for their transgression.

Wotan pleads the lovers' cause: "I cannot defeat him. He found my sword." But Fricka replies, "Remove then its magic, or bid it break! Shieldless send him to fight!" The Old Order moves blindly on, never realizing that all the forces of evolution are with the New, and that the latter's victory is inevitable

As Fricka is leaving she encounters Brunnhilde. "Wotan doth wait for thee. Let him inform thee how the lot is to fall," she says.

Wotan regrets his bondage to form in the lament: "I am less free than the earth-born. Endless regret! Infinite grief. Saddest am I among all living." In vain Brunnhilde pleads the cause of Siegmund. "He and Sieglinde represent the Future," she urges, "and unless they survive, civilization will come to an end."

There is no compatibility between Fricka and Brunnhilde; one espouses the conservative and conventional; the other, the progressive and original. Wotan, as Fricka has rightly pointed out to him, is forever bound by his own laws. He has raised up Walsung as a free spirit to choose, of his own free will and by his own unaided might, to secure the Ring for Wotan. The hero must accomplish this voluntarily and without aid from the god—for if he acts as Wotan's agent or messenger then Wotan, not the hero, is responsible. And Wotan cannot break his own laws, even indirectly. But Siegmund has already had aid from Wotan! Fricka triumphantly lays this dilemma before him and he gloomily concedes that she is right and that Siegmund must fall.

All this he explains to Brunnhilde who, deeply moved, announces that she will shield Siegmund despite Wotan's order to the contrary. He wrathfully commands that she carry out his instructions. In great dejection she takes up her weapons, prepared to obey, and enters a cavern overlooking the pass.

From the orchestra emanates the tumultuous Flight music as Siegmund and Sieglinde appear in the pass below. He is exhausted but Sieglinde, half mad with fear, urges him forward. Brunnhide watches the hapless pair and is touched with compassion by their love for one another and by their dauntless spirit in such distressful circumstances. Such are the souls dearest to Truth. A tender love scene between the two Walsungs is high-lighted by staccatos of the Flight motif intermingled with their individual soul motifs, Love and Delight.

Later, while Sieglinde sleeps, Brunnhilde promises her aid to Siegmund despite Wotan's decree—for Siegmund has already rejected her offer of the halls of Paradise on condition that Sieglinde does not accompany him thither, saying he preferred the abode of Hell to Valhalla without his loved one.

The motifs of Fate and Death are woven together as Brunnhilde tells Siegmund of his approaching death. But when she vows to aid the lovers, the minor motif of Death is changed into a major and becomes the Song of Transfiguration.

Sieglinde sleeps on, dreaming restlessly of her woeful past, while Siegmund prepares for battle. Storm clouds cover the mountains, thunder reverbrates through the passes, and Hunding's horn call is heard. The two men shout challenges to one another, Hunding appears, and the combat begins. Brunnhilde is hovering in the air above Siegmund, protecting him with her shield and whispering words of encouragement. So it is that in a crisis an aspirant to the higher life will become conscious of the abiding presence of the Angel of Truth.

As Siegmund is about to overcome Hunding there is a terrific peal of thunder, followed by a rift in the sky. Above Hunding appears Wotan, warding off Siegmund's blows with his spear. Siegmund's sword is shattered by Wotan's spear, so crippling him that he soon sinks to the ground under Hunding's mortal thrust. Siegmund's motif is sounded by trumpets; Hunding's, by tubas and lower strings. When Wotan's spear shatters Siegmund's sword half of the Walsung's motif sounds clear and challenging until Hunding strikes the fatal blow.

Sieglinde, awakened by the clash of arms, faints at her beloved's death.

There ensues a poignant silence, followed by a soft rendering of the Death motif on horns and bassoons. Light fades from the sky and an intense gloom broods over the scene.

While Wotan converses with the victorious Hunding, Brunnhilde lifts the weeping Sieglinde to her horse and disappears amid the storm clouds, pursued by the maledictions of her angry father threatening her with punishment for her disobedience.

Hunding's victory proves of small worth. As Wotan bitterly commands him to go to Fricka and tell her that he, Wotan, has avenged her, Hunding falls dead. Shouts the thwarted god, "Brunnhilde, the disobedient, vengeance upon her!" and he also disappears amid the storm and lightning—objectifications of the violent emotions motivating this entire act.

ACT III

Act III opens with the magnificent Ride of the Valkyries. Upon the summit of the topmost peak and among the clouds, a sunny plateau is sheltered by lofty pines. This is the assembly place of the Valkyries. As lightning plays from peak to peak its light flashes upon the nine warrior maidens who come sweeping through the clouds, their wild shout echoing and re-echoing down the mighty currents of the wind.

Suddenly they see Brunnhilde riding across the sky faster than Valkyries have ever ridden, and they note with astonishment that she bears upon her flying steed—not a man, but a woman! Brunnhilde alights and asks them to help her shield Sieglinde, whose life must be preserved at any cost.

Another ominous roar of thunder and Brunnhilde realizes that Wotan is approaching. She bids Sieglinde hide herself in the forest, admonishing the maid to "Bear all troubles and hurts bravely, laugh when sorrow and pain torture, for you bear in your heart the greatest hero in the world." Thus does the Spirit of Truth counsel every individual in whom New Age idealism is in process of coming to birth.

At Brunnhilde's words, the face of Sieglinde glows with new and exalted joy. She goes toward the forest, accompanied by the magnificent Redemption by Love motif.

Brunnhilde bids her to *journey toward the East,* adding that her child will be Siegfried, the Victorious One, who will one day fuse together his father's broken sword—the two halves of which the Valkyrie gives to Sieglinde. Again to the Redemption by Love motif, Sieglinde bids farewell to Brunnhilde: "Oh highest of wonders! Noblest of maids! Thou true one, holiest comfort doth give. For him whom we loved, I saved the beloved one. May my heart's deep thanks win for thee joy."

From the darkness of the lowering clouds comes the voice of Wotan summoning Brunnhilde to the punishment due her disobedience. Their meeting is a dramatic contrast between Wotan's rage and the pathetic resignation of Brunnhilde. The tempestuous music softens as Brunnhilde comes before Wotan, saying humbly, "Here am I, Father."

Wotan storms at her, declaring—in anguish as well as anger, for he loves her dearly—that it is she who has invoked sentence upon herself. In a new motif, the clear and pure Walsung's Love, Brunnhilde bids him remember his own deep love for his offspring. In aiding Siegmund she has been more loyal to his true self than he himself has been, although she has defied his verbal commands. "When Fricka thine own intending did frustrate, and when her intending was followed, to thyself wert thou false." Wotan sorrowfully admits that she has done only what he would have liked best to do, but dared not.

However bound and obligated by the Old, on occasion everyone has glimpsed something of the untrammeled splendors of the New. Wotan has previously described his oneness with Truth (Brunnhilde) in the words "What secret I hold from all others, still will remain unspoken forever; myself I speak to when speaking to thee."

Although he knows she has done no wrong, Wotan is so far enmeshed in the rules and regulations of the Old Order—figured in Fricka—that he finds himself powerless to do aught but punish Brunnhilde. He must put her to sleep (silence and shackle Truth). Therefore, in deep sorrow and sadness, he "kisses her godhood away." Moving and tender is Wotan's farewell song to his best-beloved daughter: "Farewell, my brave and beautiful child! Thou, once the life and light of my life! Farewell! Farewell! Farewell! . . . Broken now is our bond. Exiled for ages, thou art banished from bliss."

The punishment for her disobedience Brunnhilde now learns. She is to be left with the spell of sleep upon her, for any passing mortal to awaken and possesses. "Lest I fall prey to some coward," she pleads, "let my sleep be so guarded that only the most fearless dare approach me. Let fire enfold me to destroy anyone unworthy to pass through it." Brunnhilde's appeal is made to the Sleep motif, first in the minor key indicating that this proceeding has to do with inner planes; later, in the major, revealing the active relationship that exists between the inner and outer worlds.

As Brunnhilde sinks into deep slumber, the sorrowing Wotan places her tenderly beneath a great fir tree. Then he summons the fire god, Loge, and bids him spread the illusion of fire around the mountain's base. When Wotan strikes the rock three times with his spear, great sheets of golden flame spring forth, filling the night sky with a blaze of light.

With his spear Wotan then draws a circle about Brunnhilde, saying, "He who fears my weapon shall never break through this fire. Sleep until he comes who is more free than I." The motif of Siegfried accompanies these words—Siegfried, son of the Victorious One, predestined to be Brunnhilde's deliverer. Truth sleeps under the vigilance of the Old Order awaiting its liberation with the coming of the New Day.

In the celestial beauty and magic of his Fire Music, Wagner has given free rein to his great genius. This is the music of that supernatural Fire which does not burn but exalts, for it is the God-given Fire of Spirit which produces light rather than heat.

Of the four Initiations whereby man gains control of the elements, Initiation by Fire is the most exalted. When an emancipated member of our human family is ready to receive this Illumination, heaven and earth resound with angelic rapture. Wagner brought this harmony from heavenly spheres and bequeathed it to earth in the beauty of his transcendent Fire Music, a magnificent finale to the second music-drama of the Ring Cycle.

Siegfried

PREFATORY NOTE

It has been remarked frequently that a work of art is often an unconscious biography of the artist himself. This is emphatically true of Wagner's operas, and perhaps most of all in relation to *Siegfried.* The hero of the *Nibelungenlid,* in his battles, conflicts, temptations and final victory, seems to reflect Wagner's own life history.

Upon the completion of the *Siegfried* composition-score, Wagner wrote: "If my life thus far has thrown me aimlessly through storms, then my life's ship before it reached the haven had to undergo the most extreme hardships. Nevertheless, the haven has been won, and now for the first time I live joyfully and gladly." Verily, this joy and gladness finds echo in the *Siegfried* music. It sparkles and exults with the radiance of youth in nature and in man.

The score of *Siegfried* represents more than fourteen years of intermittent labor. Wagner began work on this music in Switzerland in September, 1856. At that time he completed Acts I and II, together with the orchestral sketch. He then laid it aside to begin *Tristan and Isolde.* After that he rewrote portions of *Tannhauser* and *Lohengrin.* He also wrote *Die Meistersinger* and began *Parsifal* before again returning to *Siegfried.* Almost twelve years had elapsed, years filled with hardships, disappointments and, finally, peace. It was a master who has conquered life that finally brought to the world the glorious music which concludes the third act of *Siegfried.*

In the hero's triumphant ascent of the fire-encircled crest where Brunnhilde lies sleeping, Wagner accomplished one of his most remarkable musical feats. There is nothing in music to surpass the wild glory of the Fire Music. It is at the conclusion of *Die Walküre* that it is first heard, when Brunnhilde is laid to sleep by Wotan. It is heard again in all its rich and glorious cadences as Siegfried conquers the fire and awakens the sleeping goddess.

Wagner wrote to Liszt in the year following the completion of *Siegfried*. "You must hear this last act, the awakening of Brunnhilde—my most beautiful thing!" Those who understand the real import and message of the Fire Music fully concur with this sentiment. Again, "I have also begun the *Gotterdamerung*. I must not have much time, because whatever I write down is all superlative. But I'll still hold out and then say to myself: 'Well, it's done after all!'—so out of everything I derive strength for life."

THE PRELUDE

From Lavignac's incomparable work on the Wagner operas comes the following: "If we regard the Tetralogy in its entirety as a kind of immense symphony conceived in gigantic proportions, one movement of which answers to each day, *Siegfried* appears as its Scherzo, its impetuous intermezzo."

The Prelude consists largely of themes already familiar since they appear in the two earlier operas of the Ring Cycle. The Reflection motif here gives a tone-picture of the plottings of the evil dwarf, Mime, who purposes to dispose of everyone and everything standing in the way of his acquiring the golden treasure. Again there is the continuous hammering of the Nibelungs, sounded in the kettle drums, together with the Song of the Forge. The Bondage motif emerges dark and menacing, attended closely by Wotan's Rage, the Sword, the Dragon and the Cry of the Nibelungs—the "little people" enslaved by organized greed.

ACT I

The emotional stage is thus set for the action of the drama. Act I opens in the dark and gloomy cave in which Mime lives and plies his trade.

In *Die Walkure* we last beheld Sieglinde seeking refuge from Wotan in the forest after her rescue by Brunnhilde. We now learn that Mime, the brother of Alberich, found Sieglinde in her anguish and guided her to his cabin, where Siegfried was born. He was orphaned at birth. Sieglinde left for her son, however, his father's broken sword, Nothung, which can be mended only by one incapable of fear. The prophesy of Brunnhilde declared that the child would be the hero of the world, and that his name was to be Siegfried, meaning Son of Victory.

Siegfried has grown up a child of nature, strong and beautiful. His companions are wild things of the forest he has tamed because he knows no fear.

The music of this scene is gay and charming, bright with the joyousness of youth, the freshness of the woods and the sparkle of green and growing things. Siegfried's Idyll is a symphony in which the joys of youth and nature are intricately blended.

Siegfried's own individual keynote is heard in the motif, the Son of the Woods. It is an exultant thing, vibrant with the sheer joy of living. Translated biblically, it equates with the statement: "Behold, I make all things new."

It will be recalled that when, as a substitute for Freia, the Ring, the Tarnhelm and the golden treasure were given the Giants, Fasolt and Fafner, they immediately fell to quarreling over the Ring and Fafner slew Fasolt. Then, hiding his store of gold in a cave—Neidhehle, the cave of hate—he changed himself into a dragon and lived in the mouth of the cave to guard his possessions.

Gold continues to be hoarded through the greed of man's lower acquisitive nature—symbolized by the dragon who keeps constant watch beside its massed treasure concealed within a cave named hate. Today the dragon greed is guarding hoards of gold while countless millions starve. The time is long and the accumulated debts of causation heavy since the happy carefree days when gold flowed freely through the mystic Rhine waters.

It is said that the golden veins running through the earth are magnetic channels for cosmic forces of a particularly beneficial nature; that if gold had not been misused to enslave the race, it would have attracted to the earth fertility, plenty and every material and spiritual blessing. Paradise would not have been lost.

Gold is also a transmitter of astral or psychic forces. If we think in terms of the collective soul of the world, we perceive how it is possible for gold, due to constant association with envy, hatred, jealousy, greed and war, to become a focusing point for evil so that even to possess it tends to awaken corresponding qualities in the individual soul. It is even thought by many esotericists that the veins of gold in the earth serve as mediums for explosive gases which ultimate in earthquakes, volcanoes, tidal waves and other destructive phenomena, whereby nature effects retribution upon the human race for its vandalism.

In his *Letters from a Living Dead Man* transmitted telepathically through Elsa Barker, Judge Hatch predicted that the United States would one day become the center of the world's gold supply, thus incur the envy and hatred of other nations, and so become the scene of numerous plots. Also, that this era would be the twilight of gold and the end of the age.

Gold possesses the highest vibratory rate of all metals. It is a crystallization of the sun's rays. By right use it can be man's most valuable friend, but its misuse is resulting in its gradual disappearance from the human scene.

After gold—what? The great world-drama of the *Ring* holds the answer. It not only describes the path of destruction but it also shows the way out. The gold must be restored to the Rhine. That is, it must become universally accessible and not, as now, be hoarded by individuals. Translated into terms of divine economics, it must cease to be the basis of our medium of exchange. It is money based on gold —the supply of which is limited and can therefore be cornered and manipulated by greedy, selfish, powerful interests—that is the root of all evil. The evil lies not in gold (money) itself, but in its abuse. Its deflection from free-flowing channels of commerce (the Rhine) wherein it is available for the exchange needs of multitudes, and its appropriation by giants of finance (Fafner and Fasolt) who thereby acquire power over the lives of those who lack it, violate cosmic law and bring ruin upon the social order in which such an economy is operative. The end of the system as set forth in Wagner's Ring Cycle is paralleled in the Book of Revelations where it is spoken of as Babylon, the city decked in gold—for in the ancient City of Babylon originated the monetary system based on this scarce metal. Revelation tells how "in one hour so great riches is come to nought . . . for in one hour she is made desolate . . . Thus with violence shall that great city Babylon be thrown down, and shall be found no more at all."

Now to return to the characters of the drama and their unfolding destiny. Mime hates Siegfried, though he has cared for him through his boyhood and youth in the hope that he might be able to mend Siegmund's broken sword and use it to slay Fafner, thus procuring for himself the golden hoard, the Tarnhelm and, most important of all, the Ring. Possessing these, he could with safety dispose of Siegfried.

In Act I is heard a lovely sort of cradle song rhythm in which Mime describes the infancy and childhood of Siegfried. The tuneful horn made by Mime for the child is heard for the first time in all its jubilant ecstasy. This same simple and primitive motif, though more intricate in development and embellishment, later becomes the "musical aura" accompanying Siegfried on all his varying adventures and finally sobbing in mournful cadence above his funeral bier.

The music accompanying the story in which Mime tells Siegfried about his mother, Sieglinde, about her coming into the forest and of her death, is beautifully realistic. The narrative is faithfully transcribed in the music. The pure clear tones of the Walsung motif sound softly and sadly, to be followed by the Love motif of Siegmund and Sieglinde, tender and with increasing pathos in its closing discords. The Death motif of Sieglinde is long sustained. At length it is succeeded by a theme, graceful and charming, portraying Siegfried's gay, unfettered childhood in the woods.

According to the legend, Mime forged sword after sword for Siegfried, but the boy broke each of them in quick succession. Then Mime attempted to forge the broken sword Nothung, the gift of Wotan, but could not. (Only one who is fearless, brave and daring can do this.)

Siegfried, now grown to manhood, resolves to forge his own sword. He has come to realize that it is something he must do for himself, something no one can do it for him.

Forging of the sword introduces a new and beautifully rhythmical motif, the Song of the Sword. This and the Son of the Woods are the two motifs most characteristic of Siegfried. The sword, as stated previously, symbolizes the power of Truth in manifestation. The Song of the Sword may be interpreted biblically as "Ye shall know the Truth and the Truth shall make you free."

A new and virile musical note is added by the orchestra as Siegfried enthusiastically begins forging Nothung. He sings vociferously as he works. The orchestra accompanies the scene with more of the wonderful Fire Music as the flames mount eagerly upward because of Siegfried's lusty work with the bellows. He sings: "Nothung! Marvelous sword . . . . I soon shall call thee my sword!"

There is no treasure on earth more precious to the spiritually minded man than Truth, no labor more satisfying than its quest. This is expressed by the orchestra as Siegfried begins his work. The Forging Song soars with the fires of youthful aspiration and the joy of achievement.

Wagner relates how he came to write the music for the Song of the Forge. "A tinker had established himself opposite our house," he writes, "and stunned my ears all day long with his incessant hammering. In sheer disgust at never being able to find a detached house protected from every kind of noise, I was on the point of giving up composition altogether until the time when this indispensable condition should be fulfilled. But it was the tinker that in a moment of agitation gave me the theme for Siegfried's outburst against the bungling Mime. I played over the childishly quarrelsome theme in G minor to my sister, furiously singing the words at the same time, which made us all laugh so much that I decided to make one more effort." Thus it is shown how man may learn to turn obstacles of life into blessings for himself and others.

Mime, watching Siegfried's progress, offers suggestions, to which Siegfried pays no heed. He would not be a pioneer of the New Age were he to follow ways of the Old. The voice of the Old sounds in surprise and chagrin as Mime observes Siegfried's success: "The fool is favored by folly alone."

The work is at last completed. Siegfried, having forged it anew from the very beginning, possesses a new weapon and not just a mended old sword handed down from his father. It is the work of his own hands. With the joy of successful accomplishment, he swings the sword aloft and breaks forth again into the exultant strains of the Forging Song—previously scored in the minor but now heard in the major, suggesting the externalization of a concept or ideal from spiritual planes (minor key) on the material plane (major key).

Mime recognizes that with Nothung forged, Fafner will be slain and the Hoard, the Tarnhelm and the Ring will fall into Siegfried's hands. Therefore, he prepares a poisonous brew to slay Siegfried after the youthful hero has killed Fafner and secured the treasure.

ACT II

This act is also introduced by a Prelude musically descriptive of the coming action. From the violins comes a suggestion of the soul's horror of evil and the sinister motif of the Giants subtly distorted to represent Fafner—a theme peculiarly descriptive of bestiality. By its curious augmentations, the music is representative of the downward path chosen by Fafner, aptly symbolized by the metamorphosis of his man-like form into that of a dragon. Shortly afterward is heard the triumphant shout of the Nibelungs at their work of destruction, while the motif of the Curse of the Ring is interwoven with a somber and prophetic foreboding.

Act II opens with the Annihilation motif presaging the scene to follow. Alberich sits in darkness outside Fafner's cave, waiting and watching for an opportunity to regain the Ring. Wotan enters and is angrily denounced by Alberich. He replies that he is no longer a worker, only a watcher—for the tide of the New Order now flows so fast that the Old cannot stem it.

They speak of the coming of Siegfried and the slaying of Fafner. Wotan warns the Dragon that death awaits him unless he yields up the treasure he guards; but, he adds, Fafner may keep the gold if he will give up the Ring. Fafner, blind to coming danger, replies to all warnings—conformity with current concepts of the Old Order—"I lie and possess. Let me slumber."

Wotan disappears to the Fate motif, declaring ominously: "All things go as e'en they must, and no whit may they be altered."

It is early morning. To his own Son of the Woods motif, Siegfried appears with Mime before the cave of Fafner. Mime tries to awaken fear in Siegfried by pointing out the ferocity of the beast; how he seizes all who come too near and covers them with venomous and deadly froth, or suffocates and strangles them in his coils.

Siegfried is unaffected because he possesses absolute courage. He has never known fear and cannot imagine what it is. He lies tranquilly under a great tree of the forest to await the coming of the Dragon, meanwhile listening to the birds and longing to understand their speech. He sings of his father and mother with yearning love, wondering who they were and what they were like. He is sure that his mother's eyes were clear and tender like the eyes of the roe-deer, but much more beautiful. Exquisitely the music wells up in the violas and cellos as he whispers, "Ah, might these eyes by my mother be gladdened." Here the tender motif of Freia, Goddess of Love, seems to enfold the lonely lad like a mother's protective arms.

At this point Siegfried represents the neophyte standing at the very door of Initiation, awaiting the Dweller on the Threshold. He is conscious of the vast mysteries of the life just beyond the veil of the senses. His eagerness and his sadness arise from the fact that he is as yet unable to penetrate the veil which obscures Reality from his vision.

The stupendous harmony of Nature! Since the beginning of time artists have endeavored to interpret it, and none has succeeded more perfectly than did Richard Wagner in his exquisite opera *Siegfried.* Lilting harmonies of wind blowing through the trees, trills of woodland songsters, voices of invisible airy sprites, whispered echoes of the nature Angels—he caught them all and transcribed them in his incomparable score.

The lovely Siegfried idyll was given its initial performance privately, as a birthday present for Cosima Wagner, on Dec. 24, 1870. Just eight years later, on the same date and also to commemorate her birthday, the world first received the priceless heritage of the Parsifal Overture.

A sweet bird call awakens Siegfried from his revery. When he tries to answer it with a rousing call upon the horn, the tubas reply with the bellow of the Dragon just awakened from slumber. Siegfried laughs at the loud roars of the beast. As it rushes toward him, he admires its glittering fangs and, quite unmoved, awaits the critical moment when the monster attempts to encircle him. As it does he plunges his sword into its heart and the creature sinks back mortally wounded. The Dragon, inspired with admiration of Siegfried's valor, warns him with its last breath against the treachery of Mime.

When Siegfried draws forth his sword a few drops of the blood fall upon his hand. Instinctively, he touches his fingers to his lips and, as a result of having tasted the Dragon's blood, he finds himself in attunement with all the mysteries of nature. He understands the song of the winds, the murmur of the leaves, the language of the birds. Once again he hears the sweet trill of the forest bird, and now understands its speech. The bird tells him to go into the cave and secure the Tarnhelm and the Ring. It also warns him, as has the Dragon, of Mime's treachery.

This episode illustrates one of the more profound arcana of alchemistry. Blood is, in a special sense, the medium of the ego, the selfhood. As the blood stream is purified by sustaining the body on pure food and the mind with exalted thought, the ego is better able to use its body as an instrument of spiritual activity. Thus, an individual becomes more and more attuned to the Soul of Nature and acquires an intuitive knowledge of natural law and phenomena.

This intuitive knowledge is no mere blind instinct or vague sensing. The voice of the bird symbolizes the awakened and spiritualized intuition of the heart which, in its essence, is the voice of Spirit itself, whose admonitions are never wrong. When the aspirant learns to follow this voice he unerringly walks on the Path of Wisdom.

Following the bird's advice, Siegfried enters the cave to find the Tarnhelm and the Ring. When he is out of sight, Mime and Alberich emerge from their hiding places whence they have watched his battle with the Dragon and begin to quarrel over the possession of the Ring. Siegfried reappears with the two treasures whereon Alberich vanishes into the forest while Mime fawns and flatters.

Siegfried, however, by virtue of his awakened soul powers, senses the evil and malice of his companion's dark heart. He answers Mime in accordance with the latter's thoughts, not his words. When Mime offers him the poisoned drink Siegfried slays the schemer with one blow of his sword and leaves the body beside that of the Dragon, saying as he does so: "Nothung pays envy's wage: therefore truly did I wage it." It must be remembered that the sword Nothung represents the power of Truth. It must ever slay evils which bar the upward progress of an awakened soul.

"Humanity moves in cycles—the wise ones in spirals," an ancient mystic has said. This is a true maxim of Initiation. By evolution the masses are brought certainly but slowly to illumination; by Initiation the wise ascend steeply but swiftly to the sun-lit summit.

The slaying of Mime represents overcoming the lower sense nature. When it is slain nothing of it is retained. The Dragon, however, represents powers resident in the depths of the soul itself. These powers or forces of the psyche cannot be annihilated. They can only be transmuted. When the Dweller is "slain" it is not dead but transfigured. Its powers are added to the soul, which is then free to pass unhampered into higher planes.

Now that transmutation of the lower nature is effected,

the bird sings to Siegfried of that "Far away snow mountain upon which the beautiful maiden of Truth is sleeping. If he can win through the blaze he may awaken the bride. This shall be no coward's feat, but is for the knight who knows no fear."

"A heavenly song!" cries Siegfried, "it overpowers my heart."

The bird replies: "Glad out of grief is my greeting of love. Wisely from pain I have woven my song. None save in sighs, understand." Pain has ever been the doorway to attainment. None can wear the crown who has not borne the cross.

The Song of the Bird introduces one of the most ethereal motifs of the opera, a sweetly celestial song falling in delicate cadences upon the earth in a tender and colorful rain of melody. This ethereal Bird theme motivates the entire scene. Interwoven with it are the motifs of Fire and Siegfried's Song of the Woods, suggestive of his impetuous and youthful ardor in which there is no room for fear.

As Siegfried follows the bird with intense eagerness, from the orchestra comes an exuberant burst of music that closes with a melody soaring enchantingly heavenward, like a bird on the wing.

ACT III

The Prelude to Act III recapitulates events of the preceding two acts besides foretelling what is to come. The motifs of the Ride, Lamentation of the Gods, Sleep, Fate, the Rhine and Wotan's Spear are combined in a tempestuous pattern of great beauty. Solemn and impressive, the voices of the Norns (Fates) are heard, together with the tone-cry of the Twilight of the Gods, that foreshadows the passing of the Old Order.

To the slumberous music of the Sleep motif, the curtain rises upon a barren and rocky height where Wotan, the Wanderer, stands before a cavern invoking the Earth Goddess, Erda, to arise from her "Timeless Sleep." Surrounded with a pale blue light, Erda appears, her garments shimmering as with hoar-frost. Still half dreaming, she asks who awakens her?

Wotan replies that he has come seeking counsel of her, the wisest of beings. As representative of the decadent Old Order his question is significant: how, he asks, can he *hold back the rolling wheel?*

Erda says she once bore to him a daughter, Brunnhilde, the Spirit of Truth. Why not inquire of her? Wotan is compelled to admit that he has put Brunnhilde to sleep because she disobeyed him. Therefore, he can receive no counsel from her.

After a long silence Erda muses: "Dazed am I since I awake. Wild and strange seems the world. The Valkyrie suffers penance of sleep while her all-knowing Mother slept. Doth then pride's teacher punish pride? Is the deed-enkindler worthy of the deed? He, the Truth's upholder, tramples upon the right and reigns by untruth! Let the dreamer descend again. Let sleep again seal my wisdom."

Only by giving up its own duplicity, its own wrong-thinking which inflictes punishment upon Truth for upholding Truth, can the Old Order be saved. Wotan, typical of average humanity, cannot receive the message which wisdom offers him, although he himself has asked for it.

Again he demands of Erda an answer to his perplexing problem. He says he knows his regime is ended, for he once in anger flung the world into the hands of Alberich (evil). But now he bequeaths it to another, to Siegfried, son of the Walsungs. The orchestra underlines this statement with the theme of Heritage of the World. Wotan believes that Siegfried cannot be touched or injured by the curse of the Ring, nor by the venom of the Dragon—that its sinister influences of the Old Age cannot affect higher concepts of the New. Siegfried, he says, will awaken Brunnhilde, and she will then win salvation for the world. He will be happy to yield the world to the eternally young. "Away. away!" he cries, "mother of all fear, to endless sleep, away!"

Erda disappears in waning light as Wotan goes forth to meet Siegfried, now seen approaching in the distance.

* * * * *

It is dawn. Siegfried reaches the foot of the mountain upon which Brunnhilde sleeps and begins the climb, only to find that his upward path is barred by Wotan who stretches his spear across the way. The bird has thus far led Siegfried upon his quest but now flies away, frightened by Wotan's black ravens—symbols of fears and prejudices of the Old Order with which intuitive faculties of the New are not in sympathy. Without the guidance of the bird Siegfried is no longer certain of his course, so asks directions of Wotan. Wotan questions him closely, learning of the death of Fafner, the forging of the sword and the quest for Brunnhilde. He admits that it was he who shattered Siegmund's sword and warns Siegfried that he may shatter it again if his anger is awakened.

Siegfried, thinking Wotan to be his father's enemy, rushes upon him with his sword. When the god angrily bars his way with his spear, the youth shatters it by a prodigious blow of Nothung and continues eagerly on his way toward the summit.

Here, as in the battle between Hunding and Siegmund, the Old Order has come into direct conflict with the New. This conflict is marvelously depicted in the music motifs. Wotan's appearance is accompanied by the Bondage motif, the Flame Spell and Eternal Sleep (the Sleep motif implies crystallization); as Siegfried disappears, leaving Wotan in gloomy foreboding, the themes of Fire, Sleep and Siegfried's Horn Call are blended in tumultuous glory while a curtain of flame rises shimmeringly toward the skies.

Siegfried appears to the buoyant, challenging notes of his own call, the Son of the Woods, the Song of the Bird and the Song of the Sword. The free, the unfettered, the New, is ranged in conflict with the bound, the crystalized, the Old.

When the sword of Siegmund met the spear of Wotan, it was Siegmund's sword that was shattered. The New had not yet grown strong enough to supersede the Old. As the New Age approaches, its dominant truths are emerging from an age-long sleep under the arbitrary rules of the Old. So, when the same sword, in the hand of Siegfried, meets the spear of Wotan, it is the spear that splinters.

To the challenging and exultant Son of the Woods motif, mingled with the glory and mysticism of the Fire music, Siegfried plunges into the midst of the searing flames that surround the sleeping Brunnhilde.

The curtain of flame, through which Siegfried disappears, is familiar in initiatory work as the Fire Test. When the fires of desire have been transmuted into soul power, this outer "Fire Ring" is not composed of flame that burns, but of light which nourishes and sustains, and that illumines all the pathways of life.

As Siegfried ascends the fire grows ever brighter until he steps out into the light of a loftier place.

Siegfried discovers Brunnhilde under the great fir tree, still clad in battle dress as when she fell asleep. Not until he removes her helmet and loosens her armor does he realize it is a woman who sleeps there. His love is instantaneous. As he makes every effort to awaken her but in vain, for the first time he is smitten with fear. He gazes upon her beautiful face as she lies motionless. Then, kneeling beside her inadoration, he kisses her lips, crying, "Awaken, awaken, holiest maid!" This breaks the magic sleep and Brunnhilde opens her eyes. Gazing about her she greets the light, while from the orchestra comes the soul-stirring measure—full, rapid and up-sweeping with the currents of renewed life—of the Awakening motif, a glorious, glittering call twice repeated.

Sun, I hail thee!
Hail, thou Light!
Hail, O glorious day!
Long was my sleep—
  I am awakened!
Who is the man who broke the spell?

Brunnhilde asks Siegfried his name, and greets him as the Lord of Life and of the World. Her great love for him awakens. With a cry of ecstasy he clasps her in his arms as she sings in triumph:

Oh, hero-like boy!
Oh, Warrior child-like!
Thou strongest, purest in all the world!
Laughing I must adore thee,
Laughing, blind myself for thee,
Laughing, go to death with thee,
Laughing, wait for the end!

Woven ever and anon through the gleaming, caressing measures of Brunnhilde's dedication to Siegfried's quest for light sounds the clear high rhythmic swing of her own motif, Ride of the Valkyries—the call of Truth to the Spirit of the Aspirant, that he mount ever higher, higher, higher, for Truth can know no bounds. Siegfried responds exultingly, "Hail the world where Brunnhilde lives! Brunnhilde my Star!" Eager and ecstatic is the exquisite Love's Rapture motif, followed by the supernal calm of Love's Peace.

The seeker after Truth has attained his Quest. Together, Brunnhilde and Siegfried sing their triumphant love-duet, the soul-song of high illumination:

Love illumined
Laughing at death.

The Twilight of the Gods

Die Gotterdammerung

PREFATORY NOTES

The Twilight of the Gods, finale of the Ring Cycle, is so tremendous in its implications, so far-reaching in its evolutionary scope, so magnificent musically, that no mere words can begin to convey its grandeur. In order to form a true evaluation of this opera it is necessary to have a thorough familiarity with the story and to witness repeatedly the Ring Cycle in its entirety. In none of his operas has Wagner more truly wrought the enchantment which, as often stated, causes his audience to see aurally and hear visually.

Wagner first conceived the idea for the Ring Cycle in 1848, when he was thirty-five years of age. The great work was completed on November 21, 1874, when he was sixty-one, an interval of twenty-six years. The completion of *The Twilight of the Gods* coincided with and reflected the twilight shadows of the Master's own life. After this opera was finished, there remained only the final work on Parsifal, his swan song and the most beautiful jewel in his bright crown of immortality

In *Die Gotterdammerung* Wagner shows the downfall of the Old Order in chaos and destruction; but he also points to the advent of a glorious new heaven and new earth to take its place. In earlier operas of the Tetralogy—or Trilogy, if we consider *Das Rheingold* as an introduction, as did Wagner—the maestro traces the path of material civilization to its zenith in the Aryan age; and with it, like the intertwining of a silver with a gold thread, the path of Initiation which comes to a climax in the beauty and glory of Brunnhilde's Immolation. Wagner said that Brunnhilde, by her divine self-sacrifice for the welfare of mankind, typifies one who has attained the blessed state of liberation from rebirth. Such attainment is the highest this world knows. Thus, the Ring Cycle carries us in prospect to the very end of the present Earth Period.

Liszt spoke truly when he referred to this colossal work as the "gigantic mountain chain of the Ring." But Hans von Bulow said it all in his words to a friend: "I cannot talk to you about the Nibelung. In the face of this work all the resources of expression fail one. I will just say this, nothing like, nothing approaching it, has ever been produced in any tongue, anywhere, at any time. From it one looks right down, right over everything else."

A spirit of inevitability broods over and envelops the final opera of the Ring Cycle. In place of the usual recapitulatory Prelude there is an extended Prologue of two scenes, both of which portray inner plane activities concerned with the occult forces of evolution and their externalization in human history.

THE PROLOGUE

The hour is midnight. Perched upon Brunnhilde's rock, the Norns or Three Fates (Past, Present and Future), sit spinning the golden thread of destiny. The first Norn (Past) sings of the great World Ash from which Wotan took a branch for his spear. The second Norn (Present) sings of how Wotan inscribed upon the shaft of the spear certain laws by which he rules the world; and how Siegfried broke the spear weakened by Wotan's own violation of the *spirit* of law. The third Norn (Future) sings about Wotan's fell-ing the Ash Tree and how he heaped its wood in a green pyre around Valhalla. A new motif accompanies the song of the Norns—the Twilight of the Gods, as implied and foreseen in Wotan's act.

Again the first Norn (Past) says that the threads are so much more difficult to untangle since Alberich formed the Rhinegold into the Ring. The second Norn (Present) complains that the threads are becoming frayed: "The web wavers and tears; from grief and greed rises the Nibelung's Ring, a vengeful curse gnaws at the sundering strands." As the third Norn (Future) begins to weave the threads break and the Norns cry out in terror. Binding themselves together with the broken cord they chant, "This is the end of our wisdom! The world hears us wise ones no more! Let us descend to Erda." They disappear to the solemn theme of the Annunciation of Fate.

The Three Fates represent the Law of Causation. Their song portrays the downward course of civilization when it ceases to be grounded in Truth and when the "letter of the law" supersedes the spirit, killing the creative impulse and thus bringing an end to progress

During the Norns' singing is heard Brunnhilde's magnificent Hail to the World and the Fire Music, together with the Lament of the Rhine Maidens, the sinister Adoration of Gold and the Curse of the Ring. When the thread breaks the hour of payment strikes and the Fates depart as these various motifs intermingle prophetically.

Siegfried closes with Brunnhilde and Siegfried upon the mountain-top after he had awakened the sleeping daughter of Wotan to a new day and a new love. Brunnhilde now appears to the Valkyrie note; Siegfried, to his own call sounding in the brasses. Brunnhilde (Truth) instructs Siegfried in many works of magic but tells him that he cannot remain with her forever, that he must return to the world and there accomplish heroic deeds. To the radiant theme of Love's Greeting, she bids him never forget her or all that she has taught him. The aspirant cannot remain always upon the peak of vision, but must return to the plains below to share his revelation of Truth with others.

Great Ones are never sure of the status of their disciples until their dedication to spiritual life is complete. Brunnhilde entreats Siegfried, "One sad fear doth much appease me, that I to thee am not yet wholly all." Siegfried replies, "More gavest thou me, wonder-woman, than I can yet grasp. So find not fault if much of thy wise teachings I forget! One great thing though I know—for me Brunnhilde lives! And one lesson learned I well—Brunnhilde to remember!" This dedication or allegiance to the Quest of Truth is accompanied by one of the opera's loveliest motifs, Brunnhilde's Love. This music does not contain such rapturous ecstasy as the Love Greeting that accompanied Brunnhilde's awakening. It is deeper, more serious in mood, telling of the divine contentment of soul in intimate contact with Truth.

In token of his love and constancy, Siegfried gives Brunnhilde the Ring he obtained from Fafner, while she gives him her noble steed, Grane. As he descends the mountainside she surrounds him with her musical aura of protection, Song of the Valkyries. And she hears him calling to her in his own beautiful motif, the Son of the Woods, until he plunges into the fiery wall surrounding the base of the great rock.

An extended orchestration, Siegfried's Rhine Journey, follows, in which Siegfried's outer world experiences may be traced by the variety of motifs introduced, pre-eminently the sinister Ring and Gold motifs and the sensuous Heritage of the World, prophetic of his fall. These motifs symbolize the dominant evils of modern civilization: the will to power, avarice and sensuality.

ACT I

Act I opens in a castle situated on the banks of the Rhine, stronghold of the King of the Gibichungs. Gunther, the King, is in consultation with his sister, the lovely Gutrune, and his half-brother, Hagen. Hagen is the child of a loveless union between Alberich, the Nibelung, and the mother of Gunther and Gutrune, Grimhilde by name. She has been won with his gold—for, having renounced love, he could find no woman who would accept him on other terms. Hagen, a sin-shadowed child of darkness, plots to gain possession of the Ring for his father. To this end he urges marriage upon Gunther and Gutrune, telling them the story of Siegfried, the hero without fear, who slew the Dragon and who, alone of mortal men, can pass through the circle of fire to obtain Brunnhilde as wife to Gunther. He extracts a promise from Gunther that he will marry no one but Brunnhilde, and from Gutrune that she will charm Siegfried.

Hagen's discourse on Brunnhilde's beauty is accompanied by the orchestral motifs of the Ride of the Valkyries, the Flame-Spell and the Bird. He recounts Siegfried's exploits to the accompaniment of the Call of the Woods, the Valkyries' Song and the Conquest of the Dragon.

The conspiracy has scarcely been formulated when Siegfried himself arrives upon the scene and is greeted with hearty friendliness by Gunther. But the warning of evil rises from the orchestra in the motifs of the Curse of the Ring and the Adoration of Gold, both of which are drowned out by the triumphant challenge of Siegfried's own motif.

Two new motifs are introduced in this opera: The sinister notes of Hagen's Treachery by Magic and Gutrune's Heritage of the World, a sensuous and worldly musical phrase that always accompanies her.

Gutrune extends to the hero her most cordial friendship. She offers him a drink of mead in which Hagen has distilled a love potion to make him forget Brunnhilde and her towering mountain of flame. The treachery of Gunther and Gutrune symbolize the subtlety of tests the aspirant must meet even in the higher reaches of Initiation. There is nothing objective by which to judge. He must be able to hear clearly within himself the voice of intuition, symbolized in the bird. Indeed, as Siegfried takes the cup, the Song of the Bird softly sounds an admonition, but Siegfried heeds it not. He asks tender care for Grane, then drinks to Brunnhilde, while from the orchestra comes the exquisite notes of Love Greeting—for Truth ever seeks to guard her protegees.

This lovely motif is followed by the solemn notes of Treachery by Magic. The potion accomplishes its work. Siegfried has imbided forgetfulness. Brunnhilde is forgotten and a passionate love for Gutrune awakens in his heart. Again, like the departing sigh of fragrant memories, sounds the Song of the Bird and the Flame Spell, followed by louder tones of the now triumphant Bondage and the Adoration of Gold motifs. Once more Truth has been vanquished by materiality. The day of reckoning, The Twilight of the Gods, the end of an age, draws nearer.

One precarious condition of humanity is the fact that it is ofttimes the pioneers, to whom the masses look for guidance and leadership, who sacrifice idealism and succumb to the lure of a materialistic and carnal age, as did Siegfried.

Under the spell of the love potion, Siegfried asks Gunther for the hand of Gutrune in marriage and promises to return through the fire and bring Brunnhilde to be the bride of Gunther. As he makes this promise the Curse motif is heard clear and menacing in the tubas: "Thy bride fain will I fetch—if Gutrune for wife I may gain." The Song of the Bird flashes briefly and faintly through the music and dies away, a last premonitory warning call of the higher nature.

Siegfried and Gunther take the oath of blood brotherhood. Hagen fills a drinking horn with fresh wine for them, and each man, cutting his arm with his sword, lets the blood flow into the horn. They then drink from the horn and swear the oath as the Fidelity motif is heard from the orchestra.

Siegfried asks Hagen why he does not drink. Hagen replies that his blood would poison the cup, being less noble than theirs: "My blood would trouble the draught; its flow is hardly noble enough." This statement is of deep significance. The blood is the particular channel of the ego—hence, its sacredness in ancient religions. According to the spiritual power of the ego is the condition of the blood. When the alchemical feat of Transfiguration is achieved, it becomes luminous and fiery as it courses through the body, bearing in its stream a celestial force which renders the body immortal and beautiful. The opposite occurs in such evil natures as that of Hagen, for then an evil essence fills the blood—as Hagen truthfully, if unintentionally, avers. The blood is then a poison, harmful to anyone into whose veins it is injected.

Hagen watches in diabolical glee as Siegfried and Gunther prepare a boat and start forth to capture Brunnhilde. He sings triumphantly that he will watch and ward the hall while the others, unknown to themselves, perform his secret will and gain for him possession of the Ring: "Trusty companions, laugh as ye sail on your way! Base though ye deem him, ye both shall serve the Nibelung's son."

During the night hours, Hagen, leader of the Sons of Darkness upon the earth plane, and his father Alberich, captain of the Hosts of Evil in invisible realms, commune together, rejoicing at the pitiable condition into which mankind—represented now in Siegfried—has fallen. Alberich speaks: "If thou art fearless, fierce and false, those whom we fight in nocturnal feuds shall surely be harmed by our hate." He adds exultantly, "Mine and thine! We will master the world."

So plot and plan the Sons of Darkness through the night hours. Siegfried returns with the dawn and announces his betrayal of Brunnhilde, the Spirit of Truth. Hagen gives vent to his jubilation in a wild chant, which may well be described as the Victory Song of the Brothers of the Shadow —a victory that is no victory but merely its ephemeral caricature:

Heiho! Heiho! Heiho! Weapons! Weapons! Goodly weapons, sturdy weapons, sharp for strife. Woe, Woe is here! Waken! Waken! Waken! Heiho! Heiho! Heiho.

The music accompanying this chant of destruction is menacing with hate and vengefulness. Siegfried fares forth on his ill-fated journey to his motif, the Son of the Woods, but he is now bounded by the motif of Bondage. Throughout this tone picture of tragedy is woven the solemn and relentless measures of the Fate motif.

In the next scene Brunnhilde still sits alone upon her rock, rapturously kissing the Ring and dreaming of Siegfried's return. Her solitude is interrupted by one of her Valkyrie sisters, Waltraute, who relates all that has occurred in Valhalla during the time she slept. From the day when Wotan returned home with his spear broken, Waltraute says, he has given the Valkyries no heroic commissions. Nor would he eat of the golden apples that Freia (Vision) offered him. More than this, he has cut down the great Ash Tree, and now seems only to wait and watch for the end. Yet, he has spoken of Brunnhilde, saying that not until the Ring is returned to the Rhine maidens can the curse be lifted from gods and men. "End the grief of the gods!" Waltraute entreats, "cast it far from thee; to the Rhine daughters give it!" Her mournful plea continues:

Hear me! heed my distress!
The world's trouble
hangs upon it, I trow.

Whirl it from thee
Far in the water,
woe from Valhalla averting;
Cast the foul thing away
in the flood!

Brunnhilde refuses to accede to her sister's request, Waltraute, uttering a great cry of woe for the world's impending fate, gallops away, disappearing among the clouds. Truth cannot of itself redeem humanity. Man must save himself by finding Truth and manifesting its powers in his daily life. Brunnhilde remains watching the twilight scene and the flames that burn at the foot of the mountain. As night shadows deepen about the fire-encircled peak, Siegfried's call is heard. Brunnhilde springs up in glad anticipation of his coming, but only the image of Gunther comes toward her through the flames—for Siegfried has assumed the likeness of Gunther by means of the Tarnhelm, and in Gunther's name claims her as his bride: "I have come to claim you as my wife and you must follow me willingly." Truth can never unite with man's lower nature, so they struggle for mastery until Siegfried, in the image of Gunther, obtains the Ring from her as she falls unconscious in his arms.

Pathos and tragedy are here. A Son of Light has become an instrument of the Sons of Darkness. Truth has again been betrayed. The powerful motif of Destruction rumbles through the music as Brunnhilde swoons under the fatal spell of the Ring.

ACT II

A brief orchestral introduction to Act II is animated principally by the Annihilation motif. Hagen has summoned all the little earth spirits, the dwarfs and gnomes, and commanded them to prepare a wedding reception for their new mistress. Hagen is exultant over the prospect of victory, for his father, Alberich, has appeared to him and promised that by possession of the Ring he may rule the world. A new motif, Murder, is here introduced as the theme of Hagen's plotting; it reaches its climax in Siegfried's death.

Wedding festivities go forward to the deep and persistent rhythms of the Work of Destruction, together with the Nibelung's Cry of Triumph and the motifs of Bondage, Curse of the Ring and Doom of Valhalla. The act as a whole is dominated by the earthly, sensuous music of the Call to Marriage. Subdued and protesting, Brunnhilde's motif accompanies her into the hall of the Gibichungs and interweaves sadly with the wedding music.

Gunther leads Brunnhilde in the wedding processional, saying, "Two happy bridals bless we together, Brunnhilde and Gunther, Gutrune and Siegfried." Brunnhilde gazes in perplexed amazement at Siegfried as he, having no memory of his love for her, presents Gutrune with the words, "Gunther's gentle sister, won by me as thou by him." Then, seeing upon his finger the Ring which she thought Gunther had taken, she divines the truth instantly and denounces him as having betrayed her who is his wife. To Gunther this appears as betrayal of his own claim upon Brunnhilde. Siegfried swears upon Hagen's spear-point that he has not been guilty of betraying his blood-brotherhood, whereupon Brunnhilde strikes the spear from his hand, crying, "Holy spear, witness my oath . . . I pray that he may perish by thy point, for here he has sworn falsely." Siegfried cannot understand her wild outburst. He cautions Hagen to care for her because she is still distraught and knows not what she is saying.

A new motif foretells events to come. It is the Covenant of Vengeance sounding in the background.

Hoping that rest and quiet will calm Brunnhilde, Siegfried bids attendants proceed with the wedding festivities and then leads Gutrune away.

Brunnhilde, Gunther and Hagen remain alone in the great hall. Gunther sits, sad and dejected. After a silence filled expressively by the orchestra with music in which the themes of Bondage, Heritage of the World and Fate predominate, Brunnhilde speaks sadly: "What evil power has woven this misfortune? . . . Who will bring me the sword that will sever my bond?"

Hagen offers to help her get revenge upon Siegfried. Brunnhilde reveals to him that by her magic she has made Siegfried invulnerable except for a point between his shoulders, deeming this adequate since she knew he would never turn his back on an enemy: "If at his back thou strike —never, I knew, would he retreat, and so no spell did I set there."

Every aspirant, despite great attainment, retains some mortal weakness. It was the heel of Achilles, a thorn in the flesh of Paul. Brothers of the Shadow are alert to discover this point of vulnerability in all who aspire.

Brunnhilde, Gunther and Hagen express the inevitability of karmic law by which wrongdoing brings about its own destruction: "Siegfried falleth for sins of himself."

Hagen demands of Gunther the death of Siegfried. Gunther hesitates, thinking of his brotherhood oath and his sister's love for Siegfried. "Blood brotherhood I swore with him," he protests. Hagen realizes that only by Siegfried's death can he gain possession of the Ring, so continues to demand it. "No help from hand, no help from brain," he cries, "there helps but—Siegfried's death!" Gunther, still thinking of Gutrune, reluctantly replies, "What were we worth in her eyes, with her husband's blood on our hands?"

Brunnhilde turns upon Gunther contemptuously: "Low indeed has fallen the race that bore such faint heart as thou!" Hagen insists that the oath of brotherhood has already been broken and calls for revenge. Gunther yields to their persuasion, and the three plot Siegfried's destruction. "Tomorrow we hunt . . . a wild boar shall kill him!" Thus they hoped to appease Gutrune, masking murder as accident.

The voices of the conspirators unite in a call upon the gods, and Hagen murmurs, "Father, Alberich, again shalt thou be lord of the Ring!"

The brilliant music of the marriage feast resounds in splendor from the orchestra. Gutrune's motif and the colorful Call to Marriage accompany the bridal procession as it moves through the great hall. Gutrune is carried in a chair and Siegfried upon a shield, while youths and maidens pass before them scattering flowers in their pathway. The procession moves on. However, it is no longer accompanied by the marriage music but by Hagen's sinister motif, Covenant of Vengeance.

ACT III

Act III opens with a woodland scene on the banks of the Rhine where Rhine maidens sing of their lost gold as from the distance comes the sound of Siegfried's horn call. They rhythmically play about in the water until the horn is heard close by, when they disappear into the depths to confer and await Siegfried. He soon appears alone upon the banks of the river, having lost his way in the hunt. The Rhine maidens know him. Coming to the surface, they call him by name and attempt to cajole him into returning the Ring he wears upon his finger. Failing in their cajolery, they warn him that "It is for your own undoing that you keep the Ring. As the dragon fell, so shall you fall unless it be restored." Again he refuses, since fear is to him completely unknown and their warning moves him even less than their coaxing. "Farewell, Siegfried!" they cry, "today a noble woman will inherit your hoop and return it to us!" With this they swim away, intoning their lament for the Rhinegold.

The Rhine maidens make a statement applicable to average humanity when they say of Siegfried that "He fancies himself as fearless and wise, as he truly is trammelled and blind." When so speaking the Curse motif sounds forth ominously from the trombones.

As the Rhine maidens disappear, horns of the hunting party are heard and Siegfried answers their call. Hagen and his company join Siegfried and pile up the spoils of the hunt under the tree. Siegfried owns that he has found no game, only "water-fowl who foretold my death."

Is it true, Hagen asks, that he can understand the language of birds? Siegfried laughingly replies, "I put that away a long time ago. Since I have listened to the singing of woman, I have quite forgotten the little bird." A man cannot serve two masters. The intuitive voice of the soul—Song of the Bird—is stifled and silenced when personality yields to the allurements of sense life.

Hagen gives Siegfried a drink containing a potion with the promise that it will restore his memory. This it does. Siegfried now recalls Brunnhilde, the bird which led him to her, and the consummation of their love. Reminiscent melodies enfold him: "Brunnhilde! Holiest bride!" he calls out in ecstasy. Gunther is enraged. At this moment two black ravens circle about Siegfried's head and Hagen cries, "What say these ravens?" As Siegfried turns to look at the birds disappearing in the twilight, Hagen plunges his sword deep into the hero's back, shouting "Vengeance they say to me, and now treachery is avenged!"

Darkness falls as Siegfried is breathing his last, while

the music suggests his life in retrospect. As an ego leaves its body at death, all the events of its earthly span pass before its inner vision. Such retrospection is detailed musically in a recapitulation of the principal motifs of Siegfried's career: the Forge, Bondage, voices of Mime and the Dragon, the exultant Song of the Sword, Victory over the Dragon, followed by the exquisite strains of Forest Murmurs and the Song of the Bird. With his dying breath, and to the ecstatic accompaniment of the Love Duet and Brunnhilde's exaltation motif of Hail to the World, he cries: "Brunnhilde, my bride of heaven, I come to thee!"

The Curse of the Ring thunders forth in malevolent fury. The Fate theme follows, its half sobbing tones and the earthly life of Siegfried ebbing away together.

The funeral march has been described as a musical oration without words. Again, all Siegfried's motifs pass in review, not joyous and exultant as at the beginning, but halting and heavy with the burden of his failure. Through this passage flows softly the ecstatic Love Song of Siegmund and Sieglinde while the stirring call of the Valkyries echoes and re-echoes in subdued cadence from peak to peak. Siegfried's special motif, Son of the Woods, begins in happy youthful adandon, struggles, falters, and soon loses itself. In the uncertain light of the moon amid storm clouds, Siegfried is borne back to the castle.

Gutrune awaits the return of the one she truly loves. She is full of anxiety for during the night she has had many premonitory dreams. Hagen enters abruptly and announces Siegfried's death, calling for a processional of torch bearers to accompany the bier. The body is brought in. Gutrune repulses Gunther's effort to comfort her, and he remorsefully admits that Hagen murdered Siegfried.

The Ring still gleams upon the hand of Siegfried and Hagen immediately claims it. When Gunther forbids him, he draws his sword and slays the King beside Siegfried's remains. He then attempts to take the Ring, but fails as the proud sword by Siegfried's side, which flashes with magic light, bars his progress—a circumstance portrayed musically by a majestic and stately movement in the brasses.

Brunnhilde commands the withdrawal of Gutrune to the accompaniment of Heritage of the World. She bids the women decorate the bier with sweet-smelling herbs and asks the men to gather faggots for the funeral pyre, and to place the body of Siegfried thereon in state. Her final order is for her steed Grane to be brought to her.

When all is in readiness, Brunnhilde takes the Ring from Siegfried's hand and places it upon her own: "Now I take my inheritance for my own! O fatal Ring, I take you in my hand so I may cast you away. Wise Sisters of the Waters, laughing daughters of the Rhine, I give you back what belongs to you. Take it for yourselves, the flames shall purge the Ring and the curse shall be washed away in the river." Then, mounting Grane, she catches up a torch from one of the men, saying to two ravens fluttering near, "Fly home, ye ravens! Tell Wotan what ye have seen, and bid Loge hasten to Valhalla, for at last the day of the gods reaches its twilight! Thus casting my torch, I kindle Valhalla's Tower."

Urging Grane into the blazing funeral pyre to her own wild and splendid Ride of the Valkyries, Brunnhilde cries out, "Siegfried, Brunnhilde greets thee in bliss." The music and the flames sweep higher and higher until all the earth seems to be held in a quivering, surging sea of sound and flames until they are lost in space. When the blaze dies down and the smoke drifts slowly away, the waters of the Rhine creep up over the still glowing embers. Upon the waters, where the burning pyre was last seen, swim the lovely Rhine maidens. Hagen leaps into the river shouting, "The Ring is mine! Back from the Ring!" He is too late. The Rhine maidens have recovered the Ring. Two of them catch him and hold him under the water while a third restores the Ring to its rightful place. For the last time the

Curse motif sounds feebly and then is heard no more. The Rhine maidens swim away, singing joyously.

As noted in *The Rhinegold*, thus it is that Truth inevitably brings about the destruction of the Old Order so as to make way for the in-coming New.

The motifs which dominate this scene are the Flame Spell as Brunnhilde catches up the torch, the Ride of the Valkyries, the solemn Fall of the Gods and the Lament of the Rhine Maidens.

The spirit of our age of materialism is centered in *me* and *mine;* the New Age will be centered in *we* and *ours*. The Old is egocentric; the New, altruistic; the Old emphasizes separate selfhood; the New, collective unity.

Brunnhilde's Immolation is the universal call of Truth to the divinity which sleeps in every human being, regardless of appearances to the contrary. "What sunny light outstreams his looks! . . . Siegfried, the Star of my life!" Thus Brunnhilde describes the Christed mankind of the New Day.

The Rhine returns to its course, the waters subside and, to the majestic motif of Valhalla, a red glow is seen on the distant horizon. It is Valhalla burning, the Old Order coming to its final, fiery doom.

It is a *way of life,* not life itself, that comes to an end—a way of life so impeded with obstacles to progress that it must be destroyed in order to clear the path to a better future. Wagner states this musically by introducing at this point a note of promise, pure and beautiful, above the tumult. This motif, Redemption by Love, is shimmeringly trancendent in quality, the most beautiful of all music in the Ring Cycle. It proclaims the splendor of the New Age that is to be. Its harmonies rise and spread until the scene of wreckage and devastation is enveloped in a musical benediction, and grows more ethereal and lovely as the fires of dying Valhalla merge into the rosy dawn of a new day. After the "Twilight of the Gods" the sun rises on a clear sky, heralding an era when man will travel ways of peace and joy and brotherhood.

The character of Brunnhilde is a composite of the noblest qualities, both masculine and feminine in principle. As such she is the ideal Spirit of Truth. She typifies the manifestation of Truth in life's varied experiences, notably in circumstances which demand the highest form of self-control, decisive action, courage and divine self-sacrifice.

In all Wagner's widely diversified characters he has given us nothing quite so commanding and magnificent as Brunnhilde. Solemnly significant is the tremendous import of her final act as she returns the Ring to its rightful place in the river and climaxes the dissolution of the Old Order by applying to it her burning torch, saying as she does so, "So cast I my brand in Valhalla's wonderful Burg," then dashing into the fire and disappearing.

As the Spirit of Truth, Brunnhilde embodies the ideals of service and sacrifice. Inspiration and illumination are hers. She reflects qualities of both the finite and the infinite, the tangible and intangible. She projects the light around which all humanity revolves.

By his mystical touch, Wagner presents in the character of Wotan another extraordinarily revealing psychological study of man and the world. In him play forces belonging to the past and forces that will prevail in the future. Earlier phases of his life represent a glad young world as voiced in the mystic Song of the Fates:

By the World's Ash-Tree wove I once,
There tall and strong the sacred branches,
Rose in their dress of green.

The "Spring of Wisdom" flowed from the roots of this mighty Tree, for it is the same as the Tree of Life found in biblical lore. The decline of civilization begins when Wotan loses one eye, the one giving insight into spiritual realms.

He then cuts a branch from the Tree to make himself a spear. On this spear are engraved laws and treaties governing the age that is passing. These inscriptions so weaken the spear that Siegfried, herald of the New Age, is able to break it.

The Old Order is dying for want of that inner life by which it was originally sustained. Sing the Fates:

Drearily ceased then the flowing spring
Heavy-hearted sang I my song.

Wotan is no longer a creative worker but a passive onlooker as the envolutionary forces supplant him in the world scene by a successor who can wield powers belonging to the New. Says Wotan as he contemplates his loss of power, "No longer a worker, a watcher am I."

The Curse of Gold which, through the instrumentality of Alberich, is loosed upon the world, causes greed, selfishness, separateness and materiality to so flourish that Brunnhilde (Truth) is put to sleep upon a fire-girt mountain top. This seals Wotan's fate. From this time on his power rapidly declines and he moves swiftly toward his inevitable doom. Entirely demolishing the Great Ash Tree, he heaps the faggots made from its wood in a circle around Valhalla, the realm from which Brunnhilde has been banished and whose laws have become outmoded and impotent (the broken spear). There, amid deepening shadows, he himself finally awaits the twilight of his rule.

Wotan (civilization) loses spiritual insight and destroys the great Ash (Tree of Life) that once sustained him. He exchanges the life and light of the spirit for the acquisition of gold (material possessions) that leads to separateness. By so detaching himself from free intercommunication with life in its universal aspects, he brings to an end his own existence.

The culminating work of Brunnhilde (Truth) is the destruction of Valhalla (crystallization wrought by giving supremacy to material possessions) and her divine immolation in order to bring mankind complete emancipation from that bondage to self into which it has erringly fallen.

At the completion of the Ring Cycle, Wagner said, "My precious knowledge I bequeath to the world. It is no longer gold, nor pomp, houses nor courts nor lordly magnificence, nor the deceit of dark treaties, nor the hypocritical law of harsh manners, but only one thing which in good or evil days is worth while . . . and that is Love."

Upon the keynote of love Wagner depicts the passing of the Old and the birth of the New. Love will be the motivating power of the coming Aquarian Age—all-encompassing and all-enfolding love that will bring fulfillment to the poet's dream of an age in which all men shall know the Fatherhood of God and the Brotherhood of Man.

The New Age has no heritage more precious than the immortal works of Richard Wagner. As a modern Orpheus he comes to us, saying, "God has left for us an eternal memorial of Himself, our music which is the living God in our bosoms. Hence we will preserve our music and ward off from it all sacrilegious hands, for if we harken to frivilous and insincere music, we extinguish the last light God has left burning within us to lead the way to find Him anew."

Corinne Heline

1882 ~ 1975

The pattern of destiny was apparent from early childhood in the life of Corinne Heline, author of 28 volumes of Esoteric work.

As a tiny tot with advanced consciousness and inquiring mind she spent many hours visiting and admiring the beautiful statue of Mary in the Catholic Church across the street from her own Methodist Sunday School. Later in life she realized this was her first conscious touch with the beautiful Madonna whose over-shadowing presence was to be the love and inspiration of all her writings. Corinne's inner life-long dedication was to the Madonna.

Corinne recognized her mission at an early age. As a child of four she would put her head on her mother's open Bible and remain there for long periods, explaining, "There is something wonderful in this Holy Book and one day I will know what it is". With an advanced incarnation and preparation from childhood, her soul could easily impress the conscious mind of work to be done in this incarnation.

When in her teens her destiny was further shaped by the discovery of occult literature in the extensive library of an understanding neighbor and Theosophist, Mrs. Little. Already an avid Bible reader, the young Corinne now devoted many hours to studying occult books, borrowing one each time she visited Mrs. little. The books on reincarnation opened a new world, answering many of her inner questions. Later Mrs. Little's gift of the Rosicrucian Cosmo-conception by Max Heindel, was to change her whole life.

Corinne was born in Atlanta, Georgia, August 13, 1882, to the well-to-do Smith family. Her mother died when Corinne was 16, leaving her a comfortable inheritance which was later to be used in book publishing. Corinne mourned the loss of her mother deeply until one night her mother came to her telling her of her happiness in Higher Worlds and asked her to stop sorrowing and bring some joy to her father. She also told Corinne to look in an old trunk where Christmas money was hidden. With this money Corinne bought herself a new Bible, which is the same one she used in her New Age Bible Interpretation work. It was given to Corinne's friend, Adrienne Ashley, a beloved teacher who carried on the Bible work and compiled a 63-lesson correspondence course, used by the NEW AGE BIBLE & PHILOSOPHY CENTER, in Santa Monica, for students from all over the world. This Bible is a cherished gift with an aura which will ever sparkle with Divine Light.

Corinne moved to California after her mother died, where she met Max Heindel, and spent 5 years under the tutelage of this famous man. He saw her potential and encouraged its development. Eventually she became a lecturer, teacher, author, in her own right.

It was not until Christmas Eve in 1922, 3 years after Max Heindel's death, that Corinne knew she must begin the work for which she was destined. She got her INNER COMMISSION to interpret the Bible in the Light of the esoteric tradition, in addition to Max Heindel's asking her to undertake the work.

Corinne had had a vision of being present at the Last Supper. There were two celebrations: One for Jesus and His disciples in one room, and another room for the women where Mary sat at the head of the table giving assignments to other people who were to carry the work forward. Corinne was shocked when she was told she was to write an interpretation of the Bible, and said, "Why me? I'm inadequate". But Mary came to her, kissed her cheek, and said, "I will help you". This vision verified her INNER COMMISSION for her Bible work.

This was a monumental task, the central focus of her work in this incarnation for which students will ever be in her debt. Her works are texts for understanding the plan of evolution and initiation for the Piscean and Aquarian ages, as set forth in the Bible.

After Max Heindel died in 1916 Corinne developed a strong association with Theodore Heline, who came to be editor of the RAYS OF THE ROSE CROSS, an esoteric magazine. Theodore was a Shakespearean actor, author, and lecturer who had the ability to correlate current events with the unfoldment of man's consciousness in the light of ageless wisdom. He had an inner reality that served him in writing about the allegorical meaning behind Shakespearean plays. Later he became editor and founder of the NEW AGE INTERPRETER, an esoteric periodical, and started the NEW AGE PRESS publishing house.

Corinne and Theodore travelled extensively, lecturing to large audiences throughout the United States. They often filled the Sanctuary to over-flowing at the New Age Bible and Philosophy Center in Santa Monica, where they both were ordained as ministers. They were married in 1938, when Corinne was 56 years of age. Theodore set aside his talents to make Corinne's life work available to the world. He, like Corinne, was a New Age pioneer, prepared by previous life experiences with the qualities required for this challenging work.

After Corinne's father died, the Helines bought a hilltop home in California, and named it Madonna Crest.

It was here that Corinne did much of her writing, dictated at the rapid rate inspired by her thoughts. A pupil once asked after class, that Corinne repeat a segment from her lecture, and was told in Corinne's charming southern accent, "Ah caint remember, it came thru me so faist". Madonna Crest was a beautiful sanctuary of peace and tranquility, and in its garden was a special place, among a profusion of trees and flowers, for the Madonna.

Her book, MAGIC GARDENS immortalizes the functions of flowers in the evaluation of human consciousness. Corinne tells of the mission of the flowers and the Devas, or Angelic Hosts, that use the flowers as a means of impressing man with the inner significance of the beauty of the inner world and of the soul. The flowers, trees, and associated Deva hosts were an important part of her life expression. Because of her understanding of the four Holy Seasonal celebrations - the Solstices and Equinoxes, they were always celebrated at Madonna Crest. She knew that the many lovely trees were inhabited by the nature spirits which pour life currents into the roots, reshaping the limbs and trunks and coloring leaves and blossoms. In her book STARGATES, there is a chapter about these architects of nature, describing their appearance and the colors involved.

In addition to the seven volumes of NEW AGE BIBLE INTEPRETATION, Corinne wrote books on music as it relates to the unfoldment of the human spirit. These works serve as outlines for the New Age researchers who will help to manifest on the physical plane Temples of Music and Healing, which will be part of the new expansion of consciousness and natural healing methods of Aquarius.

Corinne was able to visit these ancient Temples by using her clairvoyance and extended consciousness, and to bring the principles used there into her writings. Her deep interest in music led to the study of the effect of music on human evolution and the true inner purpose of the life and works of such great composers as Beethoven, Wagner, and Schubert. She favored Wagner, and lectured across the country on the esoteric significance of his operas. Selections from Wagner were played in her home much of the time; they became the theme music for the sacred festivals she celebrated.

Among her other works is MYSTIC MASONRY AND THE BIBLE, which Corinne completed after a long and scholarly research at the Masonic Library in Boston. Corinne was the first woman given access to this library, and as a result she has given to the world the Bible's significance in Masonry, restoring feminine aspects in that discipline, and in Tarot, Astrology and Numerology.

The seven volumes of NEW AGE BIBLE INTERPRETATION were completed in 1954 when she was 72 years of age. She herself said, "The Bible, the supreme spiritual textbook of life, is above all creeds, dogmas, and differences in religious beliefs. It is written to meet the needs of both the wise and the simple. There are surface truths, and wisdom that is veiled. There is guidance to the spiritual life in its pages for every degree of understanding. As consciousness unfolds, its revelations multiply. It is indeed the Wonder Book of all time. The deepest wisdom contained in the Bible is accessible only to those who have attained a personal first-hand knowledge of the Spiritual world and the fundamental laws operative in them".

Corinne's task is now completed, and with love, courage and dedication. The Bible is the most important instrument by which man can measure himself for the passing age, as well as the age that is unfolding. The keys to its understanding have been given, and now the inner truths of the Bible can be taught. Her works will be textbooks for future generations.

Corinne wrote from the first-hand knowledge that gave access to the deepest wisdom in the Bible. She was divinely inspired. To our knowledge, no other writer has interpreted every one of the 62 books of the Bible in their mystical meaning. Her teachings give special clarifying details and rich images.

Theodore Heline made his transition suddenly in 1971. Corinne made her transition at the age of 93, in 1975. Her beloved friend, Reverend Gene Sande, teacher for over 50 years at the New Age Bible & Philosophy Center gave the memorial service. Those who had inner vision could see the welcoming throng greeting Corinne, along with Max Heindel and others that had participated in the cycle now closed. She is now continuing her work as a senior disciple of the Hierarchy. Her unique gift to humanity is the inner revelation of the work of the DIVINE FEMININE and her earthly representative, the MADONNA. Corinne's last book was the BLESSED VIRGIN MARY, Her Life and Mission.

The New Age Bible Center is the sole publisher of Corinne's seven volumes of the NEW AGE BIBLE INTERPRETATION, and the correspondence lessons. This Center is dedicated to keeping them in print and available for those students and aspirants of the New Age who will be instrumental in bringing ordered beauty to the age now dawning.